# For your Opponent
## Carbon Shinai カーボンシナイ

CF-TYPE
DB-TYPE
K1-TYPE
K2-TYPE

Always check the surface of your Carbon Shinai before use. If you see any damage to the surface of your Carbon Shinai similar to these photographs, stop using it immediately and buy a replacement slat.

### WARNING

Do not use anything other than our official rubber stopper on your Carbon Shinai

**When using your Carbon Shinnai**

1. To prevent injury, please use our official rubber stopper. Do not use stoppers made for conventional bamboo shinai in your Carbon Shiai, as there is a risk of injury to your opponent if the tip breaks through and enters their men grill.

2. When choosing a sakigawa (leather tip), make sure that it is more than 5cm in length and completely covers our rubber stopper. If the sakigawa is shorter than 5cm, there is a risk of injury to your opponent if a slat slips out and enters their men grill.

3. Do not shave the plastic surface of your Carbon Shinai. If you shave the surfaace, the black carbon fiber will be exposed, causing damage that may result in injury to your opponent.

4. Always check the condition of the surface of your Carbon Shinai before and during use. As soon as you notice any cracks, or peeling of the surface, or if black carbon fiber is exposed on any part of the outside, inside or edges of the Shinai, or you notice any other damage, stop using the Shinai immediately. There is a danger of injury to your opponent if your Carbon Shinai is split or broken.

5. When tying the nakayui (leather binding), either tie a knot in the tsuru-ito (cord), or tie one end of the nakayui to the tsuru-ito, or by another means ensuring that it does not move up and down during use. If there is any damage whatsoever to the sakigawa, tsukagawa (hilt), rubber stopper, tsuru-ito and so on, replace them immediately.

6. If the tip of the Carbon Shinai is damaged, or a slat is protruding out of the sakigawa, there is a danger that it could enter your opponent's men grill and injure them.

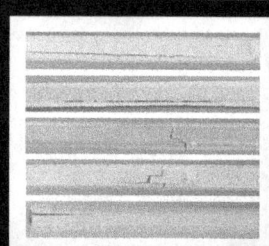

Carbon Graphite core revealed /breaks/cracks

We have improved the official Carbon Shinai rubber stopper
**The NEW official rubber stopper.**
¥300 (domestic Japanese price)

# Kendogu Revolution

## For Yourself
### 武楯 Mu Jun

### WARNING!!

1. Under no circumstances should organic solvents (such as thinner, alcohol, benzene, toluene, acetone, gasoline, kerosene, etc.), acidic or alkali chemicals, domestic cleansers, car cleansers, or anti-mist sprays, be used to clean the Shield. These substances will cause the Shield to deteriorate, leading to clouding, cracking or breaking, thereby resulting in danger of injury to the face.

2. Should the Shield develop deep scratches or cracks on either the outer or inner surface, discontinue use of the Shield immediately, and replace it with an undamaged Shield. If the Shield is used in such a condition, there is a danger of its breaking, causing injury to the face.

3. It should be fully understood that, as with the traditional Japanese Kendo-Men (mask), there is still the danger of injury to the face through fragments of broken bamboo or Carbon Shinai pieces entering through areas not covered by the Shield.

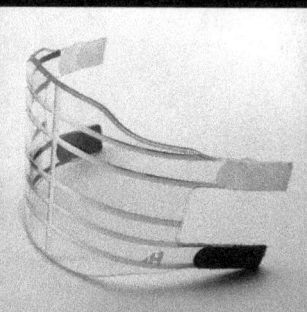

SG-TYPE

Technology: Bringing safety to sport
**HASEGAWA**
HASEGAWA CORPORATION

Homepage http://www.hasegawakagaku.co.jp
E-mail webmaster@hasegawakagaku.co.jp

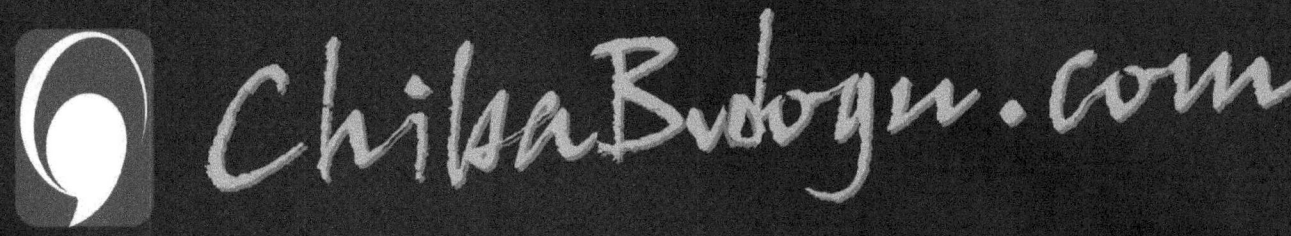

# ChibaBudogu.com

... Custom Made Bogu in Japan.

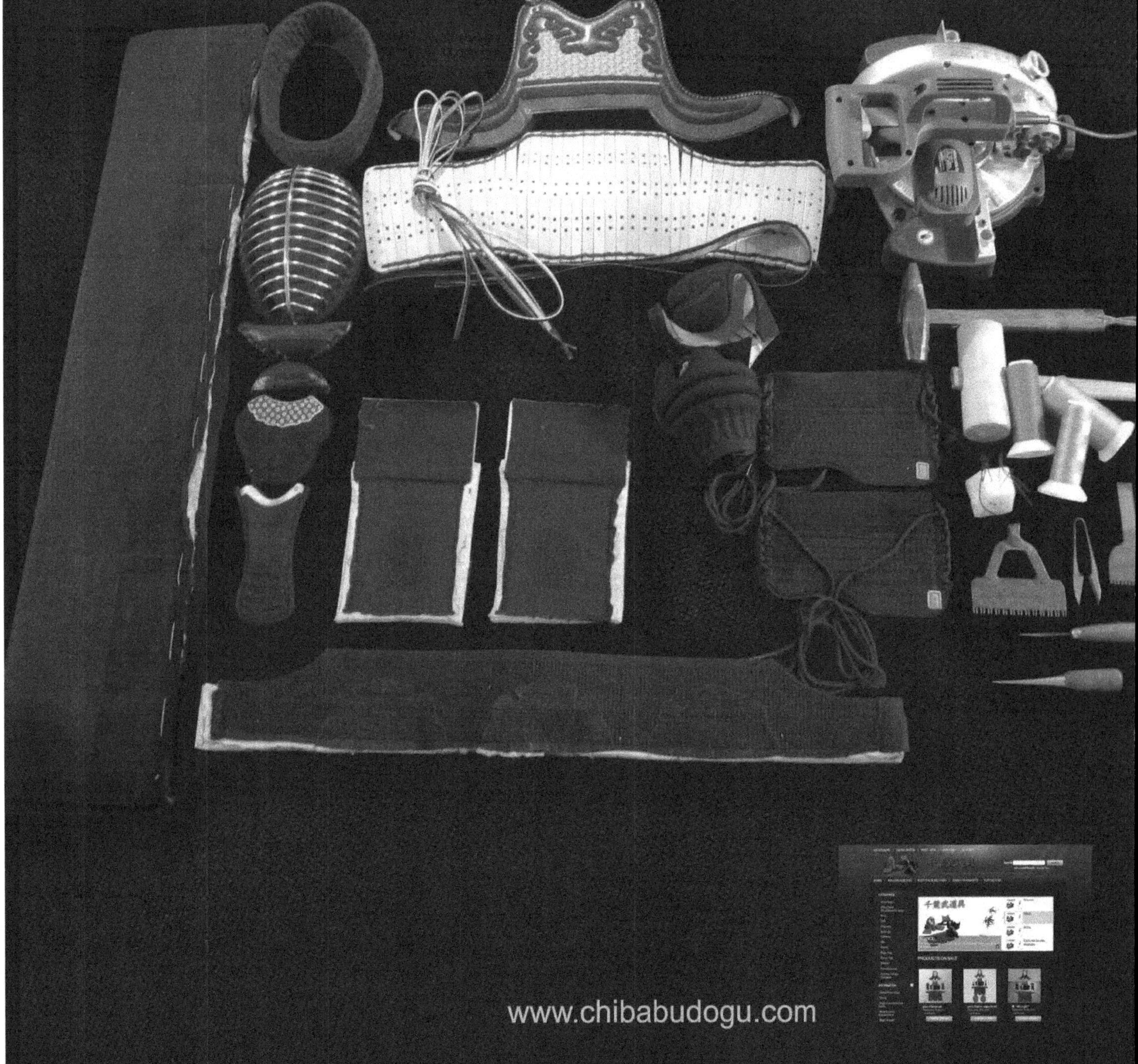

www.chibabudogu.com

# KENDO WORLD Volume 6.1 December 2011 Contents

Editorial _____ 2

**Hanshi Says** Tahara Hironori (Hanshi 8-dan) _____ 4

The Great Wall of Four & Five _____ 8

The Nuts 'n' Bolts of Kendo
Zanshin and Sen _____ 14

Jidai-geki and Chambara
A Discussion with Ishimatsu Yoshihiro _____ 16

Nonsense and Origins:
An Inspiring Conversation with Victor Harris _____ 20

Reidan-jichi Part 12 **Kihon Dōsa** _____ 23

Kendo That Cultivates People
Part 11: Further Development _____ 27

Shinai Sagas
Management Secrets of the Samurai _____ 33

Kendo's Not-so Common-sense **Kamae** _____ 36

**Bujutsu Jargon** Part: 1 _____ 38

sWords of Wisdom
"The first cut is everything" _____ 40

Unlocking Japan: Part 21
Kendo & Football _____ 42

The Kendo Coach: Sports Psychology in Kendo
Part 6 — Aggression in Kendo: part 1 _____ 44

Interview with Jodo Hanshi 8-dan
**FURUKAWA Shinya** _____ 50

Recent Developments in Korean Kendo
"Video Interpretation Appeals"
According to the Korean Business Kumdo Federation _____ 55

Strength to Strength
Continuing Growth and Success _____ 60

The PNKF Women's Tournament _____ 62

The 10th Otsū Cup _____ 64

The History of Women's Kendo _____ 66

Smile Kids Japan _____ 69

A Reflection on Reigi _____ 71

Historical Sightseeing
Part 06: The Shinsen-gumi _____ 73

Argentina:
New Kendo Wave & Why it Matters _____ 79

Book Mark 9
Kurikara: The Sword and the Serpent _____ 82

Jukendo no Kata
– Final part: TANKEN TAI TŌ NO KATA – _____ 83

Kendo World
A Cumulative Table of Contents _____ 90

---

*Kendo World Staff*
- Bunkasha International President— Michael Komoto
- Bunkasha International Vice President & Editor-in-Chief— Alex Bennett PhD
- Bunkasha International Vice President & Graphic Design— Shishikura 'Kan' Masashi
- Bunkasha International Vice President— Hamish Robison
- Senior Consultant— Yonemoto Masayuki

*KW Staff Writers / Translators / Photographers / Graphic Designer / Sub-editors*
- Aurélien Lainé
- Axel Pilgrim PhD
- Baptiste Tavernier MA
- Blake Bennett MA
- Bruce Flanagan MA
- Bryan Peterson
- Charlie Kondek
- Gabriel Weitzner
- Honda Sōtarō PhD
- Imafuji Masahiro MBA
- Jeff Broderick
- Kate Sylvester MA
- Lockie Jackson PhD
- Michael Ishimatsu-Prime MA
- Miho Maki
- Paul Benson
- Saitō Yukie
- Sergio Boffa PhD
- Stephen Nagy PhD
- Steven Harwood MA
- Stuart Gibson
- Taylor Winter
- Tony Cundy
- Trevor Jones
- Tyler Rothmar
- Vivian Yung

*Guest Writers*
- Elizabeth Marsten (2001 Women's Team USA Member, 11th WKC)
- Katō Jun'ichi (Prof. Bunkyo University Kendo Kyōshi 7-dan)
- Nagao Susumu (Prof. Meiji University; Kendo Kyōshi 8-dan)
- Nakano Yasoji (Now deceased. Kendo Hanshi 9-dan)
- Ōya Minoru (Prof. International Budo University; Kendo Kyōshi 7-dan)
- Ozawa Hiroshi (Prof. Tokyo University of Science; Kendo Kyōshi 8-dan)
- Scott Huegel (MaSC, RF Engineer living in San Francisco)
- Sumi Masatake (Kendo Hanshi 8-dan)
- Tahara Hironori (Kendo Hanshi 8-dan)
- Trevor Chapman (Dojo Leader – Kashi-no-ki Kenyukai, UK)

*KW would like to thank the following people and organisations for their valuable cooperation:*
- All Japan Kendo Federation
- Chiba Budo-gu
- Hasegawa Teiichi - President, Hasegawa Corporation
- *Kendo Jidai* Magazine
- *Kendo Nihon* Magazine
- Nippon Budokan Foundation
- TOZANDO
- Miyako Kendogu

**COPYRIGHT 2011** Bunkasha International Corporation. No part of this publication may be reproduced in any form whatsoever without written permission from the publisher, except by writers who are permitted to quote brief passages for the purpose of review or reference. Kindly contact Bunkasha International Corporation at info@kendo-world.com.

**Editorial Conventions Used in KW** Inevitably in a magazine of this nature, many non-English words appear in the text. All Japanese words are italicised and include macrons (ū, ō) etc., apart from common place names and nouns, and words in some captions and headings. As a general exception, KW treats all the martial arts (budo), such as kendo, iaido, jodo, ranks, and so on as Anglicised words without using macrons. Japanese names are written in accordance to the traditional Japanese manner of family name followed by given name. Traditional *ryūha* are written with capitals and therefore are not italicised. 'Kata' with a capital 'K' refers to the set of Nippon Kendo Kata, and *kata* refers to set forms in general. The masculine personal pronoun is used throughout the text in some articles in the interest of readability, and is in no way meant to slight the significant contributions made by female kendoka.

"Be heedful even if you have a branch of the cherry tree in hand, for the wind will scatter the blossoms"

# Editorial   Alex Bennett (KW Editor-in-Chief)

Finally 2011 has come to a close, and I am personally happy to be heading into 2012. This is the year of the 15th WKC, and it promises to be another tightly contested event with more countries in attendance than ever before. In August, I was fortunate to visit Novara in Italy, the venue for the next championships. It is a quaint little town not far from Milan, and will surely be a popular setting for some settling of scores.

As the world's kendo matures, I am looking forward to observing excellent matches by competitors from countries other than the usual powerhouses, and an appreciation shown by all to the protocols of good kendo deportment. This may sound like a rather sanctimonious statement, but I have noticed a careless trend among young kendo competitors in Japan of late. As I work for a Japanese university (Kansai University), and spend a fair portion of my time in the university's dojo with the students, I think I am qualified to warn of the waning concern shown to what I consider the most essential element of any budo art – *zanshin*.

*Zanshin* is a key part of budo culture, although it is more prevalent in some than others. Perhaps kendo and kyudo include the concept with more enthusiasm than say judo or karate. Any self-respecting kendoist knows that *zanshin* means maintaining a state of readiness after an attack, and being physically and mentally prepared to defend and counter-attack if necessary. In fact, it is clearly stipulated in the rule book that for a point to be deemed valid, the strike must be concluded with *zanshin*. That is why it is not good refereeing practice to raise the flags as soon as the *shinai* impacts the target. There should always be a slight lag between the hit and the call, to check for the presence of *zanshin*.

Real *zanshin* is not something that you consciously make, but is born naturally when you throw body, heart and soul into the attack. It is sometimes compared to a cup of water that is drunk dry. There are always a few drops left in the cup. These remaining drops are likened to *zanshin*. In a psychological sense, it means to be in total control of one's emotions and be constantly aware of what is happening in one's surroundings. It is not to get excited, but to be calm and collected, and keep your mind in the game. It means to win with humility and lose

graciously. It also means to have a feeling of respect for your opponent.

If a goal is scored in soccer, a try in rugby, or a home run in baseball goes flying into the grandstand, these are all reasons for celebration. Players perform their little victory poses and routines to the absolute delight of their adoring and ecstatic fans. Herein lies a significant difference between kendo and other sports. Victory poses in kendo are unthinkable. Showing elation in the event of scoring an *ippon* will result in the ultimate humiliation – *torikeshi*, or the point being revoked. Why? Because it is a demonstration of a lack of maturity, lack of self-control, lack of preparation, lack of respect – i.e., a lack of *zanshin*.

If you have *zanshin*, you don't have time to be happy. By the same token, you don't have time to be sad in defeat. Kendo ideals dictate that decorum is maintained at all times, and that one is gracious in defeat and humble in victory. Can you imagine what would happen if a soccer referee rescinded a goal because players were hugging each other? All hell would break lose. There is no time or place in kendo for the shameless Greek tragedies that take place on the *tatami* mats in Olympic judo. The Way of kendo is far more important than a single *shiai* result.

At least that's what we kendoists keep telling ourselves and the rest of the budo world. After all, that's what makes kendo great, right? Self-control and respect… Alas, I feel that this aspect of kendo is being increasingly belittled by sheer narcissism or a lack of self-control seen in *shiai* these days. Broadly speaking, abjuration of *zanshin* takes two forms: there are those who, as soon the flags go up, purposefully lower their guard while running through as if to say "you are so dead because of my fantastic strike that I don't even need to show *zanshin*…" They ooze arrogance, and you can almost smell it. The other form is not so much born of arrogance more than the inability to control emotion. They say that there are no victory poses in kendo, but there are. We just don't see them because the perpetrator has two hands on the *shinai*. Take the *shinai* away, and their fists would shake furiously in jubilation, not dissimilar to a striker scoring the winning goal in a FIFA World Cup final. This is not *zanshin*.

Some may ask, what is wrong with this? Why can't we show our joy or woe at the end of a match? Isn't emotion what makes us human? I don't disagree with these sentiments, and if you had seen my less-than-seemly state of delirium when the All Blacks defeated the French in the final of the Rugby World Cup in 2011, I may well be accused of total hypocrisy. My point is that kendo promotes a different set of values, and these should not be compromised. *Zanshin* is an integral element of kendo's moral principles, and more than anything else, has the potential to greatly contribute to our development as human beings.

Perhaps a good example of the profundity of *zanshin* can be found in something totally unrelated to kendo. It is well-known in climbing circles that eighty per cent of accidents occur on the descent. The thrill of reaching the summit after an arduous, careful climb upwards means that even more vigilance (*zanshin*) is required on the way down. In kendo we are not going to die in the literal sense if we fail to demonstrate *zanshin* after a strike, but we do in a metaphorical sense. The word *zanshin* and its underpinning wisdom has been handed down to us from samurai culture through the medium of kendo. The question of life and death was very much a reality for samurai, and the idea of *zanshin* touches on the key to survival for people in any age. The real battle for survival starts after the initial battle has been won. Just because you think you have achieved your objective, don't believe it for a second. It may be done, but it isn't dusted. This is the *zanshin* attitude.

We should be grateful for such a succinct concept that can basically explain most of our failures throughout life. How many times have you blamed others for your misfortune? A little time spent engaging in objective self-reflection will often reveal an embarrassing and uncomfortable truth. That is, most of your rotten luck could have been avoided if only you had shown a bit of *zanshin*. This is precisely the kind of lesson we can take from kendo and apply in our lives. Ultimately, you are responsible for your successes and failings in life, and the lack of or presence of *zanshin* will often be the deciding factor.

Kendo provides us with a wonderful framework for life, which is there for the taking if we choose to use it. Having experienced natural disasters firsthand in 2011, I have learned the importance of being prepared for the unexpected. It has served to heighten my appreciation for the insightful lessons that can be gleaned from kendo if we care to look. On that note, have a great 2012, and don't forget your *zanshin*.

# HANSHI SAYS

*A series in which some of Japan's top Hanshi teachers give hints of what they are looking for in grading examinations based on wisdom accumulated through decades of training.*

Translated by Alex Bennett - *Kendo World* would like to thank Tahara-sensei and *Kendo Jidai* Magazine for permission to translate and publish this article.

## Touch the hearts of the examiners with the best strike you can conjure...

### TAHARA HIRONORI (HANSHI 8-DAN)

*Tahara Hironori-sensei was born in Kumamoto Prefecture on March 15, 1940. After graduating from Yachiyo High School where he first started kendo, he entered the Keishichō and studied under kendo greats such as Ogawa Chūtarō, Morishima Tateo, Abe Saburō, and Yuno Masanori. Tahara-sensei served as the vice Shihan for the Keishichō and also as a professor of the Kantō Police Academy. Tahara-sensei has competed successfully in many of the major tournaments in Japan, including first place at the National Sports Meet (Kokutai), and runner-up at the Hachidan Invitational Tournament in Yamanashi. He currently serves as the honorary president of the Musashi Budokan, honorary Shihan of the Kantō Police Academy, is on the board of the directors for the AJKF, and is Shihan of the Mitsui Sumitomo Insurance Company Kendo Club. He passed the hachidan examination in 1990, and received the title of Hanshi in 1998.*

### Suburi and an unbreakable kamae...

I have been learning kendo for many years, and I know how difficult it is to master. This is the same for all matters of study. If you are in pursuit of improvement and an understanding of the deep truths that underlie what you are studying, then it is never easy to make progress, or make it to the next level. People travelling the road of kendo feel such hardships and frustrations constantly. Kendo can be summed up as "having a beginning, but no end."

Compared to other budo and sports, the number of techniques in kendo is remarkably limited. In fact, there are only four basic target areas. Using a *shinai*, exponents face-off with each other and move around in all directions trying to score valid strikes on the targets. But, if you are only in pursuit of technical proficiency to score points, you will never be able to scale the high wall that stands in the way of your progress.

When I am faced with a wall impeding my progress, one thing I always tell myself is to "go back to basics". That is, to return to having an "honest heart" (*sunao na kokoro*). When engaged in the process of learning, having an honest heart is the only way you will be

able to take on board the advice and teachings you need in order to improve.

My *sempai*, Yuno Masanori-sensei expressed the meaning of kendo to me in one sentence. "To learn kendo is to learn the Self." The greatest enemy for people learning kendo is the Self, and your own state of mind and feelings. If you can return to your original form without pretence, you can use this "honest heart" to improve your kendo.

If you can maintain this attitude, you will always have the mind of "*kyūdōshin*" – conviction in search of the Way. I think that the old teaching "*sanma-no-kurai*" from the Yagyū-ryū (classical school of swordsmanship) is very pertinent to modern kendo. It refers to the three stages of the learning process. The first step is to find a good teacher. This is probably the most important thing. Most people who continue kendo have their own *sensei* who they continue respecting throughout their lives, and whose teachings they place great value in. This is the same for beginners and high-ranked experts alike. "Reaching an impasse in training, and hitting a wall…." is a fact of life in kendo. When you come to a standstill, it is your *sensei* who offers the right words of advice to help you go on.

All people like to think that they are always right, but it is difficult to achieve one's objectives if you go about something the wrong way. The Shinkage-ryū also teaches "*kufū*" (to devise ways) and "*renma*" (training). Even though you may be training intensively, things may not be going as planned. For example, you may have difficulty trying to pass a grading examination. When this happens, you need to take a good look at your kendo with an honest mind, question what is wrong, and then start again. Also, you may be training persistently but are unable to shake some bad habits that you have developed along the way… The best advice for people facing such a predicament is to go back to the basics. However, kendoists with high grades (6 and 7-dan) tend to ask what level of *kihon* they should return to. Applied techniques (*ōyō*) derive from learning proper *kihon*. If you think that simply reviewing advanced techniques means going "back to basics", then you will fall into a hole. When I say back to basics, I really mean way back to the most fundamental elements of kendo.

Kendo basics were originally found in *kata*. During the Tokugawa period three or four hundred years ago, fencing with protective armour was developed as a training method to supplement *kata* training. However, the thrill of actually being able to strike opponents took over, and *kata* (*kihon*) was neglected. This is still the case now. It is always prudent to reflect on your basics, and go back to kendo's roots.

I think that these roots, the most fundamental aspects of kendo, are found in *suburi* and maintaining an indestructible *kamae*. We are able to do kendo because we have a *shinai* (*katana*). If there was no *shinai*, then there would be no kendo. This is a very simple concept, but many people seem to forget that total familiarity with the *shinai* is the only way to improve in kendo. When you are stuck, *suburi* is an extremely effective way for breaking through the wall. "*Suburi* for life" is an old adage that great *sensei* from the past lived by. You should do *suburi* to the extent that the *shinai* feels like an extension of your body. The old maxim "*hyakuren jittoku*" means to practise a hundred times to acquire a skill. It means to practise over and over with an honest heart…

## *Do you have the kendo manner?*

Regardless of what you are studying, it takes a great deal of perseverance and discipline to continue it throughout your life. My teacher, Ogawa Chūtarō-sensei, always used to ask me, "Are you sitting?" He was referring to *zazen* (seated meditation), and encouraged us to engage in its practice. He told us to continue doing it, and I have come to understand that continuation is a very important thing indeed; that is, if you want to improve and reach a higher level in anything, following through is a prerequisite. You must keep your heart in what it is that you are searching for. Try not to let your dedication waver.

In April 1960, I joined the specialist budo department in the Keishichō (Tokyo Metroploitan Police Department). This was the first time I was able to meet the kendo teachers who taught at the Keishichō. There were many great kendo masters and they took us through our paces every day. The honorary Shihan at the time were the legends Saimura Gorō-

# Hanshi Says

sensei (Hanshi 10-dan) and Mochida Moriji-sensei (Hanshi 10-dan). This was an incredible time to become involved with the Keishichō instructors through kendo, and I consider myself very lucky to be admitted into their tutelage. All of the tenets of wisdom that they imparted to me remain securely in my mind. Their advice helped me get to where I am in life now, and I continue to cherish their gifts of knowledge as my personal treasures.

Ogawa Chūtarō-sensei was in charge of my tuition in my first year in the budo department. The year I joined the Keishichō in 1960 was a time of social unrest, and there was much ado about the Security Treaty. Although we were supposed to be training every day to become kendo teachers, for the first few months we were dispatched to the Diet building. When we had a free moment between our guard duties, Ogawa-sensei came to talk with us.

"You fellows all came to the Keishichō as specialist students [for kendo]. As you can't do kendo at the moment, I suspect you are all feeling a little apprehensive. Don't be. So long as you complete your duties here with dedication, your kendo will not weaken. Work hard. If you slack off and lose your focus and motivation, your kendo will also suffer."

I listened intently to what our master told us, and took notes whenever I could. The older I get, the more I realise what wonderful advice he gave us. People who are not in the police, or do not belong to kendo clubs at universities cannot be expected to do kendo all day every day. They have other responsibilities. Most people who do kendo have to go to work and look after their family. Kendo is something many people do in their spare time, after taking care of other priorities. You can still keep your kendo level up when you are not able to train by focussing on your work and duties, and doing them to the best of your ability. It worked for us.

Kendo is not just about going to the dojo and hitting people with *shinai*. You should also do *suburi* and train by yourself to chip away at achieving your objectives. Continuing in this vein will enable you to get out of ruts, and naturally develop the special kendo manner known as *kurai* (pride). Rid yourself of weakness and apathy, value the connection you have with kendo, and keep on doing it as best you can. If you can approach kendo with this kind of attitude, it will bear fruit in the long run, and you will experience much enjoyment in the process.

### Are you training with kihon in mind at all times?

Continuing kendo with an honest heart, you will feel the need to seek knowledge, and visiting any dojo will be an enjoyable experience rather than one that causes trepidation. If you are in search of something, training becomes a pleasure not a chore. But, you must never neglect *kihon* as this forms the very foundation of kendo. You must practise it over and over.

When you get lost, go back to basics… I have already emphasised this point repeatedly. If you do not maintain your basics such as *suburi*, you will find the wall will be an even bigger hurdle to climb when you eventually crash into it. If you practise *kihon* properly and diligently the wall will be easier to overcome.

It will do you little good if you think to do *kihon* because an examination is looming. Your body will not deal well with the sudden shock of *kirikaeshi* or *kakari-geiko*. Basic elements such as how to hold the *shinai* properly, *ashi-sabaki* (footwork), body movement and so on, are fundamental aspects that should be continually checked as you go up the ranks.

Still, when people think of *kihon*, the first thing that pops into their minds is *uchikomi* or *kakari-geiko*. I must reiterate that *suburi* comes before this, and should be done as much as possible… Practise *suburi* over and over so that your *tenouchi*, and the distribution of strength between the two hands is even. Persist until the superfluous strength from your arms dissipates… I often see people doing *suburi* simply as a part of their warm up before *keiko*. *Suburi* is more important than

# Tahara Hironori (Hanshi 8-dan)

that. You should make time to do it properly for its own sake, not just as a convenient way of loosening up.

You should also do *suburi* together when teaching the children or juniors. The same can be said of *kirikaeshi*. Upon reaching higher grades (5-7-dan) people mistakenly think that they only need to receive *kirikaeshi* rather than actually do it. Engage in as much *kirikaeshi* practice as you can. Also, be sure to receive properly when you are *motodachi*. As *motodachi*, you must execute this role with even more feeling and determination than the attacker (*kakarite*), and understand the heavy responsibility and hardship involved. Your kendo mind and techniques will develop and strengthen naturally through conscientious *kihon* training.

I have noticed that *shidō-geiko* and *gokaku-geiko* have changed a lot over the years. Nowadays, it is hard to tell who the *motodachi* is. Younger fencers sit and wait for the *sensei* to strike, and then try and sneakily pick their *kote* off in a rather cynical way. This is the wrong way of going about training with a *sensei*. Regardless of whether or not you constantly get hit or deflected, you must try and attack as much as you can. You should challenge yourself and see which is stronger – your *sensei*'s *shinai*, or your chest which is ramming into it. Attack with total conviction (*sutemi*), harbouring no concern about your own wellbeing.

Recently I had an opportunity to train with Yuno Masanori-sensei at the Nippon Budokan. When I stood up from *sonkyo* and let out a long *kiai*, I moved to the right. When I did this, Yuno-sensei immediately crouched down into *sonkyo* again to finish the bout. The whole engagement lasted for about thirty seconds. After the *keiko* had finished, he remonstrated me in the following way.

"When you stood up, you found my *kensen* threatening, which is why you moved over to the right. What else could it mean? Here you are ready to take on your teacher, and you move away to save your backside, and look for a sneaky way in to attack. That is no good at all. You have to face your *sensei* with a feeling of 'do to me what you will', and fight as hard as you can from front-on."

I value each and every *ippon* in *keiko* as if it were a competition. In the case of high-ranked examinations such as *nanadan*, each candidate has had to wait a set number of years since passing *rokudan*, and most opponents are all basically the same age. In this sense, the examination system is quite fair. There is not so much disparity in terms of technical ability. But the four kendo targets cannot be struck robotically. True techniques are born out of an intense situation where the practitioner is totally absorbed in the engagement with absolute sincerity, and the *waza* is let loose spontaneously. Such *waza* strike the hearts of the examiners.

I think that grades are useful for kendo's popularisation and development. Practitioners who seek to attain higher ranks dedicate themselves to training so that they can cultivate good posture, form, striking technique, deportment, and pride for the rank they are aspiring to. Efforts made by individual kendo practitioners for this purpose are vital to the survival of kendo culture into the future.

My grandfather used to say that "You only keep growing until you are 25. You have to work hard to build up while you can." I think that technical development in kendo is similar. People who apply to sit high ranks such as 6, 7, and 8-dan have already reached a ripe age. They realise that they are not at an age where they can continue to expand technically, but have to try and maintain what *waza* they have already mastered, and reach an even more profound layer within each technique.

In an examination, particularly for the higher grades, you should be able to demonstrate to the examiners that you have dedicated yourself to training in *kihon* throughout your life, and attempt to strike their hearts with flowing, correct kendo execution. This is the kind of kendo that we want to convey to the next generation. Let's all aim for correct kendo built on a solid diet of *kihon*. Good luck to all!

# The Great Wall of Four & Five

By Alex Bennett

For many non-Japanese practitioners of kendo, it seems that the ranks of fourth and fifth *dan* are enormously problematic. In Japan, a good university student in his or her fourth year will usually manage to take the rank of *yondan*. With the current regulations, the earliest anybody can take the examination for *yondan* is twenty years of age. If they continue with their kendo after entering the workforce, *godan* is usually attained by the age of thirty, the earliest age being twenty-four.

*Godan* is the last *dan* grade to be examined at a local level in Japan. *Rokudan* onwards is conducted nationally under the auspices of the All Japan Kendo Federation. It is widely acknowledged that *rokudan* upwards has become increasingly difficult to pass in recent years, and as such, prefectural federations have also tightened the clamps on the pass rate for *godan*. Thus, it has become quite a hurdle for many Japanese practitioners as well, despite the abundance of opportunities to train together with high-ranked *sensei* for guidance.

The situation outside Japan is even more challenging as *yondan* or *godan* holders will often be the highest rank in their dojo, or even country in some cases. This means that people aspiring for these ranks probably don't have many people they can seek guidance from, or emulate in their *keiko*. You can usually get through to *sandan* with determination and a good fighting spirit, but *yondan* and *godan* require a lot more finesse in terms of technical refinement and repertoire, and an understanding of how to pressure your opponent to create and identify openings.

I have been asked with increasing frequency recently to offer guidance on what is required to pass these grades. Also, as I will be sitting on a grading panel as an examiner for *dan* grades up to *godan* soon, I thought this would be a good opportunity to get my thoughts in order, and hopefully provide some advice for people who are struggling with these ranks, or are almost ready to sit them for the first time.

What exactly are examiners looking for in each rank? Of course, it is very difficult to quantify what is required as every candidate is different, as are the subjective experiences of the examiners. There will always be examinees who stand out from the rest, and pass the grade as a *fait accompli*. However, often there is very little obvious difference between the candidates, so what is it that allows some of them to pass and others to fail? Obviously, an element of luck is involved, and there are many external factors that come into play, but as long as the following criteria for each grade are met by the candidate, then success is within reach.

# The Great Wall of Four & Five

| Rank | Required Years of Study Between Ranks | Age Requirements |
|---|---|---|
| Shodan | Must have the grade of *ikkyū* (1-kyū) | 15 years and above |
| Nidan | One year or more since passing *shodan* | |
| Sandan | Two years or more since passing *nidan* | |
| Yondan | Three years or more since passing *sandan* | |
| Godan | Four years or more since passing *yondan* | |
| Rokudan | Five years or more since passing *godan* | |
| Nanadan | Six years or more since passing *rokudan* | |
| Hachidan | Ten years or more since passing *nanadan* | 46 years and above |

| Rank | Criteria |
|---|---|
| Shodan | Someone who has trained in the basics of kendo and has acceptable technique |
| Nidan | Someone who has learned the basics of kendo and has proficient technique |
| Sandan | Someone who is accomplished in the basics of kendo and has good technique |
| Yondan | Someone who is accomplished in the basics and applied skills of kendo, and has excellent technique |
| Godan | Someone who has mastered the basics and applied skills of kendo, and has outstanding technique |
| Rokudan | Someone who is accomplished in the true meaning of kendo, and has exceptional technique |
| Nanadan | Someone who has mastered the true meaning of kendo, and has superior technique |
| Hachidan | Someone who has reached the inner-secrets of kendo, has maturity, and has attained total mastery of kendo technique |

Even in the Japanese, the wording is somewhat vague and ambiguous in places, but I'm sure readers get the idea. I helped translate a short document for the AJKF a few years ago which attempts to make the criteria a little easier to understand for examinees and examiners alike.

1. The central concern for evaluation in examinations for the grades of *shodan*, 2-dan and 3-dan is the level of *kihon* (basic techniques) demonstrated by the examinee. The examiner assesses whether the candidate has learnt and correctly acquired the basic kendo skills.

2. The central concern for evaluation in examinations for the grades of 4-dan and 5-dan is the level of basic kendo techniques and advanced techniques (*kihon* and *ōyō*). The examiner assesses whether the candidate has fully acquired and is able to utilise basic and advanced kendo skills.

3. The central concern for evaluation in examinations for the grades of 6-dan and 7-dan is the ability to demonstrate *jiri* (事理 technique and theory). Besides the basic and advanced kendo techniques, the examiner assesses whether the candidate has acquired sufficient knowledge and understanding of *jiri* – the techniques of kendo accompanied by theory or principles.

4. The central concern for evaluation in examinations for the grade of 8-dan is whether or not the candidate has reached the highest stage of *jiri* referred to as *jiri-itchi* (total integration of *ji* and *ri*). The

candidate will be assessed on their ability to demonstrate a profound understanding of *jiri-itchi* in addition to the aforementioned points for 7-dan and below.

Each examiner is required to make a decision after paying careful attention to the following points in accordance with the above criteria:

### Shodan, 2-dan, 3-dan

① *Chakusō* and *reihō* – The candidate's appearance and whether they are correctly wearing the *kendō-gi* and *hakama*, and are holding the *shinai* correctly (*chakusō*); Appropriate manners and deportment (*reihō*); ② Correct posture; ③ *Datotsu* (strikes and thrusts) in accordance with the correct basic kendo techniques; ④ Strong spirit (*kisei*).

### 4-Dan, 5-Dan

① *Chakusō* and *reihō* – The candidate's appearance and whether they are correctly wearing the *kendō-gi* and *hakama*, and are holding the *shinai* correctly (*chakusō*); Appropriate manners and deportment (*reihō*); ② Correct posture; ③ *Datotsu* (strikes and thrusts) in accordance with the correct basic kendo techniques; ④ Strong spirit (*kisei*); ⑤ Level of proficiency acquired in advanced kendo techniques; ⑥ Level of mental and physical discipline demonstrated; ⑦ Strategic skills to control and win the match.

### 6-dan, 7-dan, 8-dan

① *Chakusō* and *reihō* – The candidate's appearance and whether they are correctly wearing the *kendō-gi* and *hakama*, and are holding the *shinai* correctly (*chakusō*); Appropriate manners and deportment (*reihō*); ② Correct posture; ③ *Datotsu* (strikes and thrusts) in accordance with the correct basic kendo techniques; ④ Strong spirit (*kisei*). ⑤ Level of proficiency acquired in advanced kendo techniques; ⑥ Level of mental and physical discipline demonstrated; ⑦ Strategic skills to control and win the match; ⑧ Understanding of *riai* (the candidate must be able to execute *waza* and move in a way that is rational and purposeful); ⑨ *Fūkaku* and *hinkaku* (demonstrating one's own style which is dignified and elegant).

Chart 1 below may offer more concrete clues as to what is required for each grade. The higher up you get the more criteria that need to be satisfied to pass the examination.

*Yondan* and *godan* require a firmly grounded understanding of the basics (*kihon*) and also applied skills in kendo. The first three grades are usually referred to as "lower ranks". *Yondan* and *godan* are lumped together as so-called middle grades (*chūdansha*), and 6~8-dan as high grades (*kōdansha*). In this sense, the criteria for *yondan* and *godan* are clearly different from the lower ranks, but the *godan* candidate will need to show even more finesse than *yondan* for basically the same criteria. This should be a natural progression after passing the previous grade, which is why there are a set number of years required between each rank.

Correct attire and *reihō*, posture and so on are fundamental components of *shodan* gradings, so there should be no need to go into the importance of these aspects here. If you do not have a grasp of these absolute basics, then there is no way you will be ready for a *yondan* exam, or a *shodan* exam for that matter. The criteria "Skill in applied *waza*" (see Chart 1) is the first big difference to *shodan-sandan* level. In a nutshell, this means that the candidate must show that they have learned how to control the opponent through *seme*. Rather than merely striking the opponent randomly as if in an *uchikomi* session, candidates for these two ranks must demonstrate that they can also coax their opponent into making an attack, and then capitalise with more advanced techniques such as *kaeshi-waza* and *debana-waza*. Just attacking *men* every chance (or non-chance) you get will not help you pass *yondan* and *godan*. If anything, it will show that you are impatient, and unable to identify proper striking opportunities.

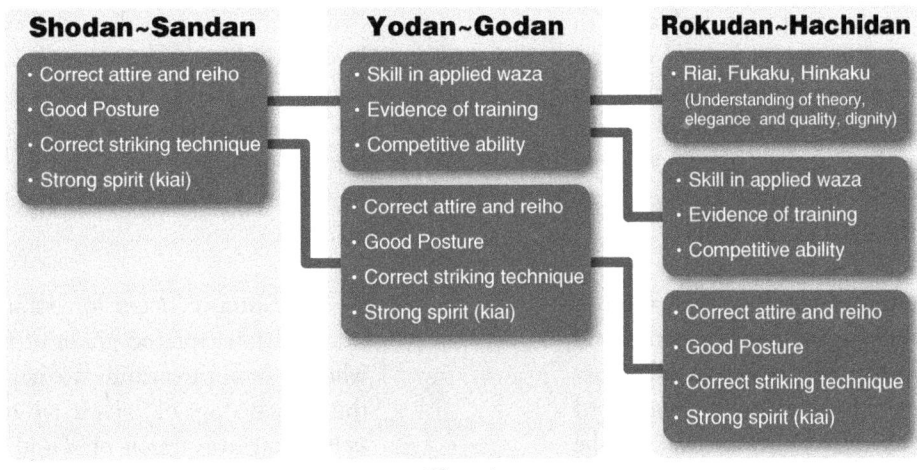

*Chart 1*

# The Great Wall of Four & Five

Of course, scoring a decent *men* is mandatory in an examination for any rank, but from *yondan* upwards it is requisite that you demonstrate the skill to apply pressure on your opponent's centre first, and strike with resolve rather than arbitrarily. A couple of these strikes made in this way will guarantee a few ticks on the examiner's mark sheet. It is important to remember, however, that *men* is not the only valid target in kendo, and a balanced approach to the targets you strike will demonstrate to examiners that you are proficient in all the basic *waza* and *ōji-waza*. Having said this, *men* should be your staple in examinations, and of course, *keiko*. Remember that if you can't do something properly in *keiko*, you will never be able to do it in an examination. If you can *seme* and strike a *men* well, other opportunities should manifest themselves for the picking.

This presents the question of how to take control in training. Here is the real secret to successfully passing your exam. It's all about attitude. Assuming you have trained hard in developing your technique, which is a given if you have been doing kendo long enough to be eligible to sit the exam, the real problem to overcome is actually believing in your skill. This will come naturally to some people, but others will have to work hard to tap into that submerged, often suppressed confidence. How do you do this? The are no easy answers, of course, but here are a couple of tips that can help you get your head in the right space in *keiko*.

First, if you are fighting your *sensei*, or somebody higher in rank, REFUSE to let them call the shots. When you are a lower grade, and your *sensei* opens up for you to strike, you usually do so without question. At the fourth and fifth *dan* level you need to be more resilient, even rebellious. You need to stand up for yourself at this stage and say, "No! I'm not hitting you because you are offering it to me. I'll hit you when I'm ready and because I earned it." Hold on and don't go. Be primed and ready to attack front-on, but wait, wait... and then hit them not when they are offering it to you, but when they are fully engaged. This may sound easy in writing, but evoking this kind of attitude is surprisingly difficult against somebody who is so much higher in rank than you. Inevitably, the engagement will end up in a round of *kakari-geiko* as it always has, but standing up to your *sensei* like a rebellious teenager standing up to his or her parents is the first step into the adult world of kendo. This is essentially what *yondan* and *godan* equate to.

The other side of the coin is your attitude towards your peers and juniors. You must remain steadfast and in control of each bout at all times. If they attack and you are not ready, do not get suckered in and strike frivolously. Keep your centre and say "No way in hell!", deflecting the strike if necessary. If you are pressured into making a reactionary strike that you did not initiate, this will fail, and look bad. Not only that, it means that you are being controlled rather than the other way around. Pressure, pressure, pressure and then strike. Or, pressure, pressure, "come on in..." and counter-strike.

In either case, you are always trying to call the shots. One thing vital for success in nurturing this kind of attitude, is to NEVER be afraid of being struck. It happens, and it HELPS you overcome the fear that is actually subduing your true confidence. Training with this mind-set will gradually emancipate your spirit, and foster true belief in yourself. Ultimately, you have to believe you already have the grade before you sit it. You have to sit the exam KNOWING that it is a mere formality. You will only be able to achieve this by training with an attitude. Remember though, there is a fine line between confidence and arrogance. Understand the difference and avoid falling into the latter.

Candidates for *yondan* and *godan* examinations must be able to show that they are able to apply effective offensive techniques and counterattacks. This requires patience, and a good understanding of your optimum striking distance (*maai*). If you are too close, the engagement will look stifled, and the techniques will either be too small, or too deep – either of which leaves a bad impression. Ideally, you should engage from *tō-ma* (distant interval) and apply pressure by edging into *issoku-ittō-no-ma*. When you do make a strike, be sure that it is made from a distance that allows you to maintain a straight balanced posture on impact. If you need to lurch forward, you are too far away, and are not striking with *ki-ken-tai-itchi*.

If you have an annoying opponent who just keeps coming at you, this is where you need to maintain your composure and overcome him or her with *ōji-waza*. It is also permissible to keep your *kensen* in the centre and let them run onto it if they are persistent in making random attacks. The point is to keep in control of yourself and your opponent, and not get drawn into a mutual *kakari-geiko* session. Show that you know how to take charge. You will not be able to achieve this under the pressure of an examination if you do not approach your regular training with the same attitude. This connects to the next point, "evidence of training".

Evidence of meaningful training is seen through the way in which you complete your strikes. Does the strike make a nice crisp sound (*sae*), or a rattling thud? The nice crisp sound is proof of appropriate strength in the striking movement – not too hard, and not too soft. Are you striking at suitable opportunities, or just haphazardly? Persistently blocking the opponent's attack without

countering is a no-no, as is having your attacks blocked. This shows that there was no opportunity to strike in the first place. This may happen one or two times during the exam which is not too much of a serious offence. However, if it is a regular occurrence, then the ticks on the examiners' mark-sheets may be replaced with crosses. Also, never, ever tussle from *tsubazeriai*. If you end up in *tsubazeriai*, you are best advised to quickly strike *hiki-men* and move back, or immediately retreat back to *issoku-ittō-no-ma* for meaningful engagement. Do not strike *hiki-dō* or *hiki-kote* as it will most likely be too weak, and look half-hearted. Avoid feeble attacks at all costs. Each attack should be made with total conviction.

Obviously, the way in which you approach an examination may be different to how you would fight in a *shiai* in this respect. In the case of a grading, you have limited time to show the level of kendo you have reached. Still, you shouldn't go into the examination without an element of competitiveness. One of the important points for the *yondan* and *godan* gradings is the interaction you have with your opponent, and how you deal with them. You need to show that you can read, control and defeat your opponent. If you are LUCKY enough to have a strong opponent in the examination, the chances are they will hit you. This is not necessarily a bad thing as a strong opponent will make you look good too, so long as you strike with well-timed conviction. It is not a *shiai*, and you will not be failed if you get struck, but you must also strike your opponent too. And, whatever you do, never block. Deflection with good *tai-sabaki* (body movement) is okay, but no blocking.

Once you have passed your two bouts, you will then have to sit the Nihon Kendo Kata test. International Kendo Federation regulations require people sitting the *sandan* examination to do all ten *kata*. In Japan, however, the *kodachi-no-kata* are only tested from *yondan*. In any case, make sure that you are able to do each *kamae* correctly (angle of blade etc.), and that you understand the concept of *irimi* for the *kodachi*. Nothing more really needs to be said here as *kata* is the same no matter where you are and who you do it with. You just need to learn it properly, preferably not out in the car park like so many people in Japan do just before the examination!

Finally, you will have to sit the written examination. A significant point here is that the nature of the questions tend to be more philosophical than earlier grades. This is because a higher understanding of the psychological and philosophical aspects of kendo is expected from *yondan* onwards. Each country or region will have its own set of questions for the written exam. The list of *yondan* and *godan* questions is published by the All Japan Kendo Federation in a useful booklet that comes with the answers as well (Japanese language only). Anybody who has been doing kendo long enough to be sitting the *yondan* and *godan* examination should be familiar with the concepts in these questions. I highly recommend that anybody at this level purchase a copy of the *Japanese-English Dictionary of Kendo* from the AJKF. It can be obtained online for 2,100 yen, and will be an invaluable resource for your understanding of kendo. The revised edition was released in 2011.

In conclusion, preparation for the examination should be the same as for any other grade: spend time reviewing your *reihō* and appearance in a mirror, practise Nihon Kendo Kata relentlessly, and study hard for the written exam (you might actually learn something new). Also, be sure to seek advice from as many people as possible about your strengths and weaknesses in training. I also find that taking a video of your *keiko* every now and again is an extremely effective way of identifying problem areas. Another important thing to remember is that the time for each bout will be quite short. In most cases it will never exceed two minutes. It is advisable to get accustomed to this length of time in your training so that you know how to pace yourself in the examination. The following bullet points are a summary of the main things to think about in the actual examination.

- Don't move in too quickly from the start.
- Don't get too close. Make sure that you strike from your optimum striking distance.
- Always have a straight posture when striking.
- No half-hearted strikes. They must be crisp and decisive, and not simply a reaction to your opponent's attacks.
- Hands and feet MUST be consolidated at this level.
- No right-handed strikes!
- Remember that getting hit does not mean a fail, but failing to hit does.
- But, it is not *kakari-geiko*! You only need to score three or four clean, crisp points in the set time.
- Include a few *ōji-waza*, especially *debana-waza*, *kaeshi-waza*, *nuki-waza* (but not too many). Balance is the key.
- As a general rule, no *hiki-waza*.
- No rushing in and striking randomly.
- Take your time and create opportunities before striking.
- Always try to maintain control and take the initiative.
- Remain unfazed if you get hit, and keep your *kensen* steady.
- Be confident. Sit the examination as if you already have the grade. It is not a lucky prize for your efforts, but affirmation of your actual skill level.

Finally, if you fail, try and try again. For whatever reason, too many people tend to give up at this level. This is a terrible shame. Believe me, kendo really starts to get interesting from here.

# AKJF 4-dan and 5-dan Examination Questions

## I. Theory
1. Write about the "Concept of Kendo" and the "Purpose of Practising Kendo".
2. Write about the requirements for improvement in kendo.
3. Write about the points to remember when engaging in *keiko* with lower grades.
4. Write about the mind-set of an instructor.
5. Write about the importance of warming up.
6. Write about the importance of cooling down.

## II. Technical
### [*Kihon*] (Basics)
1. Explain *kamae* and *metsuke*.
2. Explain the various *ashi-sabaki* and points to remember when instructing footwork.
3. Explain the objectives and benefits of *kirikaeshi* and points to remember when teaching it.
4. Explain how to receive *kirikaeshi* and points to remember when teaching it.
5. Explain *taiatari* and points to remember when teaching it.
6. Explain how to receive *taiatari* and points to remember when teaching it.
7. Explain what is correct *tsubazeriai* and points to remember when teaching it.
8. Explain *yūkō-datotsu*.

### [*Ōyō*] (Applied)
9. Explain the concepts of *seme* and *kuzushi*.

### *Shikake-waza*
10. Explain *ippon-uchi-no-waza* and points to remember when teaching them.
11. Explain *nidan* and *sandan-no-waza* (consecutive techniques) and points to remember when teaching them.
12. Explain *debana-waza* and points to remember when teaching them.
13. Explain *harai-waza* and points to remember when teaching them.
14. Explain *hiki-waza* and points to remember when teaching them.

### *Ōji-waza*
15. Explain what *ōji-waza* is and the representative techniques.
16. Explain *nuki-waza* and points to remember when teaching them.
17. Explain *suriage-waza* and points to remember when teaching them.
18. Explain *kaeshi-waza* and points to remember when teaching them.
19. Explain *uchiotoshi-waza* and points to remember when teaching them.

### [Technical Terms and Psychological Factors]
20. Explain *maai*.
21. Explain *kentai-itchi* (offence and defence combined).
22. Explain *hasuji*.
23. Explain *tenouchi*.
24. Write about the importance of *zanshin*.
25. Explain the concept of *ichigan-nisoku-santan-shiriki*.
26. Explain *kyojitsu*.
27. Explain *shikai*.
28. Explain *heijōshin*.
29. Explain *fudōshin*.

### [*Keiko-hō*]
30. Explain *uchikomi-geiko* and points to remember when teaching it.
31. Explain *kakari-geiko* and points to remember when teaching it.
32. Explain *gokaku-geiko* and points to remember when teaching it.
33. Explain *hikitate-geiko* and points to remember when teaching it.
34. Explain the meaning of *keiko*.

## III. Nihon Kendo Kata
1. Write about the importance of learning the Nihon Kendo Kata.
2. Explain correct handling of the *bokutō*.
3. Write about the important things to keep in mind when performing the Nihon Kendo Kata.

## IV. Shiai
1. Write about the mind-set of *shinpan*.
2. Explain the correct way for *shinpan* declarations and using the flags.
3. Write Article 1 (Objectives) from the *Regulations and Subsidiary Rules of Kendo Shiai and Shinpan*.

# THE NUTS 'N' BOLTS OF KENDO
By Nakano Yasoji, (Kendo Hanshi 9-dan)    Translated by Alex Bennett

# ZANSHIN AND SEN

**IT IS OFTEN SAID IN KENDO THAT ZANSHIN, OR THE CONCEPT OF CONTINUED PHYSICAL AND PSYCHOLOGICAL ALERTNESS AFTER AN ATTACK, IS IMPORTANT. HOW IMPORTANT IS IT?**

Originally it was said that chances occur when you throw it all to the wind. My teacher, Takano Sasaburō-sensei, often taught that *zanshin* was something akin to throwing water out of a cup, and when you put it down again, there is always a little bit left in the bottom. This is true *zanshin*... In the case of kendo, this state is achieved by striking with abandon (*sutemi*), and the remaining psychological and physical residue is *zanshin*. It is born through totally throwing oneself into the attack. If you think that *zanshin* is merely to turn and face the opponent after the strike, this is really only a lukewarm interpretation.

Now that competitive kendo is popular, *zanshin* is used to describe the final element in the process of scoring a point, not stepping out and such. This is why it always ends up by turning around and facing the opponent. This is also an important consideration, but *zanshin* is more than just form.

**HOW DOES ONE 'LEAVE ONE'S HEART'?**

It is best left naturally. Completely throwing yourself into a strike doesn't mean to say that you have nothing left at the end. There is a little bit of excess left from the strike which remains naturally. Hence the analogy with a cup of water. This 'leftover heart' provides the driving force for the next action if required.

**IN CONCRETE TERMS, HOW FAR SHOULD ONE RUN THROUGH AFTER THE STRIKE TO DEMONSTRATE ZANSHIN?**

In the old days when samurai actually cut each other down with real swords, they would never have showed their back to the fallen enemy. They would face their opponent at all times, even after the decisive blow, just to make sure. In this sense, there is no definite number of steps one should take after striking, but it shouldn't be too many. I would think three steps would suffice. A strike which requires conscious cantering through afterwards is not a good strike in my opinion.

**WHAT DO YOU THINK OF PEOPLE WHO DEMONSTRATE ZANSHIN BY LOWERING THEIR KENSEN OR TAKING ONE HAND OFF THE SHINAI?**

I really don't think that taking your hand off the *shinai* for *zanshin* is a good idea. Why would you do this? It just means that you have to re-grip your *shinai* if your opponent counterattacks, and this will be too slow. Kendo is a traditional sport with ancient ideals based on mortal combat. I think that you should always have your *shinai* in the prepared position ready to face the opponent at any time, with a sense of urgency.

**IF YOU ATTACK THE OPPONENT FROM THE FRONT, THEN YOU WILL INEVITABLY END UP CRASHING INTO HIM OR HER AFTER THE STRIKE. DOESN'T THIS MAKE IT DIFFICULT TO DEMONSTRATE ZANSHIN?**

All you can do is *taiatari*. If you make a straight attack and they are standing in the way, clash with them.

### WHAT ABOUT 'HIKIAGE', EXAGGERATED MOVEMENTS AFTER AN ATTACK?

This is just for show, and would never happen if fighting with serious intent. In the old *gekken-kōgyō* fencing shows that were popular towards the end of the nineteenth century, it seems that some of the fighters did flashy *hikiage* performances after striking to please the spectators. But this is not real kendo.

### DOES HITTING THE FLOOR WITH THE SHINAI AFTER STRIKING HIKI-DO MEAN THAT THERE IS NO ZANSHIN?

More than whether or not the *shinai* hits the floor after the strike is the question of posture. If it is a firm strike made from the hips, then it matters little if the *shinai* hits the floor afterwards. The real issue is to judge whether or not the strike is good or not…

### THOSE WHO FIGHT FROM JODAN WILL REGULARLY STRIKE WITH ONE HAND, AND THE POSTURE FOR ZANSHIN IS OFTEN DISRUPTED. HOW SHOULD A JODAN FIGHTER DEMONSTRATE ZANSHIN?

A *jōdan* fighter should never step back for *zanshin* after completing a strike. After striking, you should go straight inside with one hand off the *shinai* to close the gap on the opponent. If the opponent tries to strike while retreating, continue forward and strike again. Nowadays, we see some *jōdan* fighters holding on to their opponents after striking, but this should be penalised as it is not *zanshin* but simply interference. If you miss from *jōdan*, just go straight into *tsuba-zeriai*, and start looking to strike immediately. If the opponent takes the initiative, it will be difficult to strike when you want to, and it will be hard to move back and assume *jōdan* again.

### SEN

#### IT IS SAID THAT SEN, OR TAKING THE INITIATIVE, IS THE MOST IMPORTANT STRIKING OPPORTUNITY.

It is well known that there are three *sen* in kendo, called *mittsu-no-sen*. These are *sensen-no-sen*, *senzen-no-sen* (also simply known as *sen*), and *go-no-sen*.

First of all, *sensen-no-sen*. When facing an opponent, you feel their will to strike. They may be about to strike *men*, but you strike ahead of them. Just as they are about to attack, you sense their intention and strike it down before it can manifest. This is not easy to achieve, and is said to be the highest level of kendo technique. *Sensen-no-sen* is very clear in the Nippon Kendo Kata. In order to succeed, you need to be able to read your opponent's mind and body movements to know when to attack. This is very difficult, and although we aspire to reach this level in our *keiko*, it is not common.

The most common kind of technique comes from *senzen-no-sen*. When the opponent starts an attack, you strike back before it can reach fruition. If they strike *men*, you strike them instead before their technique is able to be completed. We use this *sen* a lot in *keiko* and matches.

*Go-no-sen* is when the opponent makes an attack, but you counterattack after doing *suriage* (parry) or *uke* (block), or *nuki* (avoiding) their strike.

There are many modes of thought with regards to the question of *sen*, but these are the accepted interpretations. *Sensen-no-sen* truly is sublime, and it is a wonderful achievement even if one technique in this category is executed during a match.

In the case of *go-no-sen*, this is generally a counterattack following an opponent's completed strike. However, it is sometimes not as simple as this. What say, for example, the opponent starts an attack, but then it is knocked down and countered in quick succession (bang-BANG), just like a spark off a flint? In form, it looks like *go-no-sen*, but the feeling behind the technique could well be different as the opponent is coaxed into making the attack which is rendered ineffective as it starts, and countered. In this sense, it could also be *sensen-no-sen*. If the opponent attacks and this is blocked first, then followed with a counterattack in a clearly separate movement, it is considered to be *go-no-sen*.

### DO SHIKAKE-WAZA FALL INTO THE CATEGORY OF SENZEN-NO-SEN, AND OJI-WAZA INTO GO-NO-SEN?

If you clearly block the opponent's attack and then immediately follow up with a counterattack, then this is called *go-no-sen*. If your opponent attacks and you strike them first without blocking or receiving in any way, then this is called *senzen-no-sen*. Anything with a block first is usually *go-no-sen*.

### ALL OF THE THREE SEN ARE IMPORTANT, BUT WE ARE NORMALLY ENCOURAGED TO TRY AND STRIKE WITH SENSEN-NO-SEN. THE REALITY IS THAT SENZEN-NO-SEN IS MORE COMMON.

*Senzen-no-sen* is common, but so too is *go-no-sen*. But in order for these techniques to work, you have to have the attitude of attacking with *sensen-no-sen*, i.e., always taking the initiative and trying to see through your opponent. Always try to attack with *sensen-no-sen* in the course of your daily training.

# JIDAI-GEKI AND CHAMBARA
## A Discussion with Ishimatsu Yoshihiro

by Michael Ishimatsu-Prime

*The Mikogami Trilogy* (*Mushuku-nin Mikogami no Jōkichi*) is a series of *chambara* (sword fighting) films based on the novel by Sasazawa Saho (1930–2002), and made by the Tōhō film production company between 1972 and 1973. It is comprised of *The Trail of Blood* (*Kiba wa Hikisaita*), *The Fearless Avenger* (*Kawakaze ni Kako wa Nagareta*), and *Slaughter in the Snow* (*Kōkon ni Senkō ga Tonda*), and stars the recently deceased Harada Yoshio (1940–2011). He plays Jōkichi of Mikogami, a drifter and hired sword who, attempting to go straight, gets married, has a son, and starts work as a craftsman. However, when his wife and son are murdered by gangsters whom he had encountered earlier, he sets out for revenge. These films are a wonderful example of 1970s Japanese *chambara* cinema, but they are also significant to me personally. The screenplay for *The Trail of Blood* was written by my father-in-law, Ishimatsu Yoshihiro, and *The Fearless Avenger* was co-written by him and my wife's uncle, Ikehiro Kazuo, who directed the trilogy, and is one of Japan's foremost directors of *chambara* films.

Ishimatsu Yoshihiro is the eldest of six children and was born in Fukuoka Prefecture, on the southern Japanese island of Kyushu in 1932. His high school years coincided with World War II, during which it was

compulsory for him to practise kendo and judo. Upon graduating high school, he attended the prestigious Tokyo Imperial University (Tokyo University) where he studied literature. After graduation he went to work as a screenwriter at Daiei. In 1971 when they went into bankruptcy, Ishimatsu-san became a freelance writer, a job he still does and loves even at the age of 79. He has written for some of the great directors of Japanese cinema including the aforementioned Ikehiro Kazuo, as well as Fukusaku Kinji (1930–2003) and Masumura Yasuzo (1924–1986), with whom he co-wrote *A Certain Killer* (*Aru Koroshiya*, 1967) which starred Ichikawa Raizō (1931–1969), one of Japan's greatest *chambara* actors. He also wrote *Black Test Car* (*Kuro Tesuto Kaa*, 1962) which was directed by Masumura Yasuzo. In a career spanning more than 50 years, Ishimatsu-san has to date penned around 50 films, over 700 hours of TV programs, and a guide to *kabuki*. Included in this vast body of work is some that falls into the category of *jidai-geki* (period dramas) and *chambara*. Furthermore, under the pen name of Munakata Shō, Ishimatsu-san has also written three *jidai-geki* novels: *Sōshin*, *Sengoku Aruki Miko*, and *Ōnogunemon* – a story related to the 47 Rōnin.

One Sunday evening in October, 2011, when my wife and I visited her parents for dinner, I asked Ishimatsu-san about writing *jidai-geki* and *chambara* films, TV, and books.

\* \* \* \* \*

**MIP** *Is there a particular period of Japanese history that you find interesting to write about?*

**IY** – At the present time I am writing a novel set in the Edo period (1600–1868), but in the past I have written about the time from the Bakumatsu period [the end of the Edo period, usually referring to the time from in which Commodore Perry opened Japan in 1853] to the Meiji period (1868-1912). My interest now is in the Edo period and that can be divided into a few different times. For example, at the start of the Tokugawa Bakufu (the Tokugawa military government) from Ieyasu, the first shogun, to Iemitsu, the third shogun, things looked settled and stable, but they actually weren't. It still had the feel of the Sengoku period [the period of constant civil war from the mid-1400s to the start of the Edo period]. I like to write about that time and atmosphere.

Another era of the Edo period that is interesting is the Genroku era (1688–1704). This was after the third shogun and was a period of real peace. There was no conflict and it was a time when the arts and culture started to flourish – for example theatre and *kabuki*. I write human drama about people who were involved in the arts at that time. Also, because it was so peaceful, the samurai didn't have much to do. Before that, warriors were influential because of the chaos and fighting. However, in the Genroku era, the people who had money became powerful. While the samurai were still at the top of the *shi-nō-kō-shō* [samurai-farmer-artisan-merchant] strata, it was the merchants who had the money and power that came with it. It was a great time for artists and business people but for the samurai, they were left alone. They had a job that didn't really mean much – all they had was their pride. They were frustrated in these times of peace. I also write about people in this period and situation, as there is drama in that gap – the difference between samurai and the others – and it's what I'm writing about in a novel now.

**MIP** *Is there a thematic difference between writing about, for example, the Edo period and the Sengoku period?*

**IY** – For me, the themes and the characters stay the same, but the situation and story are completely different, as well as the point of view from which the story is told. The Edo period was a time of peace, but in the Sengoku period there were many who lived and thrived because of their strength of arms. In the Edo period though, it was not just about having power. Humanity was important. In peaceful times there may have been an undercurrent of fear and people having ulterior motives, but the Sengoku period was not like this. There were many strong samurai, and they would cut down their opponents in any way that they could – it was about winning in battle. It was a harsh but simple time.

**MIP** *What is difficult about writing jidai-geki?*

**IY** – With regards to film and TV, it's the audience – they are made for people to come and watch. These films and TV programs need to have value to the people who watch them. They have to be something that ordinary people are interested in. This is very important. Also, for TV, the viewing figures are important, and for films, how many people come to the cinema. Commercial viability is always the main issue. What I really want to write, and what could be a hit film are sometimes very different. They are made for different audiences, and this can be a restriction while writing. It needs to be popular, or might need to be watched by a particular target group. The producers might choose to use a popular actor or singer, or even decide on how the story proceeds. This is all because of the ratings it receives – in the end its success is judged by numbers.

***MIP** How do you choose the topics to write about?*

**IY** – Of course, writing films is very difficult if I have no empathy with the main character or hero, and even the villain, especially as I may have to spend up to six months writing about them. Having empathy for the characters is the most important thing. This is also the same for modern day dramas, but it is especially so for *jidai* films, as nobody really knows what those types of people were like back then. In contrast, in films about modern times the characters are easily understood by viewers.

***MIP** What does your writing process involve?*

**IY** – There are two patterns. First somebody asks me to write about something or someone. I still need to be interested in the topic to take it on. The second is that I find a character I'm interested in and want to write about. It's not a time or an event that I start with, but always a human being.

I spend a lot of time researching the period in which the character lived. Buying history books costs a lot of money, as you can see from the huge collection I have. [His study actually resembles a library]. I also look into specific historical events that may be of interest. This is the time consuming part.

When I have the character and the time period decided, I then create the story – I spin a fictional narrative around them. You can't change history, but you can change the way in which you look at something. Through looking at an event through the experiences of the character, you can make many different stories without changing the facts.

When I write about recent times, everybody knows about the current circumstances and situation, and there are restrictions because of that. When I write about events set way back in history, I have more freedom of expression. Some aspects need to be historically accurate, but apart from those, I am free to create and put my own spin on things.

***MIP** Daily customs now are very different to those of the Edo period or before. How do you make sure that people behave in the correct way in your stories?*

**IY** – Once I have decided the theme, I go to the library and check through many different materials, resources, and books. I also look through original documents from the time I intend to write about. After doing my research, I work out an angle for the story. If you just write things as they were, it's not a drama – it would just be history. I try and make an interesting story from various historical elements. The result is fiction, but with a firm historical basis.

***MIP** With film and TV, how do you write a fight sequence? Are they generally left to the director, or do you have a lot of input?*

**IY** – The director usually decides how the scenes play out for films. I do study about *kenjutsu* to get information about the techniques – I'm reading a book now about Yagyū Shinkage-ryū, so I have a rudimentary understanding of the basics. For example, if the swordsman in question is from the Yagyū Shinkage-ryū, I know that they hold the sword in a certain way. I don't go into too much detail but write that he's standing in such-and-such a *kamae*, and I am aware of the idiosyncrasies of the schools. When it comes to the actual fight, the *tateshi* (the sword fighting choreographer) and director consult with each other about the scene, and then start filming it. They tend to choose actors who are usually skilled in kendo or other sword arts. There are skilled *chambara* actors who are very famous, such as Konoe Jushirō (1914-1977), who was a friend of mine. He is the father of Matsukata Hiroki (b. 1942), who himself is a famous actor and appeared in *13 Assassins* (2010, dir. Miike Takashi). The success of a fight scene is in great part due to the actor's adeptness in using the sword.

***MIP** What is the situation with jidai-geki films and TV programs now?*

**IY** – TV programs cost a lot of money to produce, and recently there haven't been many *jidai-geki* made. *Mitō Komon* was on for many years, but that has now finished. Sometimes on Fuji TV they make specials of *Onihei Hankachō* – maybe a one-hour special like a film.

There are still quite a few samurai films being made, but there are a few problems surrounding the genre nowadays. In the past, there were different styles of *jidai-geki* movies, and lots of people who specialised in making them. Now there aren't so many being made, even if a top writer and director come together to collaborate on a project. The problem is that expert staff who are able to make these types of films are getting fewer, and it costs an awful lot to produce. Still, there have been a few high quality productions recently such as *Ichime* (2011, dir. Miike Takashi), *13 Assassins*, and *Saigo-no-Chushingura* (2010, Dir. Sugita Shigemichi). These movies are well worth seeing. *Jidai-geki* are still relatively popular with viewers, but the problem is finding the money and the staff for production.

Ishimatsu Yoshihiro, 79, writer of *jidai-geki* and *chambara* films, TV and novels, talks to Kendo World writer Michael Ishimatsu-Prime in his study at home in Kawasaki. He has written for Fukusaku Kinji and Masumura Yasuzo.

**MIP  Finally, please explain what the Chambarist Club is?**

**IY –** The main person in the Chambarist Club is Nagata Kazuo, the number one literary critic of *jidai-geki* novels in Japan. He is young, but very well-known. The Chambarist Club is for people who like samurai movies. We are basically *otaku* (geeks) – old age *otaku*! We meet once or twice a month in Shinjuku and Sangenjaya, or other places where we can show videos, and watch *chambara* films, not TV programs. About 20-30 people regularly attend the club meetings, but there are about 60 members in total. Many of them are collectors of films and posters, and other memorabilia that are very expensive these days. They bring them to the meetings to show the other members.

\* \* \* \* \*

Before I finished speaking to Ishimatsu-san, he gave me a few details of the novel that he is writing at the moment which will probably be of interest to the readers of *Kendo World*. It is a fictional story centred on Yagyū Munenori's son Jūbei, the strongest adept of the Shinkage-ryū who works as a page for Tokugawa Iemitsu. The other protagonist is a female martial artist who guards one of the shogun's concubines, and whose speciality is using a *kodachi*. Without wishing to give too much away, they are working together to fight against the *ninja* of Iga who were used as guards throughout Edo castle. This is a good example of what Ishimatsu-san mentioned earlier – he has taken real people, situations and history, and created an interesting story around it. Ishimatsu-san is having trouble writing the final climactic scene, but it should be ready for publication in 2012.

I would like to thank Ishimatsu Yoshihiro for taking the time to talk about his work, and to Chie, his daughter (my wife), for her assistance.

# NONSENSE AND ORIGINS:

## An Inspiring Conversation with Victor Harris

By Scott Huegel

Speaking with Victor Harris brings you face to face with modern era kendo. It is not that he positions himself this way, or by any measure wants to be a spokesperson, but when discussing kendo he has an undeniable skill for communicating a clear representation of where he believes things have been, where they are now, and where they should be going.

Whether we want to admit it readily or not, the kendo of today is in a strange place. It exists with its roots in tradition, and yet is evolving in a modern world which bears little semblance to the time of its creation. Even within the last fifty years, change throughout the globe has been more dramatic than the hundreds of years preceding this time. As this type of change leaves its mark on everything, kendo is no exception and change imprints its influence accordingly.

It is difficult to argue that the kendo we practise now is having an easy time applying itself to the traditional precepts that it was based upon. As it grows in popularity, it also grows in its regulations, associations, and rules. This is a natural path for any martial art that has existed for hundreds of years; however the basics, *kihon*, can sometimes be momentarily lost along the way.

Certainly, we as *kendōka* try our best to remember and apply the basics of kendo and the philosophical side to our practice. It is generally agreed that kendo exists outside the realms of normal sport, however most of us no longer live in a world where we can train in kendo all day and everyday. We live and work in busy societies, and the fact that we create time to study kendo in the first place is testament to our commitment. In short, we are very busy people

and it is easy to forget the basics, the *kihon* on which kendo is founded. Of course, we all have moments of clear realisation in regards to the truth of kendo, and do our best to hold onto these moments so they resonate throughout our training, but they can become muddied more than we would like.

You might be thinking "Where is he going with this?" "Isn't this supposed to be about Victor Harris?" This is the only way I can begin this article as it ties in with what his life, and his beliefs, represent.

He is the man most renowned for his translation of Musashi's *Gorin-no-sho*. It has become staple reading for *kendōka*, and Harris' translation of this work has proved to be the most widely read. There have been statements from others saying that particular inclusions or translations in Harris' work are misinterpreted or even incorrect, but he does not hold his translation as some kind of sacred cow. If you approach Harris with any kind of reverence about what a fine job he has done with translating such a delicate work, he remains modest and honest about the origins of his desire to undertake the task in the first place.

"I put the *Gorin-no-sho* into English so that I could read it more easily", he states simply.

Simplicity is a good adjective when it comes to Harris' approach to kendo. Indeed, he is uncomfortable in an interview situation as he does not want to be portrayed as a purveyor of truth, or that he has done something quite incredible by introducing the English speaking world to Musashi. Although what he has done is incredible and has opened the thoughts of Musashi to thousands of readers, he is more concerned with the work itself and what Musashi has written in it. While some authors or translators would rest on their laurels and enjoy the acclaim and attention they receive by what they have done, Harris will not be distracted in getting to the point of what is important. Musashi's work is important. Kendo is important.

"Everything in Musashi's book is true", he says. "Let go of the nonsense, and go to the origins."

Nonsense and origins. Two factors that figured prominently in our discussion.

The origin for Victor Harris' inspiration goes back at least to 1953. He was at school then, and remembers going through Victorian-era travel books found in the library. He came across one that detailed a journey through Japan and it struck him as exotic and enticing. "It cut through the khaki-clad existence of London at that time", he jokes. It did resonate with him though, as it has done with many *kendōka*, this undeniable attraction of a first exposure to Japan. Words led to action and he then began judo, and through this began reading Suzuki Daisetzu's writings. It was Daisetzu's Zen readings that brought him to Musashi as it describes him as "an invincible swordsman".

Harris eventually began practising kendo at the Nenriki Dojo in London. It continues today as one of the oldest dojos in Britain, but it was not until he reached Japan that Victor Harris earnestly began his study of kendo and Musashi.

While in Japan, he taught English, honed his Japanese language skills, and trained hard in the art of kendo. Miyamoto Musashi's work was known to him, and after three years of residency in Japan he returned to Britain where he began working as a translator for engineering firms dealing with Japanese businesses. This was in the early seventies, so work was plentiful, but his eye was on Musashi.

Harris has already stated that he was not particularly interested in the idea of translating Musashi's book

as a kind of scholarly endeavour. He merely wanted it in English so that he could read it. It took him a year to do so, and upon finishing, coincidence led to its publication.

When Harris returned to London and to the Nenriki Dojo to carry on with his kendo, he met a fellow club member who happened to work for a publisher. Almost organically, the *Gorin-no-sho* left behind its native language roots indecipherable to most and was released to the English-speaking world. Within a year, the book was published.

Now working as the Head Curator for the British Museum's Japanese Antiquities Department, he has acquired eminence in his field through both his work and his translations, but Harris is quick to brush all of these details of his own history aside. Many times throughout the interview he wants to move the focus from himself to Musashi and kendo. This is clear even when training, as Harris does not spend time on lengthy explanations of techniques. He leads by action and places emphasis on the basics. Throughout practice he returns back to the foundations; cutting, left arm, and *tenouchi*. Watching him practise, you are aware that he is truly putting his beliefs into action and constantly works on applying Musashi's ideas to his own kendo.

I was interested in hearing what Harris would have to say when I asked how Musashi would view modern kendo. Upon hearing the question he thought for a few moments, but ultimately concluded that it is an impossible question to answer. Not because it is a question without merit, but one that transcends our own conscious thought.

"You're talking about an enlightened man", he answers. "Everything in Musashi's book is true and was written by an individual with a very different state of mind than mine."

Following this interview, I felt the need to re-read the *Gorin-no-sho* and it is easier to appreciate where Harris is coming from in this regard. Prior to the interview, I had not read anything from the work for a few years, and I realised that it is not something to read once. It is a book to be used as a constant reference. The writings seem to grow with one's own kendo. Concepts that were vague or unclear a few years ago seem to make more sense now. It comes only through practice, and practice is key to Musashi.

It is also clear that what you read has been produced by a person who has mastered his art. In some cases Musashi goes into great detail about specific techniques such as "The Five Approaches", "The Abdomen Timing of Two", etc. However, many of these techniques end on the note that the reader "must train hard to understand it", or "you must research this well". When reading the *Gorin-no-sho*, it becomes apparent that the ground rules are there, but can only be truly understood when put into practice over and over. It is this practice that led Musashi to his enlightenment, to his state of realisation.

This idea of enlightenment finds difficulty in positioning itself in today's world. It is made even more so in kendo as the basis of the art is less on words and more on action. When the concept of an enlightened person enters a conversation, most people shift uncomfortably. At times it seems an outdated idea, but Harris believes strongly in Musashi's enlightenment, and feels that "the enlightened being" is still valid in kendo today. It is refreshing to hear, and a good reminder of all that is appealing about kendo. In short, he feels that we all certainly can understand and put into practice Musashi's ideas, and is convinced that eventually modern day kendo will produce another figure like Miyamoto Musashi.

"One will appear again", he says with no trace of doubt. "Like a shining star in the sky."

REI
DAN
THE GREATER MEANING OF
KENDO
JI
CHI

REIDAN-JICHI PART 12

# KIHON DŌSA

By Prof. Ōya Minoru (Kendo Kyōshi 7-dan)
International Budo University

Translated by Alex Bennett

## 1. Clarifying Fundamental Movements (*kihon-dōsa*)

*Kihon-dōsa*, or basic movements, refers to *kamae*, footwork, and manipulation of the *shinai*. In other words, it entails all of the principles behind the striking and thrusting movements for scoring *yūkō-datotsu* (valid attacks) in kendo. From the *seme-ai*, or the mutual probing stage, even when the optimum opportunity is seized, if the preceding movements are not satisfactory, or the *hasuji* is incorrect, it will be impossible to score a valid point.

When somebody has reached an impasse in their training, they are often advised to "go back to basics!" If there are any defects in the way you execute the basics in kendo, this will hinder overall technical improvement. *Kihon-dōsa* is not only connected with *kihon*, but must be applied to interaction with an opponent. In other words, if all of the movements are broken down in the process of training, and practised independently, it will be difficult to know how to apply them in the midst of an engagement with the opponent. *Kihon-dōsa* should be practised as a unified whole, taking care to check the components while repeating continuously. The content should be broadened step by step, and the quality improved incrementally.

## 2. Chūdan-no-kamae

When assuming *chūdan-no-kamae*, the kendoist must be ready to move from *seme* (probing or applying pressure) to *waza* (executing a technique). Technically speaking, this means that the way the left hand grips the *shinai* in the *kamae* is paramount, as is the posture and physical readiness to instantaneously leap into action with the *shinai* and body in unison as soon as a striking opportunity manifests. With this point in mind, this article will analyse the various technical factors and correct form of *chūdan* as well as internal senses.

### 2a. Readying the Feet

*i. The Left and Right Feet, and Centre of Gravity*
The positioning of the feet and location of the centre of gravity is an essential consideration in order to be able to move freely in *chūdan*. The best foot positioning for easy movement is when the toes of the left foot are separated from the heel of the right foot by approximately 10cm behind, and to the left. Both feet should be parallel. The centre of gravity should be situated in the middle of the space between the two feet.

The position of your centre of gravity will change with movement. Movement is initiated by a change

in the position of the centre of gravity. If the distance between the feet is narrow, the stance will be unstable, and conversely too settled and difficult to move in an instant if the space is wide.

It is easy to get the mistaken impression that a wider stance is conducive to more explosive movement. In actuality, it just makes you more fixed in that position, and unable to move freely. On the other hand, a narrower stance gives one the feeling of instability both in body and mind. This feeling is alleviated by "forging the gut". It is hard to move if the feet are too wide, and difficult to fight if they are too unstable. It is important to develop an internal sense where stability and instability in the feet coexist and work together. It is a matter of finding the perfect balance between the two.

### ii. The Left Foot

The muscles around the ball of the left foot should be firmly planted on the ground. The left ankle should also be taut, the heel slightly twisted inwards, with the arch of the foot stretched. This will induce slight tension in the hamstring, the hips will be pushed forward, and tenseness in the lower abdomen will result providing stability. If the heel is too high, tension will dissipate from the hamstring and the kick off will be weak. This will prevent effortless movement in the desired direction, meaning the body will open up during the process of striking. As a result, the left foot will fly up at the back as the strike is made, or the right side of the body will lurch around making the *hasuji* (trajectory of the blade) of the strike incorrect.

If the heel is planted firmly on the floor, it will be difficult to move quickly. The left heel, left hamstring, hips, *seika-tanden* (abdominal region), neck, and chin are all connected, and if any one of them is not arranged or primed properly, it will have an adverse effect on the other parts of the body. The *seika-tanden* refers to the region just below the navel where bodily energy collects. It controls body movements and emotion.

### iii. The Right Foot

It is difficult to move when your centre of gravity is too far forward and your weight is on your front (right) foot. When you do need to lunge forward to attack, it will be like trying to uproot a post out of the ground first. Your movement will consequently be slow and clumsy. Your right heel should be slightly elevated as if it is floating above the floor. This will enable smooth, rapid movement. Furthermore, the right foot is the main player in the process of *seme*, and is also the foot that "decides the strike". Namely, when applying pressure on the opponent and probing for openings, the right foot slides across the floor, adjusting the *maai*, and suddenly transforms into the stamping foot as soon as a striking opportunity appears.

*Using the Right Foot*

Adjust the *maai* while probing ("*seme* foot")
↓
Stamp (*fumikomi*) when a striking opportunity appears ("strike-deciding foot")

If the opponent steps back when you apply *seme* with the right foot, immediately bring the left foot up behind the right. This means that you have advanced a step. The way in which the right foot is poised in *chūdan* is crucial in the process from *seme* to execution of the strike.

## 2b. Priming the Lower Limbs

The left hamstring should not be too tense, nor should it be too relaxed. This way, you will be able to move without hesitation when necessary. As the right foot

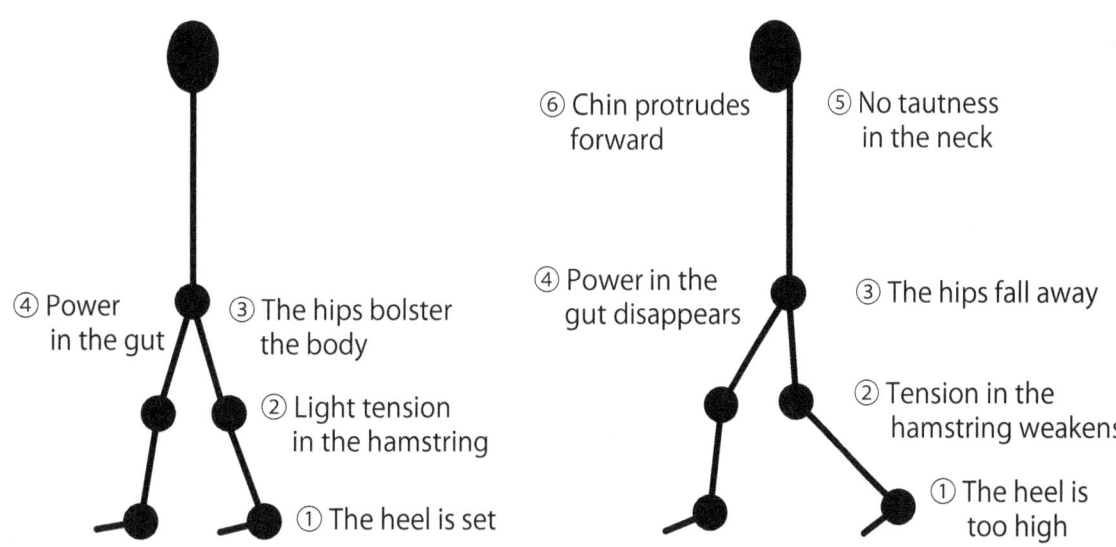

is the "*seme* foot", the right knee should be lightly stretched and ready to move swiftly into action. There is a teaching to "encase the scrotum with the inner thigh" (*fuguri wo uchimata de tsutsumikomu*). This means making sure the lower body and hips are steady and primed, with the toes and knees pointing in the right direction.

## 2c. Preparing the Torso
### i. The Buttocks and Lower back
The lower back or waist is situated in the centre of the body and serves as the platform for the upper body. A settled lower back region ensures that the upper body is also steady. Another teaching suggests that one should "tighten one's anus". This is achieved by squeezing the hollow between the right and left buttocks towards the pubis so that the pelvis lifts up, and the lower back becomes secure. A suitable amount of tension will manifest in the left leg by doing this. The lower back and the *seika-tanden* are inextricably linked; so the *seika-tanden* will also become replete if there is pressure centred in the lower-back. Have the feeling of pushing the hips forward, and the *seika-tanden* will become replete through tensing the abdominal cavity.

The quickest way to understand the above explanations is to bring your feet together and lift both heels off the ground as high as you can. Your lower back region will then become tense and the lower abdomen firm. Keeping the tenseness in the midriff area, slowly lower the heels down to the ground, then step out with the right foot. This will prepare the torso for a strong and settled *kamae*.

### ii. Armpit, Back, Chest, and Shoulders
Your armpits should be lightly closed, your back straight, and your shoulders should not be raised, as this will impede your breathing. Also, by lightly closing your armpits, the muscles in the lower side of your arms and elbows will be readied, and your *seika-tanden* will become sated with your energy and breath. You do not need to make yourself taller. By setting your hips, closing your armpits slightly, and opening your chest, your back will straighten up as a matter of course. If you try and straighten your back only when you do *keiko*, this will feel unnatural and hamper your movements. A straight posture is a matter which should be considered both in kendo and in the course of your everyday life. Both should overlap.

If your shoulders are raised, this means that you will not be able to breathe from the *tanden*. If your shoulders are tense, this will prevent the flow of *ki* and respiration into the lower-abdominal area. It used to be said that yakuza fought by squaring off at the shoulders, but samurai fought with their stomachs. Also, puffing the chest out unnaturally (external pressure) will encumber proper respiration. If your hips are set, your armpits are closed, your back is straight, and shoulders down, your chest will open up naturally. Breathing will be made easier when the internal pressure is greater than the external pressure applied to make your body unnaturally big.

## 2d. Suspending the Head
### i. The Neck and Chin
Straighten your neck and pull it slightly to the rear. This will have the effect of pulling your chin in and stably resting your head right on top of the spine. As a useful indicator, a line should appear in the skin between the chin and throat. The relationship between the neck and the head is like the two sides of a coin, and is vital in the maintenance of a rational posture in the *kamae*

| Distribution of Strength | Striking movement → | Even distribution in the left and right hands |
| --- | --- | --- |
| | Internal sensation → | *Ki* is concentrated in the *seika-tanden* and the opponent is pressurised with the left hand |

and while making an attack. If your chin sticks out, this ruins your posture and opens the trachea up so that a large amount of air is breathed in instantly, but the tension in the *seika-tanden* dissipates as a result.

### ii. Lips and Tongue

If your lips are tightly shut, it will be difficult to breathe properly. Conversely, if your mouth is wide open, you will inevitably take in too much air in one breath. When exhaling, be sure to have your mouth lightly closed, but not shut. Also, pressing your tongue against the inside-top gum will close the oral cavity causing you to breathe out through your nose. This is incorrect. Attaching the tip of your tongue to the bottom gum, slightly widening your mouth to each side and exhaling in a thin drawn out manner will enable your exhalation from your mouth to last longer. The longer you can extend your exhalation the better. "When you breathe in, this is '*kyo*' (falsehood)"; i.e., you will be unable to move when inhaling. "When you breathe out, this is '*jitsu*' (truth)"; in other words, this is when you are in your strongest, most replete state. The lips and tongue dictate the way in which you are able to breathe, and are an important aspect to learning correct respiratory method in kendo.

## 2e. Preparing the Arms

### i. Gripping the Shinai

The little finger of the left hand should fully grip the *tsuka-gashira* (bottom of the *shinai* handle). The *tsuka* is firmly (but not too powerfully) clasped in the order of the little finger, ring finger, and the middle finger as if holding onto an egg. The forefinger and thumb grip the *tsuka* lightly. Too much strength in the forefinger and thumb will make the arms tense, and it will be difficult to generate smooth *waza* with *sae* (crispness or decisiveness). Pointing the thumb towards the middle finger will relax the muscles on the upper side of your arm. Furthermore, the bottom knuckle of the thumb is positioned just in front of the navel, one fist out from the body, and turned gently in and down. The right hand grips the *shinai* near the *tsuba* in the same way as the left.

The *shinai* should always be clutched from above. The intersection point of the 'V' between the forefinger and thumb of both hands is in line with the *tsuru* of the *shinai* and the seam in the leather of the *tsuka*. Gripping the *shinai* from the side will result in discord between the elbows, wrists, and *tenouchi* (grip). This in turn will hinder the execution of effortless striking, cause erratic *kensen* movement, and incorrect *hasuji* (direction of the blade). This means that the strike will not be completed with correct *tenouchi*, and will be inaccurate.

### ii. Distribution of Power in the Hands

The distribution of power in the right and left hands when in *kamae* influences the start and finish of the strike. The right hand is auxiliary, and controls the direction of the *shinai*. If there is too much power in the right hand, it will obstruct the striking process, and result in a large obvious movement (*okori*) as the attack is started. If the right hand is dominant, your posture will deteriorate, and the *shinai* will not be able to be manipulated properly, resulting in inadequate striking technique. The strength is distributed evenly in the left and right hands, and there should be an internal sensation of *ki* focussed in the *seika-tanden*. The left hand is used to direct pressure on the opponent.

### iii. Wrists, Elbows, Chest

The wrists join the backs of the hands with the forearms. The way in which the wrists are used influences all aspects of the strike from start to finish. When too much power is put in the wrists to the extent that a crease in the skin appears, the *kensen* will be too high and ineffectual, and the strikes will become rigid. The wrists and back of the hands should be smooth with no crimp in the middle. Close the armpits gently, relax the shoulders, remove excess power in the wrists and elbows so that they lightly touch the side of the body, and the muscles in the top side of the arms are relaxed and ready. Make the chest area (space between the arms) expansive, as if holding on to a globe. Take care not to stick your elbows out as your strikes will become stiff. Even though you are holding the *shinai* with the hands, try and develop the sense that you are actually holding it with the elbows; then take it to the next step, and feel as if you are holding the *shinai* with your torso i.e., your stomach and hips.

There is much to the seemingly simple middle stance of *chūdan*. It provides the foundation for all of the movements and techniques in kendo, and all serious practitioners must study it well.

# Kendo That Cultivates People

by Sumi Masatake (Hanshi 8-dan)
Translated by Honda Sōtarō

## Part 11
## Further Development

Previously I have outlined the attitude that practitioners who are approaching higher levels of training need to have in their *keiko*. In this instalment I will introduce what is required of kendo practitioners to maximise results at this stage and consider how to advance to higher levels both through encounters with others, and through training by oneself.

### Keiko is an interaction of personalities

*Keiko* begins with the formality of *rei* containing the message 'o-negai-shimasu' through drawing the *shinai* (*battō*) and *sonkyo* even if we do not voice the actual words. The mental pressure that practitioners feel during these moments facing each other connects with the feeling of satisfaction in having done one's best after the practice is over. Somebody who has not practised a martial art will most likely overlook this significance.

After exchanging *waza* with your partner in *keiko*, performing *sonkyo*, *nōtō* and then exchanging *rei*, form the habit of asking yourself, "How do I feel?" You may have practised *kakari-no-keiko*, *hikitate-geiko* or *gokaku-geiko*, so your feelings should be different after each session. I mentioned in the previous instalment that the degree to which you have learned to control your mind and develop your *ki* is evident in the manner in which you strike, and your reaction when you are struck by your opponent. Reflection on your power of will and decision making abilities in *keiko* and *shiai* will reveal to you the state of your mind. Likewise, we are also able to glean a measure of the inner state of our opponent. Insights into ourselves and our emotions come to the fore along with our will power, and take form through our physical actions. From this we can surmise that kendo is a kind of personality-interplay and that reflecting on our performances allows us to refine our own personality and know more about the personalities of our opponents.

Do you feel tired but content after *keiko*? Even after a hard *keiko* session which leaves you tired and breathless, do you feel a sense of fulfilment? If you finish feeling mentally flat, irritated or disappointed, then perhaps the *keiko* between you and your opponents was meaningless and contained nothing but acts of random and pointless hitting. *Keiko* loses its value if participants strike and thrust thoughtlessly, move further away than necessary without *zanshin*, perform nasty *mukae-zuki* or overtly show off in their striking. Most importantly, we must not lose control of ourselves or our emotions. In the midst of *keiko* we may receive a hard strike that hurts us even through our *bōgu*, or we may be hit in an uncovered area. Even under these circumstances we must control the feelings which arise in us, and face our opponent calmly if we wish to cultivate ourselves. Taking rash action based on sudden rushes of emotion seems to have become a norm in modern society but this must not occur in *keiko*. If these emotions present themselves, then this should be taken as an opportunity for post-*keiko* reflection. Do not look for the causes of this contention in your opponent's behaviour, but rather cultivate your self-control so that you are not provoked by their behaviour. You should also consider if there is something in your own actions that is causing your opponent to act that way. Even if both practitioners practise physically hard kendo and crash into one another with strong *tai-atari*, there should be

# Kendo That Cultivates People

no hard feelings if both sides are seriously pursuing proper kendo.

Simply landing your strike is not the main objective of kendo, so do not fall into the trap of obsessing over scoring points. Another mistake is to train in techniques at the expense of mental development, as your techniques are largely a reflection of your state of mind. Kendo is not about dominating your opponent and stifling their personality; if you have a true desire to improve yourself by learning from your seniors, then people will want to practise with you again, and you will not be avoided as an overly-aggressive or excessively competitive practitioner.

### A practitioner develops through contributing to their organisation

Every practitioner trains as a member of some kind of organisation. Most practitioners in Japan belong to the All Japan Kendo Federation and this membership brings with it certain types of responsibilities; basically it is hoped that members will uphold the ideals and traditions of kendo and apply them in their day-to-day lives. What you are now is a result of the efforts of the people who taught and supported you when you were young in school, sporting clubs and other institutions. These cultural connections are intangible, rather like the growth that a young plant is able to achieve from water taken in by its roots in the ground. We must not forget the contribution that these people have made in our lives. Hopefully you can look back on your training with a sense of gratitude to those individuals.

An important part of your own development is being active in supporting the development of others, for example, being involved in the management of a kendo club or federation will provide you with many opportunities for personal growth. In doing so, you demonstrate the skills that you have acquired from your seniors and teachers and have the opportunity to pass them on to your juniors and the next generation. You should gratefully serve as *motodachi* and participate in club events on a voluntary basis, working for the development of your organisation and of kendo in general. When you are in the dojo or participating in events, it is beneficial if you can work with people whose ages, lives, jobs and realities are different from yours as this kind of interaction is character-building. Making these kinds of efforts demonstrates your dedication in passing kendo onto the next generation, and contributes to the benefit of your community at large.

Another area where caution should be exercised is in consideration of ranks and titles. A particular *kyū* or *dan* grade may give you a general idea of the level at which a person's skills lie, however it is in no way indicative of them as a person. You must not speak or behave arrogantly simply because you have a high grade or people address you as 'Sensei'. We must maintain good relationships with other practitioners regardless of grade as we are all travelling the same path. Modesty is important, and so is decorum when dealing with those who do not practise kendo; we should always strive to promote kendo in a positive way so that kendo organisations can be an accepted part of society. *Kyū* and *dan* grades and *shōgō* titles provide proof of your training but they do not equate with you being a good person. Ranks and titles, as well as winning and losing, are temporary and superficial things; they should not be the focus of your training. As members of society we should deal with others in a modest manner befitting of our status, and make efforts to develop our organisation by giving willingly of ourselves regardless of our experiences or position.

When involved in a kendo organisation for an extended period of time, practitioners will generally serve in various roles at events. This may include being an official, a manager, or a referee at competitions, or even being a judge on a grading examination panel. In these positions they must pass various kinds of judgements and manage both the competitors and visiting spectators. To execute these duties proficiently, the individual must decide what kind of attitudes they wish to impart to the competitors and spectators. The individual's attitudes, speech and behaviour will shape the way in which kendo is passed on to the next generation. One must remain unbiased and completely fair in judging competitions and gradings. The results of one's decisions will directly affect the competitors' and examinees' views of kendo and impact upon the future direction of their training. To be effective referees and judges, senior practitioners must base their own training in alignment with the correct principles of kendo, allowing them to make proper judgements and manage competitions and gradings smoothly. In courts of law, careful verdicts must be passed by the jury in a dignified manner; likewise in kendo we should also consider our decisions carefully and maintain an air of dignity. Making immediate judgements about competitors' and examinees' strikes requires a high level of self-confidence, something which must be acquired through continual training and study. Naturally, being given an opportunity to referee or judge is a valuable learning experience in itself. An individual

will also not make a good referee or judge if they are overconfident in their own abilities or are stubborn in their own decisions. They will fall short of attaining all of the traits that kendo offers. I occasionally witness referees and grading panellists interacting with other officials in a condescending manner, and I believe such behaviour should not be tolerated. Everyone involved in the running of these events is connected to kendo in some way, and is therefore travelling the same path. We must all learn to respect each other's positions; ranks or titles should never dictate how we interact with others.

### Senior kendo practitioners should regard themselves as 'educators'

Kendo is a path of self-cultivation and in the course of one's training, a practitioner will have experienced various teaching methods. Later on, when they go on to teach kendo to others, they will be able to fall back on this methodology. In Japan it is not necessary to have a sport trainer's certificate to teach sport or budo. However, the majority of organisations study and devise teaching methods to best impart lessons to their participants. It is also common to conduct seminars or have an official certification system. Certificates are important as an individual should never rely solely on their own experience and intuition. Teaching is a very important activity, and senior kendo practitioners should study how to teach. It would be selfish to think that one's own perspective is enough in passing on knowledge or teachings to another. You may inadvertently distort a learner's outlook or have a negative impact on their progress or life in general. It is important to consider what you have learned so far and ask yourself how you should best pass it on to the next generation. We have all learned particular *waza* in kendo but we usually have our own idiosyncrasies which we should keep to ourselves. Even so, there are many concrete fundamentals which we should impart such as *tō-hō* (sword use) and *tai-hō* (body use). These essentials must be taught carefully and in a patient manner. There is a heavy burden on teachers when they teach students at the *nyumon-ki* level because it would not be an exaggeration to claim that the experiences a beginner has will have a large impact on the future of their training. I find it difficult to tolerate instructors who place too much emphasis on competition at the expense of basics, and ruin young people's kendo careers in the process. We all need to find a good teacher when we start out, but I feel that even many highly graded practitioners are leading young students astray from the true path of kendo.

Let us consider how a practitioner's attitudes are formed. Obviously it is not just the technical teachings they receive from an instructor that influence them; the instructor's words and behaviour play a significant role. A student observes how their instructor interacts with others inside and outside the dojo. The instructor's practice of *rei* and displays of respect and courage all fall under the student's scrutiny. There is a proverb: *shitei-dōgyō*, 'teacher and student are both travelling the same path'. This teaching should remind us to discipline our students but also to praise them when we see positive progress. Instructors must keep in mind that their students will copy their words and behaviour, both good and bad. Our students see us as role-models and we should be grateful for this opportunity and not take the responsibility lightly as kendo is ultimately about disciplining the character.

# Making Use of Kendo Training

After many years of kendo training, practitioners often reflect on their abilities and become aware of certain shortcomings. In this section I will examine *keiko* for people of advanced age and high-graded practitioners who are approaching the *jukuren-ki* (maturity) stage of their training. It is common advice in kendo to firstly practise large and straight techniques, secondly to try to expand your repertoire of techniques, and finally to try to eliminate unnecessary motions. Let us examine what kind of *keiko* is necessary for practitioners to make their movements efficient, as it is certainly no easy task to achieve this level of skill. One of our responsibilities in passing on kendo culture to the next generation is to properly impart the teachings of those that came before us. To apply the finishing touches to our training we must learn, revise, and practise, while always being honest with ourselves.

## Methods for prolonging the decline of physiological and physical strength

The average life expectancy of Japanese people has been increasing and many of the world's oldest people are Japanese. However I feel that many elderly folk would be healthier if they were able to fully afford the cost of rising medical expenses. Age brings with it a gradual loss of physical movement and, in particular, the legs and lower trunk are adversely affected. Elderly people may have problems with their knees as a direct result of this weakening process. To maintain strength, it is important to take care of yourself and develop good habits such as taking regular walks and receiving therapeutic massages. Weakening of the lower body limits upper body movement as well, and this lack of ability to exercise properly can negatively affect the vitality of internal organs and may cause ill health.

Physical exercise is vital in maintaining a healthy constitution throughout our entire life. Development of the body and mind in childhood is aided by physical activities that use the entire body. Sufficient and well-planned physical exercise is necessary to engage in many social activities while one is young. The need for lifelong participation in sports is also widely necessary as younger and younger adults are suffering from lifestyle-related diseases while simultaneously the instances of disease in the middle-aged are increasing. This is cause for the examination of various social issues and should not be overlooked.

Practitioners who have engaged in kendo for their entire lives are often noted for their youthful appearances when compared to non-practitioners of the same age. There has been a recent trend of people starting kendo as adults, or re-starting kendo after becoming less busy in later life. Starting exercise at an advanced age should not be taken lightly, and individuals should seek professional advice. Exercise based on limited experience and misinformation may do more harm than good. One should follow the four stage cycle of examination - prescription - practice - evaluation.

Reengaging in an extremely physical activity with an image in your mind of you at your peak of youthful capability is an endeavour which must be avoided at all costs. Even if you had practised since an early age before stopping your training, you should still not overestimate yourself. Holding your breath excessively or tightening your abdominal muscles should be avoided; ideally we should breathe deeply from the abdomen and aim for a condition called *jōkyo-kajitsu*, which means that our upper body is relaxed, but our lower body is charged and powerful. Although you should continue practising *suburi* and basic cutting exercises, it is preferable that you deliberately change the way you tackle *keiko* by using different methods from those you encountered when you were first at the *tanren-ki* stage. During *kihon-geiko* try to relax your upper body and control your breathing by maintaining a sense of fullness in the lower abdomen even for infrequent or short training sessions. Study the application of *tenouchi* so that you can make the *monouchi* section of your *shinai* work effectively and efficiently. When you serve as *motodachi* in *shidō-geiko* you should try not to avoid being struck, but keep mental and physical composure aided by abdominal breathing from beginning to end. At this stage it is more

beneficial to learn to 'control' your opponents rather than trying to 'beat' them. This advice should help you obtain your training goals despite advancing age. There is no need to make or receive wildly aggressive attacks when you are *motodachi*; it will only hurt your ageing body and actually deviates from the principles of kendo. Always be patient, focus on performing logical (*ri*-based) kendo, and think deeply about how you can defer the decline of your physical and physiological strength.

Stretching, bathing, having massages, rehydrating, resting, and other such post-*keiko* care will become more important than pre-*keiko* warm-ups. With age it will also become increasingly inadvisable to drink alcohol immediately after *keiko*; you should forbid yourself from drinking as you may have done when you were still young.

### The emotional highs and lows during keiko can lead to injury

*Keiko* is a medium for an interplay of personalities, and often strong emotions are aroused. When an experienced practitioner faces a less-skilled opponent, there is a tendency for the senior to shout out criticism, something of which I am often guilty myself. It is important to remember however, that losing control of the emotions may cause physical injury. Modesty is called for to avoid physical and emotional harm to yourself and your partner. Naturally, there are also positive emotions and practitioners often feel elation when they can strike well or are able to beat their opponent. However, it is possible for this elation to turn into over-excitement, and an individual may momentarily underestimate the physical burden they are placing on themselves. Going beyond one's limits in this way can result in injury.

A great kendo teacher argued for modesty in *ji-geiko* by pointing out: "If a practitioner is satisfied simply by landing a number of successful strikes against their opponent, then they are practising vulgar kendo." More often during *ji-geiko*, anger and impatience are dominant in our emotions, sometimes coming from within ourselves, and sometimes provoked by our opponent. In either case these negative feelings are a bad influence on our *keiko* and we should exercise care that this does not lead to accident or injury.

The following situations are some examples of when I personally behaved inappropriately, or displayed an attitude that I later regretted.

- I was teaching junior and senior high school students at a kendo seminar and, despite my careful explanations and numerous demonstrations, they were not paying enough attention and could not perform the exercise properly. I lost my temper and yelled at them, "Are you being serious about this?!"

- I was acting as *motodachi* during a *kirikaeshi* session with young students (I normally have young students perform three or more sets). Their negligent attitude angered me; they were just hitting each side of my *men* with no consideration of distance, *tenouchi* or breathing. I bit my tongue and continued to tolerate their lack of effort.

- During *ji-geiko* my opponent would not launch attacks against me, and just kept moving backwards and sideways meaninglessly. He was worried about being struck and just kept defending with his *shinai*. When he eventually made an attack it was careless and he showed no regard for *tachi-suji*. In disgust I lashed out with hard strikes against him.

- During *gokaku-geiko* my opponent seemed to be showing off and constantly retreated backwards after making barely the slightest touch in attack. I lost patience and made rash attacks which were counterattacked, resulting in further loss of my mental composure.

- During *ji-geiko* I made careless and haphazard counter-attacks against an opponent who attacked me in a selfish and inconsiderate manner. He avoided eye-contact and confronting me directly, so I retaliated against him with multiple *tsuki* attacks.

- I thoughtlessly yelled, "You are not trying hard enough!" at a young practitioner because he did not correct his bad footwork habit despite me giving him advice and many chances to fix the problem.

After experiences like these I leave the dojo feeling depressed, tired, and out-of-tune with my body. Even though at the time I thought that I was teaching properly, often I have not put myself in my students' shoes to reflect on the effectiveness of my instruction. I was stuck in the mindset that the teacher is the sole imparter of knowledge and lashed out at my opponents for self-satisfaction; I was old and experienced enough to have been able to control my feelings much better.

When high-graded practitioners act as *motodachi* during a training session, they generally cannot choose who

# Kendo That Cultivates People

they will be paired with, and they may end up practising with students who have many problems and bad habits. If the practitioner gets disheartened by this, or lets this affect their kendo, then they only have themselves to blame. Maintaining a positive attitude is important, as every new partner presents a new opportunity for improvement and growth.

Recently, I heard a story about a spirited kendo teacher who had just been awarded the title of Hanshi. He was teaching a group of university students about high-level techniques, and he singled out an individual student who could not perform a certain technique properly. The student was naturally embarrassed and approached the Hanshi expecting a barrage of criticism. Instead the Hanshi smiled and said, "It took me forty years of hard training to master this technique. It's not easy to do and, if you were able to do it straight away, then I would be very surprised!" At this, the student felt encouragement to carry on training. On hearing this story, I was both impressed and embarrassed at the same time because if it had been me teaching, I most likely would have lost my temper. In the previously mentioned scenarios, if I had been able to remember what it was like to be young and inexperienced, then I could have dealt with things in a better way without losing control.

Too much instruction can squash a young practitioner's feeling of independence, and we must avoid judging their performances by the standards of our own level of experience and ability. A calm and patient teacher will help students feel a sense of fulfilment in their practice. High-graded practitioners must cultivate *kurai* (dignified refinement) in their kendo. The effects of *kurai* are not immediately noticeable in the short-term, but become more apparent further into one's kendo career and life.

*Everyday exercises can improve your kendo performance*
Strikes, thrusts, and dodges are practised by all practitioners countless times since their entry at the *nyūmon-ki* level, however, at the *jukuren-ki* level, practitioners must make those motions sharp, crisp and efficient. It is fair to assume that practitioners rarely consider how to properly dodge until they reach middle age. When we are young and physically fit there are various methods of meeting an attack, such as *taiatari* or blocking and, even if our attempt at *suriage-waza* or *kaeshi-waza* fails, we are often able to stand our ground and use physical strength to keep our balance and continue the match. If an individual persists with this physical approach into middle age, there is a chance that they may be injured or, in the worst case scenario, actually be forced to stop kendo training altogether.

Practitioners at the *jukuren-ki* level should consider the physical and mental distancing factors that allow them to be within a comfortable attacking distance from their opponent, yet have their opponent feel that they cannot easily launch an attack themselves. To achieve this, one must be sensitive to the distance and time factors involved in the rhythm and flow of body and *shinai* movements. In addition, it is also important to be aware of the functions of the mind and to learn to distinguish between *kyo* (emptiness/falsehood) and *jitsu* (fullness/truth). The states of *kyo* and *jitsu* are closely connected with factors of time and, to successfully control your opponent, you need to learn how to correctly discern which of the two states you and your opponent are in at any given time.

The next skill to develop is your co-ordination of body and *shinai* movement when reacting to your opponent's attack. It is easy to coordinate your body and *shinai* when you initiate an attack after successfully reading your opponent's intent. However, as you begin to lose your physical strength, you will need to develop body movements that enable you to react immediately to an unexpected attack while avoiding crashing into your opponent. No matter what direction you move, you should keep an upright and stable posture. To do this you must have mastered moving with a stable centre of gravity, and your movements should begin from the hips. It would also be of use if you research the traditional Japanese style of walking called *nanba-aruki*. In this method of walking, the right arm and right leg are swung forward together, which is then followed by the left arm and left leg being swung forward together. I also recommend that you try to maintain good posture in your everyday life, by moving with as little up-and-down motion as possible. Even if your weight-shifting and footwork motions are small or subtle, they must still be smooth as if you were dancing. At the same time they must not be too repetitive or stop, and must not lead you to be short of breath. The way in which you approach *keiko* is connected to your everyday gait; the left and right *geta* (clogs) of great swordsmen were said to wear thin at the same rate.

Whether of advanced age, advanced grade, or both, a practitioner naturally wants to avoid things such as heel pain, knee injuries, and being knocked down by *taiatari*. Calmness and patience will enable you to develop your body movements and achieve *shin-ki-ryoku-itchi*, the hallmark of maturity in the *jukuren-ki* stage.

## Shinai Sagas
# Management Secrets of the Samurai

By Charlie Kondek

In Kendo World 5.3, a story of mine was published called "You Know What to Do". That story was about a young man learning that his skills and attitudes in kendo can be applied to the workplace, particularly in management. Like most of my kendo stories, the characters and plot are fictional but inspired by real people and events. In this non-fiction piece, I would like to share my thoughts on kendo and business in greater depth.

The title of this piece is an affectionate jab at a body of business literature that seems to be a thing of the past. When I was a boy in the 1980s, and American fascination with Japanese economic success was at its height, it was not uncommon to see articles and books with titles like this one. Such things were among my first exposures to Japanese culture broadly, and Japanese martial arts specifically. Of course, you and I can no more reveal the management "secrets" of the samurai than the esoteric business practices of Roman centurions or the unpublished wealth strategies of the Vikings. But with tongue in cheek and the same good intentions, I want to share principles I have encountered in my kendo life that have influenced my working life.

### Gratitude, Contrition and Manners

Kendo begins and ends with *rei* (etiquette, respect and courtesy) as the saying goes, so this should be the obvious starting place. In kendo, one learns to prize *rei* and to develop an instinct for it. One seeks always to understand what the proper behaviour is in any situation. As with *waza*, one copies what one sees in others, especially seniors, and applies it.

Any Japanese knows there is *reihō* in the workplace as well. Here in the States we often articulate it as "process" or "company culture" and marginalise it, but we should be as cognizant of it, perhaps, as the Japanese. In kendo, we quickly determine who is leading in any situation, and what is expected of us. We ask for permission to engage or collaborate, and thank our colleagues afterward. We apologise when we do something wrong. We even have a system of obligation between leaders and subordinates, seniors and juniors, that covers performance of tasks but also long term growth.

If in our working lives we can develop a kendo-like attitude to manners that includes an attention to detail and consideration for others, how much better would the workplace be? When I got into management, I tried to discern the *reihō* that was expected of me, and impart the *reihō* I expected from others.

### Communication and Over-communication

To do this, one must communicate. The essential need for communications is a truism repeated often at every organisation, so you'd think businesses would be especially good at it. In my limited experience, they are not. The truth is, to get the level of communication I desire, I urge the people I work with, especially any direct reports I manage, to over-communicate.

By this I mean communicate often, even to the point of redundancy. This can also mean including many people in the line of communication, even if they may not need the information, and documenting it in both written and verbal form – a duality that happens in kendo as well.

One of the things I've noticed about the information we are given in kendo is that if it's important, it gets repeated. In fact, is this not how maxims are born? They are repeated so often and express something so well it becomes a saying known by heart. Often, new meaning emerges as things are repeated and understood in greater depth over time. Frankly, I have to hear and ponder things – and practise them – repeatedly before they "sink in." So I appreciate over-communication.

### Task Management

The majority of the work in one's kendo life is in regular practice. In my experience, the responsibility for running practice is shared between teachers and senior students or club captains. Often, this has meant having a senior student run the advanced practice while the teacher works with beginners, or in some cases having senior students run practices without teachers being present.

This is the essence of working: identifying what has to be done and doing it. The essence of management is organising others to this end. Running the *keiko*, to whatever extent, allows you to do exactly this. You know you have to fill a couple of unforgiving hours with productive practice in *men*, *kote*, *dō*, *kakari-geiko*, *ji-geiko*. How you do it is up to you – but you had better get started, be efficient, and be finished on time.

### Hard Work and Camaraderie

At the end of each kendo practice, our *keiko-gi* is damp with sweat. Kendo is hard, and part of the lifestyle is strenuous exertion, even to the extent that we make things more difficult for ourselves than they have to be. We call this *shugyō* – "austere self-discipline"; we punish ourselves with consistent hard training so that we may become physically, mentally and spiritually strong.

I'm not suggesting we adopt this same mind-set in the workplace. While discipline is necessary, austerity usually is not, is even detrimental to efficiency. What should be evident, though, is an appreciation for work, for exerting one's self in the workplace, for doing one's best and, most of all, not shirking from hardship. In kendo, if your *sensei* asks you to do *kakari-geiko*, even though you are exhausted, you do it. What if you took that same attitude toward work?

Along with this hardship comes a sense of togetherness with one's fellows, the feeling that, having been through the wringer with one's dojo mates and broken bread (or, more commonly, poured libation) afterward, a bond has been formed, an appreciation for the lifestyle shared. I think some of the best times in my life have been relaxing around the table of our usual tavern after a hard practice talking kendo and life over a couple of beers. A beer simply tastes better when you've earned it through harsh physical exercise.

If you've developed similar friendships forged not in the shared fire of kendo, but by the same in the workplace, you've achieved the same thing – friends, mentors and peers for life. They will aid you on your path even if separated, which we usually are in the high turnover of today's working world in which people change jobs often. You see, kendo even teaches us that essential work skill of networking.

### The Way: A Long View

It is helpful to think of this last point in examining one's plans and expectations for either a professional or kendo career. Kendo is a capital–W "Way," a lifestyle. The understanding is that you will walk this path for life. Even though we may be impatient to acquire skill or tokens of merit such as rank or trophies, kendo takes a long view of its adherents and measures years patiently. A Way is less about arriving than travelling, less about the sum of an experience than the process of continual cultivation.

How many of us view our professional lives with the same patience and optimism? How many of us take a long view of our careers, in which we value our professional experiences as much for experiences as something that gets us closer to a professional or financial goal? Certainly in today's working world, depending on the industry, three, five, seven years is a long time to stay in one job. Also, changing jobs is often the only way to get the salary or position we need. I have for some time tried to take the long view, not just of myself, but of everyone I work with. I always tell myself and anyone I manage, that anyone you work with in any capacity can reappear in your working life later. In other words, your intern today could be your client tomorrow. Your vendor could be your next employer. Everyone that touches your work has an idea of you they take into the next phase of their life that can impact yours. What will they remember about you?

I am reminded of something I have heard many high ranking and accomplished *sensei* say at seminars I've attended: "If you keep doing kendo, you will see me again." What will you be the next time that *sensei* sees you? The same? Or further along the path?

## Context

On a flight from Detroit to Los Angeles, I sat next to a human resources executive and we talked a great deal about leadership. She recommended a book, the *U.S. Army Leadership Field Manual*, which she said was the best work on the subject she had ever encountered. I read the book, available in the business literature section of most book stores, and was struck by how it validated many of the ideas I'd already had, and articulated others I had not.

The cornerstone of the manual's philosophy is that the Army is, in the first place, highly organised and, in the second, values driven. Army leaders must "Be, Know, Do;" that is, leaders must be people of character that follow Army values, have a level of knowledge appropriate to their position that includes a thorough understanding of the roles they command and, most importantly, exemplify what they expect from others in their actions.

Naturally, and perhaps because kendo comes from distant military traditions, I found all of this very kendo-like – certainly kendo has explicit and implicit values and a kendo instructor must "Be, Know, Do". But the other idea the book supplied that resonated with me was that organisations like the U.S. Army give context to its members. That is, members of the organisation know that they belong, and know where they belong. They know they are inheriting a legacy, traditions, and that they are being held to a standard general to the entire organisation and specific to each rung in its hierarchy.

Kendo supplies this easily. The workplace? Well, it's hard to feel a sense of legacy to specific companies these days when a mercenary attitude is the dominant one of employers and employees alike. Still, I think there's a principle to be seized here, that we can create contexts in the workplace even if they are temporary. As long as you work with me, we could say, we will hold our work to a standard of excellence that is portable.

## Personal Courage and Accountability

This last item may not be one that occurs to the *kenshi* normally but if you stop and think about it, you'll see it makes sense that kendo gives us courage.

Even though we don't face actual injury in kendo at the edge of a sword, kendo is very frightening – why else would fear be enshrined among the four mental "poisons" that can upset us? We fear losing a point, a match, we fear disappointing our teachers or ourselves – we're not even sure what we fear, we only know we must contend with having a *shinai* pointed at our throat and an opponent shouting at us. Kendo, simply, is conflict, and it affords us ample opportunity to experience conflict. Therefore, it makes us more capable of conflict – it gives us personal courage that transcends the dojo and inhabits other aspects of our lives, including and perhaps especially the workplace. In large part because of kendo I am not afraid of disagreeing with someone, or taking a risk and personal responsibility for that risk.

Which is another aspect of kendo that applies: accountability, that rare coin, it seems, in the currency of the workplace. In kendo, no one is to blame for your shortcomings, your defeats. Though we are instructed directly and train communally, only you can make yourself perform in kendo. Only you fight your matches. Certainly, in the workplace, where so much work is performed by teams or dependent on the completion of tasks by others, we can find ourselves inheriting problems not of our making, and we shouldn't have to take blame for them. But someone with a kendo-like attitude in the workplace is one that takes ownership, I think, that answers boldly for his portion of the work.

\* \* \*

I've worked at a management level for about five years. When I was appointed a manager I was not given any special training. I do not think this is unique. Rather, managers are typically chosen from among existing teams to replace managers that have moved on to other responsibilities. The new manager is chosen based on seniority, familiarity with the work and the aptitude for organising projects and leading others.

If that sounds familiar, it should, because this is what happens when *sensei* delegates aspects of the dojo to others. When I became a manager I tried to figure out how to be a manager. I set expectations with my bosses, emulated others, asked for advice, sought out literature on the subject and, quite naturally, implemented concepts I had learned in kendo.

The result? The feedback to my management skills has been very positive and I have earned a reputation for management among the people I work with. I am doing something right, and I hope these ideas resonate with you, too, even if they only confirm habits you are already implementing.

# Kendo's Not-so Common-sense KAMAE

Article by Nagao Susumu
(Meiji University Professor, Kendo Kyōshi 8-dan)
Translated by Paul Benson
Kendo World thanks Nagao-sensei and Kendo Nippon Magazine for allowing us to reproduce this article

In this article, I will address a simple question that is seldom asked nowadays.

**Question: Why is it that many kendo *kamae* lead with the right hand and foot? And, what *kamae* are there besides *chūdan* and *jōdan*?**

In the rules of kendo, nowhere is it written that *chūdan* must lead with the right hand and foot, and that *jōdan* is *jōdan* only if it leads with the left foot. Moreover, looking at the subsidiary rules on strike regions and the specification of *shinai*, the rules themselves envision *kamae* other than right-foot-right-hand *chūdan* in addition to *nitō* stances. Actually, in the old styles there were many *kamae*. In Niten Ichi-ryū, there are *nitō* variants of *chūdan*, *jōdan*, *gedan*, *hidari-no-waki*, and *migi-no-waki* called the "*gohō*" [the five directions]. And, as in the Jigen-ryū and Unkō-ryū with their highly pragmatic killing blows and *aiuchi* strikes, their *kamae* were likely something close to a simple *hassō* (in today's terms).

Presumably, these schools practised with *kamae* reflecting their own style when *shinai-uchikomi* practice started in the latter 1600s through to the 1830s. For instance, in the aforementioned Unko-ryū, students wore iron *men*, went into *hassō* with a *fukuro-shinai* (bamboo sword inserted in a leather sheath). They advanced towards each other in a half-run, and struck each other's *men* (*aiuchi-gattai*). This drill was also practised in the pre-war Shōwa period.

Chiba Shūsaku also gives an idea of the look of Jikishin Kage-ryū *uchikomi* practice in the *Chiba Shūsaku Sensei Jikiden Kenjūtsu Meijin Hō*: "Take *jōdan* when facing your practice partner, and have a spirit of immediate attack, circling around start to finish. For footwork, use *uki-ashi*, where the feet are neither in the air nor on the ground. As soon as an opening manifests, jumping in and winning is called 'victory of *sen*'." The same is stated in the *Shintō Munen-ryū Kenjutsu Kokoroesho*, so these characteristics of Jikishin Kage-ryū *kamae* and practice were evidently still around up to the 1830s. However, Chiba Shūsaku points out that these characteristics faded in the 1840s, with many students using *gedan* and *seigan* stances, even in the Jikishin Kage-ryū. Following the encouragement of literary and military arts in the Tempo Reforms (1830s), the ban on inter-school bouts was relaxed which brought about rapid exchanges between styles. The decrease in cases of *jōdan* in the Jikishin Kage-ryū noted above likely resulted from coping with the Ittō-ryū featuring thrusts from *gedan*. Still, here we can see the beginning of a convergence on *chūdan* (*seigan*) which transcends school affiliations.

On the other hand, *shinai* specific *kamae* and techniques were being developed at this time, such as single-handed

*waza* from left-foot *jōdan* as seen in today's kendo. It is expressly written in the *Shintō Munen-ryū Kenjutsu Kokoroesho* that swordsmen in the Kyōshin Meichi-ryū "go into *jōdan* putting the left foot forward." Perhaps left-foot *jōdan* was uncommon at the time. Apparently it was characteristic of Kyōshin Meichi-ryū followers to pull up the *hakama* with the right hand and make lightning quick strikes with only the left hand to *men* or *kote* from left-foot *jōdan*. Left-handed strikes from left-foot *jōdan* are now common, showing the influence of Kyōshin Meichi-ryū style. Afterwards, the "Dai-Nippon Teikoku Kendō Kata" (now the Nippon Kendo Kata) were established in 1912. These use *jōdan* (left and right foot forward), *chūdan*, *gedan*, *hassō*, and *wakigamae* for the *tachi*. These stances are passed down today in the teaching guidelines (despite *gedan*, *hassō*, and *wakigamae* hardly ever being used in *shinai* kendo).

Just two or three decades ago, there were many *sensei* who adopted several *kamae*. When I was in junior high school in the early 1970s, there was an instructor in Yatsushiro, Kumamoto Prefecture, who used a right-foot-right-hand *jōdan*. Also, when I was working as a part-time lecturer at Saitama University in the early 1980s, Shidō Yoshitaka-sensei practised with me using the *hassō* he inherited from his teacher Sugawara Tōru (Tokyo Higher Normal School [currently known as Tsukuba University] lecturer, nicknamed "Peter-sensei"). As for why *nitō* culture is not mainstream in kendo, Musashi explained in the *Gorin-no-sho*: "In battles, there are many times it is better to use the sword single-handed, so one must first learn to wield the sword single-handedly." It is because of this attitude that *ittō* is central in kendo.

Still, there is the phrase "*seigan* culture" in kendo which highlights a certain respect towards *seigan* (*chūdan*) as the fundamental offensive and defensive *kamae*. With *jōdan*, at least before the war, there was an unspoken understanding that you had to practise *chūdan* substantially and be a person of excellent strength and skill to take *jōdan*. Also, if you took *jōdan* (especially towards one's superiors), it was considered good manners to bow first. For a time *muna-zuki* (thrusting to the chest as opposed to the throat) was recognised temporarily against *jōdan* and *nitō* in the 1979 rules. This was because of the notable performances of *jōdan* users in the 1960s-70s (refer to All Japan Kendo Federation's "*Sanjūnen-shi*" [30 Year History]).

As for the predominance of leading with the right hand and foot, samurai walked wearing their two swords on their left hip. Since one usually draws the sword with the right hand, gripping the sword with both hands naturally comes to a right-hand right-foot *chūdan*. This warrior culture has been carried on. There is an adage "one sword becomes ten thousand, and ten thousand swords come to one", and particularly since entering the modern age, there is this ideal of having the spirit of this "one sword", and closing the bout from *chūdan* – the *kamae* best suited for offence and defence – with one strike, regardless of the opponent's movements and attacks. I think this and the other ideas previously mentioned are the primary causes for why *chūdan* is dominant in kendo today.

**Answer: There is an attitude now which respects *chūdan* as the fundamental *kamae*; but until 20, 30 years ago, several *kamae* were commonly seen.**

# Bujutsu Jargon Part 1

Bruce Flanagan MA (Lecturer - Ritsumeikan University)
The first instalment in a series of reference articles featuring ancient and modern terminology related to Japanese *bujutsu*.

### # 01 道場破り *dōjō-yaburi*

The act of forcing one's way into a dojo (usually of a different *ryūha*), challenging the instructor and/or students to a duel, beating them, and thereby effectively destroying the reputation of the dojo. The term also referred to the person/people who perform the act. Another similar expression is *dōjō-arashi* which included tearing down the dojo nameplate (*hyōsatsu*) and demanding financial payment from the defeated instructor and/or students.

### # 02 武者修行 *musha-shugyō*

An intense period of training (*shugyō*) undertaken by a warrior (*musha*). This generally meant travelling to various dojo in order to challenge others to friendly contests or life-and-death duels. The term *shugyō* refers to austere training undertaken by practitioners of Buddhism and, with this influence, a warrior's training may have included meditation, fasting, prayer, periods of isolation or pilgrimages to temples. The concept is equated with European knight errantry and nowadays may be used in a light-hearted manner to refer to an intense period of study or an apprenticeship. See also: *heihō-shugyō*, *heijutsu-shugyō*, *bugi-shugyō*

### # 03 臨機応変 *rinki-ōhen*

Four character phrase (*yoji-jukugo*) meaning to 'take advantage of opportunities' (*rinki*) and to 'react to changes' (*ōhen*). In other words, one should maintain a flexible approach and be able to meet the requirements of the situation and any sudden changes that may occur, rather than stubbornly persisting with a pre-planned strategy. The term is in general use and is not restricted to *bujutsu*.

### # 04 格闘技 *kakutō-gi*

Generic term referring to fighting techniques and martial arts. Technically the term *kakutō* implies *kumi-uchi* (grappling or hand-to-hand combat), although weapon-based *bujutsu* are sometimes referred to as *kakutō-gi* as well. Recently the Japanese media has been using the word in reference to systems, arts or sports that involve kicking, punching or grappling such as kick-boxing, wrestling and mixed martial arts. See also: *kakutō-ka*, *sōgō-kakutō-gi*

**#05 bugei-jūhappan**

The 18 martial skills that a warrior would verse himself in for a complete combat education: archery (*kyūjutsu*), horse riding (*bajutsu*), swimming (*suiei-jutsu*), grappling (*jūjutsu*), arrest and restraint (*torite-jutsu*), stealth (*shinobi-jutsu*), firearms (*hōjutsu*), swordsmanship (*kenjutsu*), sword-drawing (*battō-jutsu*), spearmanship (*sōjutsu*), knife fighting (*tantō-jutsu*), the iron truncheon (*jitte-jutsu*), hand-thrown weapons (*shuriken-jutsu*), the glaive (*naginata-jutsu*), the staff (*bōjutsu*), the sickle and chain (*kusarigama-jutsu*), pins and small stabbing weapons (*fukumibari-jutsu*), and spiked staff weapons to ensnare the enemy's clothing (*mojiri-jutsu*).

**#06 shinken-shōbu**

Literally meant to fight (*shōbu*) with real swords (*shinken*), implying a duel to the death. In modern contexts the term *shinken* on its own means serious or intense, while *shōbu* retains its meaning of a contest or ordeal in which winning and losing are involved. Hence, the modern connotation of *shinken-shōbu* is a life-risking endeavour or a very serious undertaking.

**#07 kirisute-gomen**

During the Edo period (1600-1868) the *bushi* class were provided with legal immunity (*gomen*) from the Tokugawa shogunate (Edo Bakufu) in instances in which they killed an inferior. Under special circumstances they were not punished for cutting down (*kiri-suteru*) lower-ranked samurai (*kashi*), townspeople (*chōnin*), and farmers or commoners (*hyakushō*) that had caused them insult or injury. Occasionally referred to as *burei-uchi*.

**#08 katchū**

Armour worn in combat or on ceremonial occasions. The first *kanji* means protective covering and refers to body armour (*yoroi*). The second *kanji* is *kabuto* which means armoured helmet. *Katchu* refers collectively to the whole suit of armour and is also called *gusoku*. The term *ko-gusoku* describes armour attachments and might include *sune-ate* to cover the shins and lower legs, *kote* to cover the hands and forearms, *wai-date* to protect the sides of the abdomen and *nodo-wa* for the throat.

## Bibliography

- *Kōjien (Daigohan)*, Iwanami Shoten, 2004.
- *Bujutsu Jiten (Zusetsu)*, Osano J., Shinkigensha, 2003.
- *Nihon Budō Jiten (Zusetsu)*, Sasama Y., Kashiwa-Shobō, 2003.
- *Kendō Wa-Ei Jiten*, Zen Nihon Kendō Renmei (ed.), Satō Inshokan Inc., 2000.

*Kendo World* is a martial arts magazine. A mighty fine one, in my view. For ten years, it has disseminated quality articles on the historical, philosophical, technical and cultural aspects of a number of Japanese budo – namely kendo, naginata, iaido and jodo – in English, to an ever-growing international readership. In this issue, however, in an attempt to further expand the scope of *KW*, I've decided to introduce the traditional martial art of my homeland, Australian Rules Football, and detail the inroads it is making into the sporting landscape of Japan.

'Aussie Rules', as AFL is sometimes referred to, is a code of football that bemuses most non-Australians when they first see it. It's fast, dynamic, and indisputably rough. It is frequently confused with a sport it bears little resemblance to, Rugby Union, though many do describe AFL as a 'cross between soccer and rugby'. In truth, the sport AFL is most similar to is the Irish code of Gaelic Football, so much so that Australia and Ireland play each other annually in a hybrid competition called, ironically enough, 'International Rules' (a name like that doesn't sound nearly so embellished when you consider the Americans have been using the term 'World Series' for over a century). Some sports historians have suggested that the so-called father of AFL, Tom Wills, based the rules of the sport on *Marn Grook*, a traditional aboriginal game involving the kicking and catching of a ball made from a stuffed possum skin. Wills, legend has it, grew up with and could speak the language of the local aboriginal people, the Djab Wurrung. But I digress... Suffice it to say that AFL is heavily woven into the fabric of Australian cultural life.

Which is why I found myself standing in an Irish pub in central Osaka on the last Saturday of September last year. It was Grand Final Day, you see, the play-off match to decide who would be the champions – the 'Premiers', as they are known – of the 2011 season. What made the afternoon all the more exciting was that my beloved team, the Collingwood Magpies, was defending its 2010 Premiership against the Geelong Cats. And on this particular day last September, I had taken my son, Max, to watch the game, albeit via satellite TV.

As the start of the game neared, the pub began to fill with excited patrons – Australian and Japanese – colourfully decked out in the opposing teams' colours. It wasn't long before I had started up a conversation with members of the Osaka Dingoes – the local AFL team that is part of the Japan Australian Football League (JAFL). Many of the Japanese members of the Dingoes had, I soon learned, either studied in or spent a working holiday in Australia and had fallen in love with AFL. As we shared our predictions about how the game would play out, it soon became apparent to me that my new Japanese acquaintances were extremely knowledgeable and passionate about my national sport.

The game began, but alas, the Magpies were soon blown

# LOCKIE JACKSON
# UNLOCKING Japan

**PART 21** Kendo & Football

away. Completely obliterated. And unfortunately for me, the Collingwood Magpies happen to be the team that everyone loves to hate – much like the Hanshin Tigers in Osaka, whose colours, coincidently, are also black and white. That Collingwood was getting hammered made the majority of the patrons in the pub ecstatic. Having mouthed off earlier about how confident I was that Collingwood would win the game, I, on the other hand, was preparing for a discrete exit from the pub.

Just as my son and I were heading out the door, a couple of the Dingoes asked me if I would be interested in playing for them. At first I thought it was a joke. To use an old Australian expression, "I've been in a good paddock", and the thought of chasing a bunch of twenty year olds around a field while having my nose punched in isn't really how I had envisaged spending my early years of middle age. I politely declined the invitation.

But the boys from the Osaka Dingoes are a persistent bunch, and for reasons unbeknown to me, by the end of this short exchange I had agreed, in an apparent compromise, to serve as one of their umpires in the next week's game.

And so, there I was, one week later, standing with a whistle in my mouth on a converted soccer pitch that was the home ground of the Osaka Dingoes – the picturesque Kibogaoka Kōen. And before my eyes, one of the funniest sights known to man began to unfold. A rabble of overweight, middle-aged, balding English teachers proceeded to live out their childhood dreams of becoming AFL stars. Some of them waddled. Some

of them walked. All of them spent a great deal of time bent over with their hands on their knees. There was lots of telling other team members what to do. And in amongst this band of washed-up foreigners were a number of fit, agile, and decisively skillful Japanese players racking up possessions with apparent ease. Their disposal of the ball was generally more precise than their Australian teammates, and it was also more creative. No doubt about it. Some of these Japanese kids could definitely play.

At the quarter-time, half-time, and three-quarter-time breaks, I couldn't help but listen from a distance to the coach addressing his players. He implored his charges to pass the ball to his Australian spearhead forwards. After he finished speaking, the Australian players in the team began busily directing their Japanese teammates, telling them what they should have done better and what they needed to do next. The Japanese players listened attentively, as the Aussies barked their instructions. Considering the indisputable gulf between the Australian and Japanese players' fitness, tenacity, and skill levels, I found all of this quite bizarre.

Now I might be drawing a long bow, but my experience watching the Osaka Dingoes got me thinking. It occurred to me that what I was witnessing in the park that afternoon was not dissimilar to what I often saw in kendo dojo in Australia when I was living there over a decade ago. This might strike some as a gross over-generalisation, but I often got the impression that many Japanese who practise kendo while living overseas are motivated, primarily, by a desire to meet people and make friends with other Japanese as well as foreigners who have an interest in Japanese culture. It's a chance for some, I suppose, to network with other Japanese expats and stay connected to things Japanese. In many cases, such people had not practised kendo since their high school days, and were, in a sense, rediscovering it while living abroad. Of course, there is nothing wrong with any of this – kendo can be a wonderful way to make friends and share oneself with other people.

Yet I couldn't help feel that Japanese sometimes were put on a pedestal in the dojo simply by virtue of being Japanese. Because they came from Japan, it often seemed to be assumed, their kendo was automatically more authentic and technically developed – sometimes in instances when it actually wasn't. In my view, this was most often the case when it came to the practice of *kata*. Stated bluntly, some foreign *kendōka*, in my view, seem to have a kind of complex about being, well, foreign.

The point, therefore, that I'd like to make in this column of *Unlocking Japan* is an obvious, but in my view, all too frequently forgotten one. Merely hailing from the native country of a particular cultural pursuit or sport doesn't necessarily make one extraordinarily proficient in it. It's fantastic that budo, and sport more generally, has the potential to allow people to transcend linguistic and cultural barriers, that it provides the chance to experience rich, deep, and meaningful exchanges with people from other countries. But let's not make any presumptions about proficiency based on nationality, whether in the dojo, or on the football field.

# "The first cut is everything"

*"The sword is for defeating the enemy, not for defence.
Face the enemy, brace yourself for death, and attack."*

Tōgō Tōbei Shigetaka (1561-1643)
(Founder of the Jigen-ryū)

During the Satsuma Rebellion in 1877, there is a record in government files which describes the chilling attacks made by rebel Satsuma warriors who were students of the Jigen-ryū. They screamed like frenzied monkeys as they charged forward to cut their enemies down mercilessly. Bodies strewn on the battlefields revealed deep diagonal cuts extending from the shoulder through to the navel. The extent of the carnage was so unnerving that government soldiers shivered in their conscript boots. Some of the fallen soldiers had their sword guards firmly driven into their faces. They were probably trying to defend themselves, but the force of the cuts from the Satsuma warriors was so strong that they didn't have a chance.

The Jigen-ryū had a fearsome reputation that was well deserved. Even Kondō Isami of the notorious Shinsengumi remarked that "When faced with a warrior from Satsuma, make sure you get the first cut in." All classical schools of swordsmanship advocate the importance of making the first cut, but the Jigen-ryū took this sentiment to a new level. Even now in the Jigen-ryū, students place a log in the ground and whack it with a stick left and right with all of their might in a practice known as *tachiki-uchi*. The wood gets so hot that it is said to give off the smell of smoke. The only *kamae* they use is similar to *hassō* but is called *tombo-no-kamae* (dragonfly stance), and their blood-curdling screams are awe-inspiring. Jigen-ryū students hone their skills by striking the stake 3,000 times in the morning, followed

# SWORDS OF WISDOM

By
ALEX BENNETT
Based on the book
"KENSHI NO MEIGON" (1998)
by the late Tobe Shinjūrō
Used with author's permission.

by another 8,000 times in the evening. In line with this idiosyncratic training method, in battle they simply attacked by running towards the enemy and then cutting diagonally down on their necks and through the torso. No frills, but lots of blood and guts.

The founder of the school was Tōgō Tōbei, a warrior of the Shimazu domain. His real name was Shigetaka, but he is known as Chūi within the *ryū*. He originally studied the Taisha-ryū. In his travels he ended up in the Tenneji Temple in Kyoto where he met the monk Zenkitsu Oshō. Zenkitsu had inherited the teachings of the Tenshinshō Jigen-ryū, an offshoot of the Tenshinshō-den Katori Shintō-ryū. He studied under Zenkitsu from 1588, and was awarded a scroll of mastery. When Chūi returned to Kyūshū he was ordered by Lord Shimazu Iehisa to engage in a duel with the clan's sword master, Higashi Shinnojō. Chūi defeated his opponent before he could even draw his sword, and was thereby appointed the official domain instructor for swordsmanship. Not long after, he changed the kanji of *jigen-ryū* from 自顕流 in his master's school to his own 示現流 although they mean essentially the same thing – "reality".

Stories abound about the exploits of Chūi, and like all the other great warriors introduced in this series, it is virtually impossible to corroborate any of them. Still, the fact that his name has lasted through the centuries to feature in the pages of this humble magazine is proof enough that there is no smoke without fire. One often-relayed episode concerns the time when he sent his nephew and top student out in the dark of night to dispatch some wild dogs that were making an awful hullabaloo. They came back after their task was complete and boasted that they hadn't even scratched their blades in the canine massacre.

Chūi listened with disdain to his disciples. Quietly drawing his sword, he proceeded to slice through a thick wooden chess board. His cut was so powerful that the sword continued through the *tatami*, and the wooden floor underneath leaving not a scratch on his blade. "That", he said "is how you cut…" The pair stood in stunned silence. "The sword is for defeating the enemy, not defence. Face your enemy, brace yourself for death, and attack." That summed up his sword philosophy, and once his sword was drawn, nobody could get out of the way or stand up to the awesome cutting power of each stroke.

He did not care if he lived or died, and each cut he made was final, especially the first cut. A similar philosophy remains in modern kendo. It is often said that the first cut is the deepest, and that if nothing else, you should always try to get the first strike against your opponent. This was Chūi's message to his understudies. The mark of a true cut is not whether your blade is undamaged, but the conviction with which it is made. And it is the first cut that is everything…

# The Kendo Coach
# Sports Psychology in Kendo
## Part 6 — Aggression in Kendo: part 1

By Blake Bennett

*"Outside of wartime, sports are perhaps the only setting in which acts of interpersonal aggression are not only tolerated but enthusiastically applauded by large segments in society. It is interesting to consider that if the mayhem of the ring or gridiron were to erupt in a shopping mall, criminal charges would inevitably follow. However, under the umbrella of "sport", social norms and the laws specifying what constitutes acceptable conduct in society are temporarily suspended. In their stead is a new order of authority, namely the official rules of the sport. These dictate the forms of aggression that are illegal (e.g., a low blow) and the conditions under which aggression is unacceptable (e.g., a late hit)."* Russell (1993, p. 181)

## 1. Introduction

Considering its historical roots in Japan's medieval combat methods, it is understandable that kendo retains a large element of intrinsic aggression. It is however, the instant where the control over this integral part of training is lost, that harmful intents and unrestrained emotions and impulses come to the fore. As such, it is at this point where sincere concern for the opponent's improvement, correct technique, and the goals of ethical education are left by the wayside, and kendo potentially becomes a danger to its young participants. Therefore, even though modern kendo developed from a culmination of aggressive combat forms from

many different *kenjutsu* schools, kendo training as an effective tool for the physical, mental and spiritual development of its practitioners – as advocated by the All Japan Kendo Federation (AJKF) and the Japanese Ministry of Education, Culture, Sports, Science and Technology (MEXT) – is certainly an important aspect to safeguard.

The use of various harsh training methods in kendo, such as a rigorous *kakari-geiko* session, the use of *kuzushi* (to unbalance an opponent and create an opening), or the employment of *mukae-zuki* (thrusting at the opponent's throat as they attack) may seem to be aggressive, violent, or even appear to resemble bullying in the eyes of some observers. However, many would argue that this is not the case. According to the objectives of *shidō* (instruction) in the kendo environment, these harsh instruction methods are labelled by Sumi (2006) as *kitae* (forging) and *shitsuke* (discipline), and are a necessary element in the pursuit of character-building and strengthening the mind and body of the student.

However, certain incidents in recent decades in the world of budo (namely judo, sumo, and to a certain degree in kendo), have sparked challenges to traditional approaches to *keiko*. Injuries, and in some cases deaths, that occur as a result of the long-established instructional and disciplinary methods used in budo have received more news coverage in Japan in recent years (e.g. "Kendo Accidents", 2009; "Killing Causes Kendo Club to Call it Quits", 1999). This coupled with an apparent change in social attitudes about appropriateness in the educational environment has had an effect on the methods utilised by kendo instructors. Fear of being accused of harassment, bullying or violence has made younger kendo instructors wary of employing traditional training methods.

Changing attitudes toward harsh kendo training, and trying to find a balance of traditional methods taking into consideration the motivations of youth, is a problem faced by many kendo instructors outside Japan as well. Considering potential problems that can result from the physical nature of kendo, not to mention the utilisation of a weapon, a typical form of training such as *kakari-geiko* may easily be misconstrued as unnecessarily aggressive or violent to onlookers.

This raises the following questions: what is it that distinguishes the harsh, traditional methods of modern kendo instruction from contemporary views of aggression and violence? How are these methods justified as a legitimate means for mental, moral and physical education? Furthermore, are these traditional methods justifiable in terms of Western perceptions of violence? If not, in order to teach so-called correct kendo, how or to what extent can traditional kendo training methods be employed outside Japan. In other words, to what extent should tradition be modified or altered to suit contemporary needs both in Japan and internationally?

This series of articles will seek to investigate definitions of behaviours of aggression and violence based on Western psychological research, and will consider these findings against the seemingly aggressive or violent methods used in traditional kendo training. While developing a broader understanding of Western ideas of violence in sports, this and ensuing articles will focus on the justification of the use of aggression as a means for mental, moral and physical education through the traditional ideal of "*kitae*" (forging).

Although issues relating to both *shiai* (competition) and *keiko* (training) will be covered, the main focus will be on elements of aggression in the training environment. In contrast to *keiko*, *shiai* are regulated by strict rules adjudicated by *shimpan* (referees). These articles are based on the notion that there is a higher likelihood of uncontrolled aggression in the training environment.

Throughout discussion in these articles, the terms "harsh training" and "traditional training" will be often referred to. For the sake of clarity, it is important to first define the intended meaning of these terms.

Traditional Training:
- A form of (harsh) training that has undergone little change and is similar to what current kendo educators underwent as school students e.g. *suburi, kirikaeshi, kakari-geiko, gōdō-geiko* etc.
- For the most part, ignores much of the recent sport science/pedagogical knowledge regarding physical and mental performance enhancement utilised in other sports/physical pursuits.
- Tends to rely on long established training methods as customary approaches within a dojo.

Harsh Training:
- Activities and approaches in kendo training that aim to challenge and push the physical and mental boundaries of the practitioner (i.e. a strict approach by *motodachi* in *kakarigeiko*).
- The *motodachi*'s use of body and *shinai* to inflict a certain amount of discomfort and/or pain upon the training partner with the aim of toughening his or her body and spirit.
- May also be termed "rigorous", "rigid", "tough" etc.

## 2. Difficulties in Defining Aggression and Violence

The need to find an appropriate definition for aggression and violence in sport is critical to this discussion. However, as the terms "aggression" and "violence" are used to describe a reasonably wide range of behaviours, particularly in the sporting scene, much of the psychology literature regarding aggression alludes to issues surrounding the difficulty of finding a clear and agreeable definition (Kerr, 2005; Leith; 1991). As Leith points out, the word aggression can be used to negatively describe a fight between two athletes, yet at the same time, an athlete who utilises hard body-contact conducted within the rules and works to the benefit of his (or his team's) performance, can also be depicted in a positive sense as an aggressive player. In short, depending on various factors, people tend to be inconsistent in their views of aggression and violence (Leith, 1991).

To illustrate how individual perceptions of aggression and violence differ in certain situations, the following six scenarios – based on examples provided by much of the Western sport psychology literature regarding aggression and violence in sport – are designed to portray a series of fairly typical occurrences during a kendo training session (mainly in Japanese schools). Each example is deliberately simple, and follows no purposeful pattern of good or bad. The reader is therefore encouraged to consider each situation case-by-case, as the objective of including straight-forward examples is not to state a biased opinion of aggressive behaviour in kendo, but to evoke individual thought around this issue.

*Example 1:* In a high school kendo club training, a pupil is sparring (*ji-geiko*) with his club instructor. During the course of this *ji-geiko* session, the pupil attempts to quickly attack the instructor's head (*men*). At this point, the instructor performs *mukae-zuki* stopping the attack by placing his *shinai* into the chest/throat of the student. This happens many more times during the *ji-geiko* session, and the student is left with several large, red welts on his chest and neck.

*Example 2:* In the same *ji-geiko* session in another part of the dojo, two student club members are facing off. One attacks forwards and body checks (*taiatari*) the other, performing *kuzushi* (forcefully pushing the opponent across the side of the head). This causes the defences of the receiver to be lowered and he is consequently struck.

*Example 3:* During a high school kendo competition, one player attempts an attack at *tsuki* (the throat) on his/her opponent. The attacker misjudges the placement of the *shinai* and connects with the shoulder of the opponent.

*Example 4:* In response to receiving a painful *tsuki* to the shoulder, the receiver is angered and reacts by returning a flurry of *tsuki*.

*Example 5:* During a *kakari-geiko* (repeated striking practice designed to be physically and mentally taxing) session at the end of a training, the *motodachi* (receiver of attacks) allows the *kakarite* (attacker) to run through after each attack, and then proceeds to hit the *kakarite* in the back of the head, back, and legs.

*Example 6:* In the same *kakari-geiko* session in another part of the dojo, *motodachi* places his *shinai* on the *kakarite*'s dojo back, and in a pushing motion, causes *kakarite* to move through faster and exert more physical effort after each attack. As the engagement continues, *motodachi* begins to push *kakarite* through with the *shinai* positioned on the back of *kakarite*'s head.

As mentioned above, Leith (1991) suggests that people have a tendency to be inconsistent regarding their interpretations of various aggressive acts as tolerable or otherwise, depending on the sport and the situation. In this respect, there exists an amount of ambiguity and confusion. Certain aggressive acts can be perceived either positively as a means for achieving victory or mastery over the opposition, or negatively as unnecessary, immoral behaviour that takes place outside the rules or laws of society and the sport. For this reason, it is suggested that aggression should not be considered wholly good or bad, but rather it is better thought of simply as a kind of behaviour to be understood (Leith, 1991).

## 3. Various Definitions of Aggression

An early definition of the human behaviour of aggression provided by the mainstream psychological discipline is offered by Buss (1961). Buss suggests that aggression is a response that delivers a harmful stimulus to another organism/person. Similar to the delineation put forward by Husman and Silva (1984, p. 247) – suggesting that aggression is an "overt verbal or physical act that can psychologically or physically injure another person or oneself" – each of these descriptions cover many aspects of aggressive behaviour, including both physical and verbal actions, that may be considered objectionable (e.g. a penalty for verbal abuse).

However, many consider this definition to be somewhat

insufficient, recognising the necessity to consider complexities such as an aggressor's *intent* to cause harm or injury (e.g. Geen, 1990; Leith, 1991). Although Geen notes the difficulties associated with observing an aggressor's intent, he also acknowledges that it is necessary to draw a certain level of inference in order to actually term a behaviour as aggressive. Geen offers a definition which describes aggression as "the delivery of a noxious stimulus to another person, with the *intent* of harming that person" (1990, p. 28). Furthermore, a similar classification is provided by Leith (1991) suggesting that aggression is "any behaviour *intended* to harm another individual or object by physical or verbal means" (p. 54).

It is important to point out here that despite the element of intent, aggression is still considered a behaviour rather than an emotion, attitude or motive. Therefore, although anger and negative thoughts (i.e. wanting to hurt someone) play a part in initiating aggressive behaviour, these sentiments are not deemed to be aggressive until they manifest into directed and harmful verbal or physical verbal conduct (Leith, 1991).

Additional definitions have been provided by LeUnes and Nation (1989), who consider an extra dimension to the discussion regarding the motives of the 'victim' to avoid the behaviour or stimulus. In line with the previously stated definitions, LeUnes *et al* state that aggression is "the infliction of an aversive stimulus upon one person by another committed with intent to harm"; and additionally suggest that it is an "act perpetrated against an unwilling victim, and done with the expectancy that the behaviour will be successful" (p. 193). Further, a similar definition was provided by Baron and Richardson (1994, p. 7) some years later, stating that "aggression is any form of behaviour directed toward the goal of harming or injuring another living being who is motivated to avoid such treatment." Each of the above concerns regarding the motive of the victim to avoid the harmful behaviour eliminate any sadomasochistic and suicidal acts from the definition of aggression (Baron, *et al*, 1994; Gill and Williams, 2008).

Interestingly, the suggestion that aggression is a directed or intentional behaviour, whether it is successful or not, indicates that accidental harm is not aggression. Therefore, accidental infliction of damage on another living being may not be considered aggressive according to the literature (Baron *et al*, 1994).[1]

## 4. Violence and its Relation to Aggression

The term *violence* is often used interchangeably with aggression in discussions of this nature, and therefore deserves clarification as to how it associates with aggression. Terry and Jackson (1985) describe violence as a type of harm inducing conduct that bears no direct association to the competitive goals of a particular sport. This suggests that violent acts are therefore instances of uncontrolled aggression that fall outside the laws that govern a sport, as opposed to the highly competitive behaviour conducted within the rules that can often be termed assertive or aggressive plays in either an intrinsic, or goal-directed sense (Kerr, 2005).

Smith (1983a) further clarifies distinctions suggesting that physical *violence* is best understood as the end point on the aggression continuum; essentially rendering violence as an extreme form of aggression. With consideration to the intrinsic nature of sports such as kendo to include seemingly aggressive plays, and the rules that facilitate and monitor these techniques, Smith (1983b) provides a review of what he deems to be the four quadrants of violence that exist in sport (and in this case budo) – helping to clarify the ambiguity of some behaviours in contact and combat sports (see *Table 1*).

Following the aforementioned description concerning

*Table 1* – A Sports Violence Typology (Smith, 1983b)

| Relatively Legitimate | | Relatively Illegitimate | |
|---|---|---|---|
| ***Brutal body contact*** | ***Borderline violence*** | ***Quasi-criminal violence*** | ***Criminal violence*** |
| Conforms to the official rules of the sport | Violates the official rules of the sport | Violates the official rules of the sport | Violates the official rules of the sport |
| Legal under the laws of the land | Violates the laws of the land, however; | Violates the laws of the land | Violates the laws of the land |
| More or less accepted | Widely accepted (player norms) | Violates player norms (to a significant degree) | Violates player norms |
| | | More or less not accepted | Not accepted |

the relationship of aggression and violence as a part of a continuum, Smith's typology neatly outlines the traits of rough plays in the "brutal body contact" partition and shows that with an increase in intensity, such behaviours continue up the spectrum to be seen as out-and-out illegal behaviour – unprotected by the laws of the sport or society.

In the case of harsh kendo training, *Table 1* also shows the way in which an intrinsically aggressive behaviour may fall within a grey area, for instance, between the "brutal body contact" and "borderline violence" partitions. As certain actions can be definable as violent according to the literature or violate the written rules of the sport (e.g. deliberately hitting unprotected areas of the body in kendo), they may still remain acceptable practices at some dojo as per differing player norms and mind-sets (discussed in detail in later articles). This again illustrates the difficulties in defining behaviour as unnecessarily aggressive or otherwise.

## 5. Assertiveness and its Relation to Aggression

A further aspect to the discussion of aggression and violence in sport is that of assertiveness. Often confused with aggression, Cox (2007) suggests that although there is an element of forcefulness in assertive behaviours, the intent to harm the opponent is not present. Gill *et al* (2008) concur, stating that assertive behaviour can be defined as purposeful, goal-directed conduct, void of the intent to cause harm or injury.

Therefore, with the use of legitimate, sanctioned physical force to achieve one's aim of winning, or under the guise of teaching and forging a strong spirit in the case of kendo training, any injury that occurs to the opponent cannot necessarily be labelled as a result of aggression (Cox, 2007). That is, although assertive behaviours require the use of unusual effort and energy expenditure, assuming that the behaviour is within the rules and the intent to cause harm is absent, it is likely to be deemed assertiveness rather than aggression according to the current literature (Cox, 2007, p. 350).

Some research into this area has conceded that the decision regarding whether a behaviour in sport is aggressive or assertive, necessitates assessment of the mood of the athlete concerned. Husman *et al* (1984) suggest that hostile interactions, gestures, and overall game developments contribute to an understanding of the type of behaviour demonstrated as assertive or aggressive, however this topic remains a controversial issue in the sport psychology literature (Kerr, 2005).

Furthermore, Kerr contends that comparing aggressive behaviours with assertive behaviours not only faces limitations regarding the accurate assessment of the antagonist's intentions, he also proposes that this type of argument lacks knowledge of the true nature of some sports. According to Kerr, many skills and techniques inherent to combat and contact sports all require a certain level of aggression and therefore, trying to make distinctions whether a sanctioned body contact technique such as *taiatari* or the use of *mukae-zuki*, both intrinsic parts of the art, are aggressive or merely assertive "is simply an exercise in splitting hairs" (Kerr, 2005, p. 12).

Nonetheless, Connelly (1988) suggests that if an athlete performs with an appropriate level of performance intensity to the situation, this type of behaviour may be correctly labelled as assertive. Connelly continues by stating that "assertive players do not let opponents take advantage of them, nor are they easily dominated or pushed around, yet they are also respectful of opponents' skill and personal safety" (Connelly, 1988, p. 256).

In the next article, further consideration will be given to the issues of bullying, sanctioned and non-sanctioned aggression, and a more in-depth breakdown of aggression in sport according to the current literature in this field, and how it corresponds to kendo.

## References

- AJKF (2007). "The Mindset of Kendō Instruction". Retrieved July 1, 2010, from http://www.kendo.or.jp/news/img/kokorogamae/20070314_kokorogamae.pdf
- AJKF (2000). *Japanese-English Dictionary of Kendo* (2nd ed.). Tokyo
- AJKF (1975). "The Concept of Kendo". Retrieved July 1, 2010, from http://www.kendo.or.jp/news/img/kokorogamae/20070314_kokorogamae.pdf
- Apter, M.J. (1982). *The Experience of Motivation: The Theory of Psychological Reversals*. London: Academic Press.
- Bandura, A. (1973). *Aggression: A social Learning Analysis*. Englewood Cliffs, NJ: Prentice-Hall.
- Baron, R.A. & Richardson, D.R. (1994). *Human Aggression*. New York, NY: Plenum Press.
- Berkowitz, L. (1989). "Frustration-aggression hypothesis: Examination and reformulation". *Psychological Bulletin*, pp. 106, 59-73.
- Berkowitz, L. (1993). *Aggression: Its Causes, Consequences, and Control*. Philadelphia: Temple University Press.
- Bjtrkqvist, K., Lagerspetz, K. M. J., & Kaukiainen, A. (1992). "Do girls manipulate and boys fight?" *Aggressive Behaviour, 18*, 117-127. In P.K. Smith, H. Cowie, R.F. Olafsson, and A.P.D. Liefooghe (2002). "Definitions of bullying: a comparison of terms used, and age and gender differences, in a fourteen-country international comparison". *Child Development, 73*, 4, pp. 1119-1133
- Bredemeier, B.J. (1994). Children's moral reasoning and their assertive, aggressive, and submissive tendencies in sport and daily life. *Journal of Sport and Exercise, 16*, pp. 1-14.
- Bredemeier, B.J. & Shields, D.L. (2008). *Moral Reasoning in the Context of Sport*. Retrieved August 28, 2010 from http://tigger.uic.edu/~lnucci/MoralEd/articles.html
- Bushman, B.J. & Anderson, C.A. (2001). Is it time to pull the plug on hostile versus instrumental aggression dichotomy? *Psychological Review, 108*, 273-279.
- Buss, A. (1961). *The Psychology of Aggression*. New York, NY: Wiley.
- Connelly, D. (1988). "Increasing intensity of play of nonassertive athletes". *The Sport Psychologist, 2*, pp. 255-265.
- Cox, R.H. (2007). *Sport Psychology: Concepts and Applications* (6th ed.). New York, NY: McGraw-Hill Inc.
- Crick, N. R., Casas, J. F., & Mosher, M. (1997). "Relational and overt aggression in preschool". *Child Development, 33*, 579-588.
- Dollard, J., Dobb, J., Miller, N., Mower, O., & Sears, R. (1939). *Frustration and Aggression*. New Haven, CT: Yale University Press.
- Gakkō Risuku Kenkyūjo (2009, 12月18日), "Kendō chū no shibō jiko", retrieved October 10, 2010, from http://www.geocities.jp/rischool_blind/sports.html
- Galen, B. R., & Underwood, M. K. (1997). "A developmental investigation of social aggression among children". *Developmental Psychology, 33*, 589-600.
- Geen, R.G. (2001). *Human Aggressiveness*. (2nd ed.). Milton Keynes: Open University Press.
- Gill, D.L. & Williams, L. (2008). *Psychological Dynamics of Sport and Exercise* (3rd ed.). Champaign, IL: Human Kinetics.
- Husman, B.F. & Silva, J.M. (1984). "Definitional and theoretical considerations". In J. M. Silva and R.S. Weinberg (Eds.), *Psychological Foundations of Sport* (p. 246-260). Champaign, IL: Human Kinetics.
- Kerr, J.H. (1997). *Motivation and Emotion in Sport: Reversal Theory*. East Essex, UK: Taylor & Francis Group.
- Kerr, J.H. (2005). *Rethinking Aggression and Violence in Sport*. New York, NY: Routledge.
- Leith, L. (1991). Aggression. In S.J. Bull (Ed.), *Sport Psychology: a Self-help Guide* (p.52-69). Ramsbury, Marlborough: The Crowood Press Ltd.
- LeUnes, A.D. & Nation, J.R. (1989). *Sport Psychology: An Introduction*. Chicago: Nelson-Hall Inc.
- Lorenz, K. (1966). *On Aggression*. New York, NY: Harcourt, Brace, & World.
- *Mainichi Shinbun*. "Killing Causes Kendō Club to Call it Quits", (1999, October 23). Retrieved October 13, 2010, from http://www.accessmylibrary.com/article-1G1-56898494/killing-causes-kendo-club.html
- Nakamura, R.M. (1996). *The Power of Positive Coaching*. Sudbury, Massachusetts; Jones and Bartlett Publishers.
- Olweus, D. (1993). *Bullying at School: What we Know and What we Can Do*. Oxford, U.K.: Blackwell.
- Russell, G.W. (1993). *The Social Psychology of Sport*. New York, NY: Springer-Verlag.
- Smith, M.D. (1983a). *Violence and Sport*. Toronto: Butterworths.
- Smith, M.D. (1983b). "What is sports violence?: a sociological perspective". In J.H. Goldstein and R.F. Kidd, (eds.), *Sports Violence*. New York, NY: Springer-Verlag New York Inc.
- Smith, P.K., Cowie, H., Olafsson, R.F. and Liefooghe A.P.D. (2002). "Definitions of bullying: a comparison of terms used, and age and gender differences, in a fourteen-country international comparison". *Child Development, 73*, 4 , pp. 1119-1133
- Stephens, D.E. (2001). "Predictors of aggressive tendencies in girls' basketball: An examination of beginning and advanced participants in a summer skill camp". *Research Quarterly for Exercise and Sport, 72*, pp. 257-266.
- Sumi Masatake (2006). *Hito wo Sodateru Kendō*. Nippon Budokan
- Tanaka, M. (2010). "The History and Spirit of Kendō" in Uozumi Takashi and A. Bennett (Eds.). *The History and Spirit of Budō* (pp. 29-46). International Budo University.
- Terry, P.C. & Jackson, J.J. (1985). The determinants and control of violence in sport. *Quest.* 37, pp. 27-37.
- Tucker, L.W. & Parks, J.B. (2001). "Effects of gender and sport type on intercollegiate athletes' perceptions of the legitimacy of aggressive behaviour in sport". *Sociology of Sport Journal, 18*, pp. 403-413.

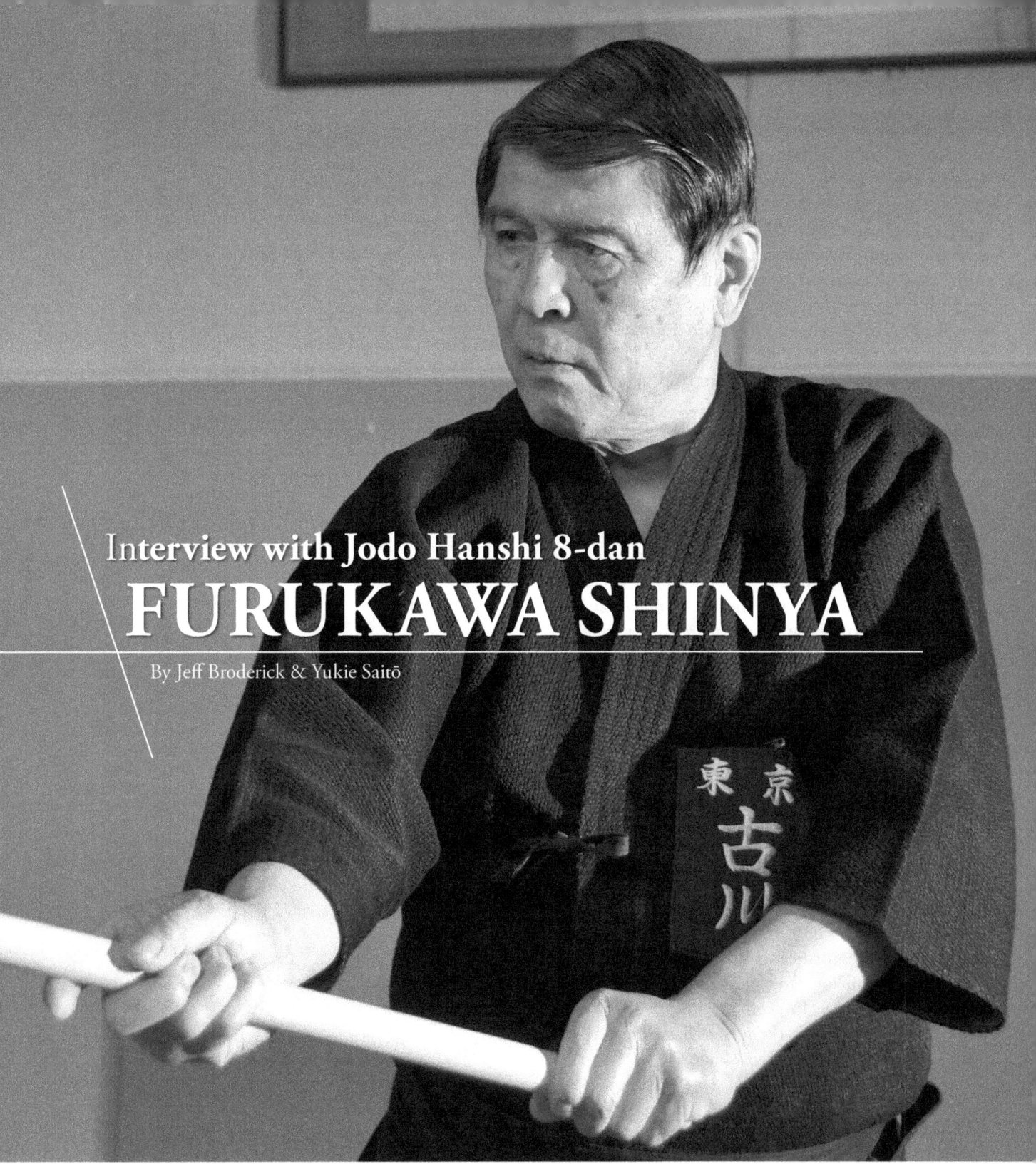

## Interview with Jodo Hanshi 8-dan
# FURUKAWA SHINYA

By Jeff Broderick & Yukie Saitō

"Welcome, come on in!" yells a deep and forceful voice as I enter the basement dojo of the *Nihon Keizai Shinbun* (Nikkei Newspaper) Dojo. It belongs to Furukawa Shinya-sensei, for over thirty years the acting instructor of this small but vigorous jodo club located in the banking district in downtown Tokyo.

As his voice would suggest, Furukawa-sensei is a forceful and committed man, but his voice also carries warmth and a casual expression that tends to put you at ease. His eyes are glitteringly observant, with a way of making you believe he is looking elsewhere, but he rarely misses anything, and he has an uncanny knack for picking up small mistakes being made by someone in the back row, on the other side of the dojo.

I can clearly recall one of the first times I practised with Furukawa-sensei. I had been doing jodo for almost ten years by that time, but he so thoroughly *schooled* me that I felt like a complete beginner again. His cuts were so effortlessly quick, I could only barely block them in time. When I was too slow, his *bokutō* whipped to a halt, hovering patiently a few inches above the target, clearly making the point, "You just died there". My strikes

seemed to do nothing; he moved his sword out of the way just to be courteous. And despite the fact that I probably outweigh him by 30 kg, I was almost unable to physically move him. Throughout our exchange, I felt a sense of wild terror, but at the same time, complete confidence that he would not hurt me. It was somewhat like riding a roller coaster – animal fear, along with the knowledge that you're not actually going to die. While I was desperately fighting for my life, Furukawa-sensei was calmly keeping one eye on the other people in the dojo, only needing to glance at me occasionally.

Furukawa Shinya was born in June, 1940 in Kitakata City, Fukushima Prefecture. Like many boys his age, he liked judo, but when he entered high school, an upper-year acquaintance recommended he try kendo. Upon joining the kendo club, he threw himself wholeheartedly into practice. "I could only do kendo for two years during my three years in high school. I practised really hard for a year, but then I took a year off. I came back to it in my third year and that was when I entered the Prefectural Championships and made it to the best 8 in the individual division. At that time, I was a *shodan* in kendo."

Financial reality put university beyond his reach. "In those days, it was really difficult to find a job. When I was ready for graduation, there was no work in the countryside, and my family was poor, so they couldn't afford to send me to university. People thought if you went to Tokyo, you would find something. So I took the test to become a police officer."

He was accepted. "After a year of police training, I was stationed at Shimura Police Station in Itabashi Ward, Tokyo. I was there for three years as a patrolman and guard at a detention center. Then, at age 23, I was transferred to the Riot Squad." Within the Riot Police is a subdivision called the 'Budō Shōtai', where select officers trained intensively to become police martial arts instructors. There, he focused his training in kendo and judo, and also *taiho-jutsu*. "*Taiho-jutsu* is a fighting style that the police use when they need to arrest someone. It includes karate, kendo, judo, and aikido, and takes the best elements from each art. You need to be able to arrest criminals without being injured or perhaps killed. The criminals can't be stronger than you are, so we learned judo, kendo, and *taiho-jutsu* to become strong. In addition, you have to try not to injure the person you are arresting. There are laws preventing officers from using more force than is necessary to apprehend someone. You have to adjust to the strength of the criminal; if he's strong, you have to be strong too, but if he's not strong, you're not allowed to just kick him to pieces! To balance that is extremely difficult." "Nowadays, we primarily use *taiho-jutsu* to arrest criminals. Kendo and judo, though, are not for fighting as much as they are for training the spirit. In other words, through judo and kendo you have to acquire mental strength – how you look at your opponent, how you must not fear or let up on him. You can't succumb to surprise, fear, doubt, or confusion."

These terms will be familiar to *kendōka*: the *shikai*, or four admonishments concerning mental weaknesses which must be overcome when facing an opponent in kendo.

驚・懼・疑・惑

The first is **KYŌ** (*odoroku*) - surprise;
The next is **KU** (*osoreru*)- being afraid;
The third is **GI** (*utagau*) - doubt, or trying to guess what your opponent might do, and wondering what you should do yourself;
The fourth is **WAKU** (*madou*)- confusion.

"You train your mental strength by doing budo. The point is not to allow these feelings to arise. If they do, you have lost."

Furukawa immersed himself in intense daily practice as a member of the "Budō Shōtai". "While normal police have a set of duties they do every day, the Riot Police were different as we didn't have set duties. We only operated when there were emergencies, or disasters. We always worked as a unit, so if there was nothing for us to do, we practised budo day in, day out." Japan in the 1960s was a place with relatively frequent civil unrest, however. "We were pretty busy. Almost every day, there was something."

It was as a member of the Riot Police that Furukawa came into contact with jodo. "In those days, jodo was extremely limited. Even among the police, it was only practised by the Riot Squad, which amounted to about 2000 people. It was a compulsory subject for us. The regular police weren't seen as needing it." Having studied kendo intensely for a number of years, he still remembers his first impressions of jodo. "Judo and kendo were practised mainly for mental training. To be honest, unless you reach about 5-dan or above in kendo, I'm not sure you can really use it practically. At least that's my opinion. The reason is that kendo nowadays is practised with repetitive hitting, over and over – it is different from old style *kenjutsu*, which taught single, decisive cuts because it was teaching how to use a *katana*. Now, kendo is just about hitting. In other words, it's not a style of 'combat' as such. So speaking for myself, when I learned kendo in those days, I was

Interview with Jodo Hanshi 8-dan
# FURUKAWA SHINYA

wondering whether I could really use it in a practical way. Jodo, on the other hand, is an art where you learn how to decisively finish the opponent off – bam, like that! You hit him and he's dead."

Another point that impressed him was jodo's physical symmetry. "Up to that point, I had done kendo, and in kendo you always have the right hand and the right foot forward. But in jodo, you use both sides of your body; I thought it was amazing, just an incredible style of budo. It was so remarkable to me, when I first saw it, I thought, how can they do that? I learned quickly because I was so interested in jodo."

Furukawa learned jodo directly from the masters. "There were five units. Shimizu Takaji-sensei was the top instructor and Azuma Morio-sensei was in charge of Riot Squad #1. Yoneno-sensei, who became a Hanshi 9-dan and has since passed away, was #2, and #3 was Hiroi-sensei, who is Hanshi 9-dan, and is still with us. Kaminoda-sensei was #4, who is still alive and is Hanshi 8-dan, and #5 was Kuroda-sensei, who has since passed away. When Azuma-sensei stepped down, I took the exam and was told I had to take over from him. That is how it happened – I was his replacement, basically." Furukawa has warm memories of Shimizu-sensei. "He was a wonderful *sensei*. It's common in Japan that as people get older, they tend to be brusque with their subordinates, but even though he was the very top teacher, his special characteristic was that he always said 'san' after people's names. He would call me 'Furukawa-san'. He addressed everybody, even if they were younger, this way. He was very kind, and came across as gentle, but his practice was very strict."

"He didn't speak or explain in words when he taught. He never said, 'Do it this way, and next do this…', not even once. If he saw you doing something wrong, he would come up beside you and just take the *jō* or the *tachi* from your hands, and show you how it should be done, like 'Bam! Bam!' and that would be it. He might show you about three times, and that would be all."

"One more thing – he was a very strong drinker!"

Active duty in the Riot Police is generally limited, but budo teachers were the exception. "In 1969, I was transferred from Unit 1 to Unit 3 as a kendo instructor. I stayed there for ten years. Because I was able to teach both jodo and kendo, I was able to stay on. I was about forty, and I was promoted to kendo Kyōshi, and began working at the Keishichō Budokan (Police Martial Arts Training Centre)."

It was around this time that he also started iaido. "I stopped iaido after reaching 5-dan. I also have 3-dan in judo, and Kyōshi 7-dan in kendo. Jodo is the only one I've kept up with, so now I'm Hanshi 8-dan. Our job was to instruct jodo, to make police officers strong, so they wouldn't be killed or injured when arresting somebody. That's what we were there for."

Up until this time, jodo had only been practised by a select number of police officers, and by the few martial artists who trained within the *koryū* traditions. This was about to change. "Jodo was originally something that was practised only in Fukuoka, originally in the Kuroda domain. Shimizu-sensei brought jodo to Tokyo with the intention of spreading it throughout Japan. He did this by bringing it first to the police, and then spreading it to the general public, by which I also mean to say that it would be spread outside the original lineage, which was started by Musō Gonnosuke, and continued for 400 years through Shimizu-sensei. He did everything he could to spread jodo."

This also involved making jodo available to the general public through classes at the Nippon Budokan. "In 1972, the Nippon Budokan started a 'Budo School', and jodo was 'allowed out' so to speak. The thinking was that it could be taught to the citizens, the people of Tokyo, through the school. Shimizu-sensei headed the school, followed by Hiroi-sensei, Yoneno-sensei, Kaminoda-sensei, and then me. We wanted to expand jodo by teaching it to a lot of people, and we continue to this day."

A practical art such as *taiho-jutsu* or jodo has obvious utility to police or military personnel, but what is the benefit of learning jodo for ordinary people – especially in a country as safe as Japan? Furukawa-sensei pointed to the other side of the dojo, where two 7-dan *jōdōka* were practising their forms. "Take Mrs Morii and Mrs Ueda for example. They are women, and obviously they are extremely good at jodo and have high ranks. In general, you find that women are particularly good at jodo. Why is this? I've often thought about it before. We men tend to have a lot of power, and if we hit with a lot of strength, like 'Bam!', well, the other guy will die, maybe. But women don't have all that strength, so they take what they are taught, and do the techniques properly. Men have this raw power, and try to do it like 'Grrr!' They often don't do it right, while women tend

# Interview with Jodo Hanshi 8-dan
# FURUKAWA SHINYA

to. So they enter competitions and do very well. These two have won the national championship before, even though they are very small, physically. So although jodo is a fighting art, there is another side to it. It has to be done correctly – at times lightly, at times softly or gently. That's one of its virtues, or perhaps I should say another way of looking at it."

Furukawa-sensei went on to explain how one's attitude or mental posture in jodo is much more important than physical strength or stature. "You have to look down on your opponent. Not in terms of your height, or meaning that you have contempt for him. I mean in terms of spiritual strength, not being afraid, pressing down on them, being strong and imposing. In Japanese, this is referred to as 'comparing bamboo' (竹くらべ). Jodo is a *kata* budo, but you must have the feeling of really fighting, or comparing your spiritual power. The forms are decided of course; you know how to move. But if you just go through the motions, there's no point. You need the feeling of 'comparing bamboo', or measuring yourself against your opponent."

Did his budo training ever have application in his police work? Furukawa denies ever having used any martial techniques in the field, but one incident echoes what he told me about not being afraid, and being strong and imposing.

"One time I arrested a murder suspect. I was quite young at the time. I was riding in a police patrol car … it was getting dark. A call came over the radio about a reported homicide. We raced to the site and were first on the scene. We were way out in the country, with farms all around. It was very dark, although the moon was out, so it wasn't pitch black.

About one hundred meters down this narrow country lane was a farmhouse where we figured the incident happened. My partner was older than me so he turned to me and said 'Furukawa! You go and check it out! I'll stay here with the radio!' I was young, you see, so I raced off down the road, nightstick in hand. I had my pistol too, but in my head I guess I was thinking, 'I'm a 3-dan in kendo!'

I ran as fast as I could and came around the corner and before I knew it, I had run right up to a man, standing there, holding a *katana*. He was still very worked up, and he said to me, 'What the hell are you looking at? What do you want? I did it! I did it!'

He was obviously very agitated. I just went up to him and said in a strong voice, 'Give me the sword!' and held out my hand. When you're in a situation like that, there's nothing else to do. You don't think about it, you just run in and do it. 'Give me the sword!' And he just handed it over, put it right in my hand, like that. I told him I was arresting him for murder."

I wondered if *sensei* had not been so fearless, if he had perhaps shown some hesitation, whether things might have been different. "I don't know. That depends on him. I think he may have been so shocked by my sudden appearance that he just gave up."

## 懸待一致

"Another important idea is '*ken-tai-itchi*' (attacking and waiting as one). The feeling is of directing yourself toward your opponent. It is no good to one-sidedly attack. The first character is 'suspend' and the second character means 'to wait'. Both sides are attacking, and you have to wait for the right moment to counterattack. It is very important to have this feeling in *kata* budo. You are waiting for the exact right moment. You don't do the movement because you know what's coming, you are waiting for the last moment. Of course we do it in the way as decided by the *kata*, but this feeling must be there. If you don't have this feeling, there's nothing."

All this talk of Japanese *kanji* made me wonder if Furukawa-sensei has a favourite saying related to budo.

## 直心是道場

"I suppose it would be '*jikishin-kore-dōjō*.'. It is originally a religious saying. '*Jikishin*' means a gentle, honest heart. It is a very important idea in the dojo. You need to have the attitude of wanting to learn. If you don't have a gentle feeling – open minded, pure – you won't learn. That of course, goes for everything in life." Having attained the highest possible rank in jodo, I asked him what his future goals might be. He answered in the humble and straightforward way that characterises him. "I want to do jodo as long as I can. I don't care until what age, just as long as I can. There's really nothing special that I want. I just want to keep doing jodo."

**Postscript:**

In July of 2011, at a ceremony held in Tokyo, Furukawa Shinya-sensei was honoured with an Imperial Award called the "瑞寶雙光章(Zuiho Soko Shō)", or "The Order of the Sacred Treasure, 5th Class with Gold and Silver Rays." The award is granted by the Prime Minister on behalf of His Majesty the Emperor of Japan, in recognition of long and meritorious civil or military service. See photo on p. 52.

# Recent Developments in Korean Kendo

By Professor Kato Jun'ichi (Kendo K 7-dan)
Department of Physical Education, Bunkyo University
Translated by Michael Ishimatsu-Prime
Photos courtesy of the KBKF

# "Video Interpretation Appeals"
## According to the Korean Business Kumdo Federation

Under the theme of the "Internationalisation of Kendo", I have introduced a variety of Korean initiatives. Some examples have been the development of the plastic *men*, the use of digital clocks in competitions, and the unique Korean style *hakama*. The Korean kumdo community has a distinct view of kendo, and they are searching for a unique way in which kumdo matches can be conducted, and how new initiatives can be put into practice. This article will introduce the new experimental system for "Video Interpretation Appeals". Rather than being created to oppose Japanese-controlled kendo culture, this idea arose from the conditions of kumdo inside Korea, and I believe the intention is to contribute to the improvement of kendo. Be that as it may, if you look at it from the point of view of the Japanese kendo world, to say that there is a feeling of trepidation that kendo, too, might finally come to this point cannot be denied. For this article, I have received from Korean kumdo officials three documents – the "Regulations for Video Interpretation Appeals", the "Report on the Implementation of Video Interpretation Appeals", and a questionnaire related to video appeals. I will use these as the basis for my analysis of the introduction of the video appeal system, and the response it received after its implementation.

### The Stages Leading to its Establishment

First, it should be noted that when the video appeal system was introduced in 2011, it was worked out by the Korean Business Kumdo Federation (KBKF), an affiliate of the Korean Kumdo Association (KKA). The KKA are not taking the lead in this matter. Furthermore, this system is acknowledged by the KKA, but to date it is only being used in tournaments supervised by the KBKF. In April, 2011, the KBKF established the "Regulations for Video Interpretation Appeals" (RVIA) and decided on its implementation at the 15th National Company Kumdo Competition.

According to the "Report on the Implementation of Video Interpretation Appeals" (Report), from 2007 the KBKF had been investigating the introduction of video judgments. At first it was known simply as "video judgment", but during the process it changed to "video interpretation". Finally, "appeal" was added to indicate that it was to address "formal objections", and it settled on "Video Interpretation Appeals" (VIA).

The KBKF is an affiliate of the KKA, from whom it was essential to get the final approval. However, according to the Report, the KBKF received an enquiry from the

KKA only a few days before VIA's implementation on March 24, 2011. When this enquiry was received, the KBKF took the plunge and the VIA was completely implemented.

## Method of Implementation

VIA will not be implemented in all of the matches in competitions where it is used. At the 15th National Business Kumdo Competition that was held from April 1-3, 2011, 89 individual matches (comprised of ten 3-dan, thirty-three 4-dan, eleven 5-dan, seven 6-dan, twenty three selection, and five finals), and eight team matches (comprised of two best-16, one best-8, three best-4, one semi-final and one final) were filmed.

Regarding the video images, there were a total of three cameras installed; one prepared by the KBKF, and one for each team taking part in the match. The KBKF camera films the match from the second floor spectator's seats facing the chief referee, and the team cameras film from each side, and these images are connected to a monitor in the interpretation desk. In the case that an appeal is lodged, the federation video takes precedence, and if it is still difficult to interpret the images, the corresponding team camera videos can be used.

## The Regulations

The Regulations, decided by the KBKF, consist of eight articles – objectives, applications, the appeal committee, the video interpretation committee, the installation of video interpretation devices, the right of appeal, the appeal procedure, and the control of video materials – and other supplementary provisions.

In "Article 1: Objectives", it first states that the purpose of the VIA is to complement the KKA's "Kumdo Match and Referee Regulations", and then, regarding the matches that the KBKF sponsors and supervises, it is to ensure the fairness of matches and to increase the level of the referees.

In "Article 3: The Appeal Committee", it states that for dealing with objections that arise during the course of a match, an appeal committee must be set up at each competition. Those committee members, composed of between six and ten personnel, are chosen no later than the day before a competition, through a consensus of the KBKF's directors.

The video interpretation committee members are chosen from within the members of the appeal committee. According to "Article 4: The Video Interpretation Committee", for each individual match, people who have no relationship to the corresponding match are chosen as members of the video interpretation committee, and in the event that an objection is made, they will interpret the video.

Article 6 is concerned with the right of appeal. The right to raise an objection is limited to the person who sits in the manager's position for the player in the match. The number of objections is also limited. In the individual competition there is a limit of two appeals per team for the whole event; and for *dantai-sen*, two appeals per team match can be lodged. However, in the case that an objection is dismissed, the remaining right to appeal is revoked.

The actual appeal procedure is explained in Chapter 7. If during a match the referee awards a point or a penalty, and if the person in the manager's chair has doubts about the decision, they raise a flag to signal this to the court judge. When the court judge receives the signal, they request the appeal committee chairman to make an interpretation. The video interpretation committee is then instructed by the committee chairman to make a decision, which is then carried out. The committee chairman then reports the verdict to the court judge, who in turn informs the chief referee. The chief referee (*shushin*) then abides by, and announces, the decision. When that happens, if the judgment is the same as the referees' original decision, the match continues without change; if the flag raised is different, it is corrected; and when the decision is different to the referees' call, the flag is lowered and the match is restarted.

## The Consistency of the KKA's "Kumdo Match and Referee Regulations"

The use of video to adjudicate matches has never been done before in kumdo matches, and observers have a tendency to focus on the fact that something new has been introduced. However, the most important point here that should not be overlooked is that competitors have been afforded the right of appeal against the referees' judgments.

The International Kendo Federation's "Kendo Match and Referee Regulations" are similar to the KKA's "Kumdo Match and Referee Regulations". Article 35 states that nobody is allowed to protest against the referees' decisions; and Article 36 states that during a match, if doubt arises relating to the application of the regulations, the manager is able to lodge an objection to either the court judge or the chief judge, before the end of the competitor's match. That is to say, it states that no-one can protest the referee's decision, and only the manager can query matters relating to the

Table 1

| Match Type | No. of Matches | No. of Appeals | % | Appeals Accepted | Appeals Rejected | Appeal Success % |
|---|---|---|---|---|---|---|
| Individual | 89 | 7 | 7.9% | 4 | 3 | 57.1% |
| Team | 8 (57) | 0 | 0 | 0 | 0 | 0 |
| Total | 146 | 7 | 4.8% | 4 | 3 | 57.1% |

administration of the rules to either the court judge or chief judge.

Notwithstanding these two articles, the KBKF is entitling the side of the competitor in question to the right to lodge a protest to guarantee the fairness of matches. At this time, the KKA has not commented about this inconsistency. One reason for this, I would guess, is that the VIA are limited only to tournaments that the KBKF sponsors and supervises, and are not used throughout the Korean kumdo community. However, sooner or later the system's consistency will probably be called into question.

## What Can Be Seen from the Report

After the recent competition in which the system was employed, the KBKF collated the following information regarding the report: 1. Progress on its implementation; 2. The applicable competition; 3. The day carried out; 4. Its method of implementation; 5. The video implementation committee; 6. The matches where the appeals were made; 7. The results of its implementation; and 8. a conclusion. A point of note in these is the number of appeals, and appeal success percentages.

The number of matches which were the object of video appeals, as shown above, were 89 individual matches and eight team matches (comprising 57 matches) making a total of 146. From these, of the seven individual matches in which objections were raised, four were approved. In the team competition, no objections were raised. From the point of view of this competition, in which the individual matches were held on the first day and the teams competition the next, it is possible to surmise that the implementation of the VIA showed itself to be beneficial in some areas. The following is from the official report.

"Some would argue that VIA diminishes the authority of the referee, but it could possibly increase the player's competitive level and the skill of the referees. In courts where videos were not taken, there was still a tendency to be dissatisfied with some decisions. In the courts where video was taken, there was considerable attention paid to the referees decisions, but the presence of the cameras also offered an opportunity for competitors and coaches to reflect and aim for qualitative improvement. As a sport, it is important to have a system in which referee calls can be scientifically verified and validated."

Through the introduction of the VIA system, a qualitative improvement in both the referees and the competitors performances is possible. In the courts in which the system was not used, there was a trend where dissatisfaction was expressed about the referees' decisions. From the content of the Report, one can infer that referees, coaches, and competitors, were given an opportunity to reflect on their level and understanding of kumdo, and could generally strive for improvement.

## Results of the Questionnaire

After the tournament, the KBKF conducted a survey related to the VIA system. 16 referees, 21 managers and coaches, and 138 competitors (175 in total) were given a questionnaire. The questions were:
1. Are you in favour of the VIA system?
2. Are you satisfied with the VIA regulations created by the KBKF?
3. Do you have confidence in the results of the video interpretations?
4. From now on, do you think that the video interpretations should continue at KBKF tournaments?
5. Do you want video interpretations to be implemented in other tournaments?

For each question, respondents were given a choice of five answers ranging from, "I completely disagree" to "I absolutely agree".

Out of the five questions it was the manager and coach group that proportionally gave the most positive replies. In fact, the proportion was higher than the competitors who actually took part in the matches. A reason for this could be that the managers and coaches were given the authority to make appeals, and so the degree to which they were satisfied became higher. On the other hand, in response to questions 1 to 3 about being for or against the implementation of video appeals, satisfaction with the regulations, and the credibility of video appeals, the competitors group was the most negative. This could be due to dissatisfaction with a legitimate decision in

response to a strike, or with an appeal that is not ratified. It is also possible to speculate that this dissatisfaction is because the competitors themselves have not been granted the authority to make an appeal. However, not all the matches were subjected to the appeal system, and it is uncertain whether or not this factor was also a reason for dissatisfaction.

Regarding all of the questions, the referee group was the much more reserved, and had the highest proportion of respondents answering "Not sure". This is obviously an expression of doubt. Although the system is accepted for the time being, more than the competitors, it is the referees who are the target of the appeals, and why competitors are not so enthusiastic.

The final part of the questionnaire was for the respondents to freely express their opinions. Many people gave their approval this time to the VIA system, and identified some areas for improvement. The content of these opinions can be divided into five categories:

1. The method of filming.
2. Shortening the time in which judgments are made.
3. Ensuring fairness.
4. The method of using the VIA.
5. Other.

The gist of the comments may be summarised as follows: With regards to category 1, efforts should be made to film from various angles in order to eliminate blind-spots, and technology should be introduced to increase the accuracy of the video judgments. In category 2 it was suggested that it is important to make rapid decisions and not waste time. For the competitors, time taken for judgments will change the flow of the match creating anxiety. Comments in category 3, especially from the competitors, suggest that the VIA staff should have absolutely no relation to the opposing team in order to increase consistency, and avoid any distrust or suspicion. It is only the manager who has the authority to make an objection, but the comments in category 4 show unease about competitors sending signals to the manager during their matches; another competitor from the same team sitting in place of the manager and raising an objection; or, objections being made to waste time. These are problems with the system, and from now on they will be investigated. A comment from category 5 said, "If the referee does not declare an *ippon*, even if it is a good strike, an appeal cannot be made." From the point of view of the regulations, an appeal can be made only when the referees' flags are raised. However, dissatisfaction can be seen with this aspect of the system.

## The Background of the Appeal Regulations and Afterword

Korean kumdo competitions are classified into two types – professional and amateur. The specialists who are called "professional" are not only working adults, but also junior high school, high school, and university students. For them, victory or defeat has a great effect on the path they take next, and their status. In other words, outcome of kumdo tournaments is far more significant for this group than in Japan. Therefore, the introduction of VIA is a necessity for them. Currently, the KKA is restricting its approval to only KBKF tournaments, and is not actively seeking its introduction into others. However, it is possible that it will eventually move in that direction in tournaments like the President's Flag Competition and the SBS Kumdo Competition (company team competitors enter them too). Also, many junior and senior high school, and university managers have had experience in business competitions. If they like it, then overall implementation may well be a matter of time.

On the other hand, when interpreting video, there are limits to what the officials are able to recognise. Judgments on the strength and sharpness of strikes and correct posture are very different from judging where a tennis ball hits the court. However, the current KBKF stance is that they are also working to clarify this from the video.

Looking only at the questionnaire, when it comes to the KBKF affiliated teams, there are points of the VIA system that ought to be corrected. At the same time, only a few said it should not be allowed. From now on the KBKF will undoubtedly continue to improve the system and methodology in an ongoing process that will be watched with interest.

Is Japan the only country with concern about the system? Preparations are now under way for the World Kendo Championships, which will be held in May 2012. I wonder how the competitors of each country would feel about this system. Kendo was created as a contest, and everyone believes that it should be carried out in a fair way. The KBKF made a bold start in the introduction of its VIA system to try and guarantee fairness and accurate calls. Instead of talking about whether this system is right or wrong, we should think about the fairness of judgments. Kendo does not only have a competitive side, but as long as this aspect remains, the problems surrounding dubious refereeing are never far away.

# Strength to Strength

**Continuing Growth and Success in Kendo through Life's Experiences**

By Kate Sylvester

*Kendo World* talks to 2003 World Kendo Individual Champion, 6-dan, Osaka policewoman, Kondō Keiko (previously Baba Keiko) about her kendo career and life experiences.

Spending time with Kondō-san, you cannot help but take an instant liking to her. It is not only her unassuming character, but also her open-hearted warmth, sense of humour and genuine enthusiasm to learn from those around her that is admirable.

I first met Kondō-san seven years ago when I had the opportunity to train at the Osaka Police for one week. She generously opened her home and life to me so that I could experience the world of a professional kendo player. I am fortunate to have remained friends with Kondō-san, and she has been a major inspiration to me for as long I have known her. Through her support, advice and friendship, I have maintained motivation to continue improving in my relatively 'unprofessional' kendo career.

Kondō-san started kendo at age six, where she became interested in it after watching some people practice in her neighbourhood. She then asked her father to take her along to a dojo to try it out for herself. She had dreamed of being a police officer from when she was a young girl and entered the Osaka Police directly from high school. At 29 years of age, she passed 6-dan on her first attempt, and is the only woman to have represented Japan at four World Kendo Championships. Judging from the results below it may have just been her destiny to live the life of a professional kendo player in the police force.

**2000** *World Kendo Championship*
—Women's Individual—**2nd place**
**2003** *World Kendo Championship*
—Women's Individual—**1st place**
**2006** *World Kendo Championship*
—Team Competition—**1st place**
**2009** *World Kendo Championship*
—Team Competition —**1st place**

She has also won the All Japan Police Championships, been runner-up twice, and 3rd place once. One title that still eludes her is the All Japan Women's Kendo Championship where she has only reached 3rd place. Kendo World (KW) asks Kondō Keiko (KK) to share with us her role as a police kendo instructor, kendo inspiration, career highlights, and life as a mother returning to kendo.

KW: **Please describe your role as a kendo police instructor**

KK: I'm currently taking maternity leave from my job as a police kendo instructor. However, before the pregnancy I taught physical-mental maintenance and improvement techniques in kendo, as well as courses in arrest and restraint techniques to police officers. I also taught kendo to children in the police dojo. My role as a female police officer also provides me with the opportunity to develop my personal traits and those of others.

KW: **Is it assumed that very few women hold positions as police kendo instructors in Japan?**

KK: There are an extremely small number of female police kendo instructors in Japan. However, the number is slowly growing in response to an increase in the number of female police officers. I think that the number of female instructors will increase in the future.

KW: **How do you see kendo developing for women in Japan?**

KK: The competitors in this year's All Japan Women's Championship were from a wide range of ages and backgrounds. The youngest competitor was a high school student, and the oldest was overall champion Murayama Chinatsu at age 37. The competitors' professions included students, police officers, teachers, and housewives, some of whom have already had children. If female competitors develop their individual strengths and apply what they have learned through kendo to their lives in and outside of the dojo, then I feel that women's kendo in general will enjoy successful growth in the future.

KW: **In your preparation for the 2003 WKC, less than a year out you suffered a serious Achilles injury. It is quite amazing that you were then able to go on and win the 2003 World Kendo Championship. Please share with us your experience.**

KK: My family, friends, colleagues and teammates gave me enormous support to help me recover from the injury, and I was extremely thankful just to be selected for the national team. My winning the championship was actually a result of all that support.

KW: **What has been your most memorable kendo experience to date?**

KK: Winning the individual division of the 2003 World Kendo Championship.

KW: **What do you enjoy most about kendo?**

KK: Kendo is enjoyable in that males and females of all ages can practise together. Also, the kind of person we are is evident in our kendo performance, which means that we have the opportunity to develop our strengths and overcome our weaknesses.

KW: **How have you been able to maintain your motivation in kendo?**

KK: It's important to set goals and gradually work towards them. Training with a wide range of people from different dojo, sharing kendo stories with them and benefiting from their advice is also very motivating.

KW: **Around the world there seems to be a trend in kendo that women do not return to kendo after giving birth. Now that you have just had your first child will you return to work as a police kendo instructor?**

KK: At the moment I'm busy looking after my son and it's difficult to train as much as I used to. But my husband (sole proprietor of the Kondō Bōgu Shop) helps out so that I can have time to visit the dojo. I will go back to work next April and resume my position as a police kendo instructor.

KW: **Can you offer any words of advice to encourage women to return to kendo after childbirth?**

KK: This was my first childbirth, so I have also been receiving advice from those who have been through the same experience. People say that a woman becomes mentally stronger through having a child, so I'm going to do my best with this in mind.

We may yet see Kondō Keiko deservedly take the title of the All Japan Women's Championship, but there is undoubtedly plenty more success and growth to come...

# THE PNKF WOMEN'S TOURNAMENT

By Elizabeth Marsten

The Pacific Northwest Kendo Federation's North American Women's Taikai is both a mouthful of a title and is the official tournament started in 2001 by Jeff Marsten-sensei (Kyōshi 7-dan), and is held every three years in the greater Seattle area. We in the PNKF lovingly refer to it as "chicks with sticks" or just the "women's Taikai."

### Why & Who?

PNKF has a long history in the promotion of women's kendo, and was the first federation (the Washington State Kendo Federation) in the United States to create a women's division back in the 1970s. This tournament's creation was due to a perceived lack of women's activities in USA kendo outside major events like the national championships or the WKC, which can only be participated in by a small fraction of the population. The women's Taikai includes competitors from Canada, as well as Hawaii and Mexico. In fact, any federation or dojo in North America that wants to enter has been welcomed. Don't let the name fool you – even if you're in the middle of France and want to come, the door is open.

In addition to the tournament, there is a week-long seminar prior to the event which is open to any women who wish to take part for a small fee (approx. $50 USD). The fee covers the expenses of the guest instructor chosen specifically for their *shiai* abilities, and also for their role in the promotion and encouragement of women's kendo.

### The History

At first, the ladies of PNKF tried various fund raising activities to generate the money needed for the large cost of bringing over and hosting a guest *sensei*, and running the tournament. Activities ranged from selling kendo equipment at anime conventions, car washes, rummage sales and candy bar sales. The tournament began by being funded through the ladies themselves with some seed money from the PNKF to be paid back through fund raising and entry fees. Over the years, the PNKF officially adopted the event, and it continually operates at cost with seminar fees replacing fundraising activities and donations from

members of the PNKF and surrounding areas. (The ladies of the PNKF much prefer the seminar fee to washing strangers' cars.) The guest instructor is put up in a homestay for the week of the seminar, and a hotel suite the night before and after the tournament, serving as the guest of honour at the *taikai* and at the post-*taikai* party.

### The Instructors

Each instructor is carefully chosen as *shiai* specialists. They practise with each and every participant, and provide coaching during matches over the week. The instructors work with the PNKF Women's Team coach to determine the seminar schedule, topics to be covered, and to keep an open dialogue on what the seminar participants need, how they are doing, and how to adjust for each training session. PNKF has had the honour of hosting Mayumi Otsuka (6D) in 2001, Kumiko Hoshina (7D) in 2004, Mark Grivas (7D) in 2007, and Mayumi Katsura (6D) 2010.

### The Men

The men (not just in PNKF) look forward to this event every three years just as much as the ladies do. They serve as court staff throughout the day for the event, and are placed in charge of various duties as kitchen staff, party coordinators, keg tapping, and serving or cleaning up. Most, if not all, stay afterwards to attend the after party. PNKF has never had a shortage of volunteers for this event.

### The Shinpan
The *shinpan* are hand-picked not only from within PNKF, but also from Canada, Hawaii and from visiting *sensei* that come with their respective women's teams. Each *shinpan* must be at least 4-dan or above, and they are arranged in groups that rotate between courts. A *shinpan* assigned to Court A will do a round of six matches on that court then move to Court B. This way, a point on Court A is the same as a point on Court B, and the *shinpan* remain fresh and consistent throughout the day.

### The Tournament Format
The focus of the women's *taikai* is the team event. The team competition goes ahead of individuals, and 5-people teams can borrow up to two players, and can enter as a federation or a dojo. Teams start in round robin pools of 3-4, and pools are decided by past records, team composition, and geographical location. Teams submit their initial lineups ahead of time, but can change them up throughout the day as needed. Once the round robin is complete, the top two teams go into single elimination round brackets. The championship team gets to take home the perpetual trophy for the next 3 years donated by Jeff Marsten-sensei.

PNKF tries to get every woman into a team. Individuals or federations without enough players can submit requests ahead of time to be placed on a team or to have a spot to be filled. For individuals, there are two divisions – *kyū* and *dan*. The individual event takes place after a lunch break, and is single elimination with players being installed in the ladder ahead of time based on win records, rank and geography.

### The Little Things
In order to make it a "fun" tournament, we not only put the men to work for the day, but strive to bring in small touches to really make it a memorable event for the ladies. This includes providing unusual trophies, plaques or medals. The 2010 Taikai awarded cut glass medals etched with the competition details strung on brightly coloured ribbons: brilliant purple for 1st, bright red for 2nd, white for 3rd and peach for 4th. PNKF has also brought in tournament sponsors such as Phiten USA, Eguchi Kendo and Maruyama Kendo in the past. These sponsors have donated prizes to award winners in the form of product or gift certificates.

PNKF has also started a commemorative *tenugui* for the event, with each competitor receiving one as a keepsake. The 2010 *tenugui* was bright purple instead of the usual white, black or navy blue. Then there is the after-party. Party goers donate throughout the day into a "drinks" fund which often includes a keg from a local brewery, various bottled spirits and beers picked up by PNKF members. PNKF members also provide a potluck style dinner for all out-of-town participants to enjoy. If you'd like more information on the *taikai*, its history, past winners, format, or just on how you could come yourself, visit: www.womenskendo.com

2010 Participants

# The 10th Otsū Cup

A Report by Trevor Jones

October 23, 2011. On this date the tenth "Miyamoto Musashi Kensho Joshi Kendo Taikai" took place at the Musashi Budokan in Ohara (now part of Mimasaka City in Okayama Prefecture). This tournament has continued to grow, not only in the number of participants, but also in importance as a sign of the popularity and increasing level of dedication and skill shown by women *kenshi* throughout Japan and the rest of the world.

Having reported on the first "Otsū Cup" in Vol. 2.1 (2003) then the fifth in Vol. 3.4 (June 2007), this tenth event seemed an appropriate time for *Kendo World* to catch up with the tournament. With over 300 people taking part in *keiko* on the Saturday afternoon, this gave a good indication of what to expect the following day.

The format followed the same pattern as that established at the 5th Otsū Cup, as the increase in numbers up to that time had led to separate categories according to age groups. The five individual events were age 18–29 (191), 30–39 (109), 40–49 (157), 50–59 (70) and 60

The Musashi Budokan

and over (32). 559 participants registered for individual competition.

The two 3-person team events were total team age "up to 100" (66 teams) and total age "101 and over" (122 teams). *Shiai* were limited to three minutes, with a *hantei* decision being given if an individual bout was

still drawn at the end of a 1-minute *enchō*, this not being necessary in the team events.

The staff of the Musashi Budokan along with a small army of volunteer helpers once again provided a very smooth and well-run operation throughout the day's proceedings. The main arena housed 12 *shiai-jō*, up from the 9 courts required in 2006, and this allowed all bouts, trophy presentations and closing speeches to be concluded by 5.00 p.m.

The day began at 8.30 a.m. with the opening address followed by a demonstration of Nippon Kendo Kata by *uchidachi* Miki Yoko (Kyōshi 7-dan) and *shidachi* Fujino Tamae (Kyōshi 7-dan). At 9:30, the individual competitions were under way....

Finland, whose kendo has a long association with Tahara-sensei, the head of the Musashi Budokan, was represented this time by Saara Poyhonen, Emilia Vuorinen and Numata Fumiko, fighting as a team and as individuals. They were unfortunate not to get through their first team round with one win, one draw and one loss (and equal points) with Emilia Vuorinen succumbing to a *kote* in the play-off.

Australia also had a strong presence at this event, with six people in attendance, all of them presently residing in Japan: Rebecca Marshall in the Nara-Ken team (Nara) "under-100" team, Viennessa Wimborne fighting for Joshi Kendo B (Kochi), Hayami Aboutaleb with Yugijuku B (Tokyo) and, as Australia, Jinny Lai, Chiaki Kobayashi and Kate Sylvester. Kate Sylvester, in her second appearance at the Otsu-Hai, made a strong showing in her individual bouts, especially with a fine *debana-kote* in her second-round match before being defeated in the third.

Once again, some strong *jōdan* fighters were in evidence, but many eyes were on Ishimura Ako (6-dan) of the Yamaguchi-Ken "101+" team who fought *nitō* to great effect. She reached the quarter-finals in her 40-49 individual competition and helped her team to 3rd place.

Panasonic Denko Sunx A (Aichi) took on Panasonic Denko Honsha (Osaka) in the "younger" team final, taking the lead with two wins before the Honsha *taishō* Hirayama Tomoka pulled one back, but to no avail.

In the "101+" final, Nara-Ken Kendo Renmei (Nara) faced Kasamatsu Keimusho A (Gifu) in a very close-fought match, starting with a scoreless draw followed by the Nara-Ken team taking the lead through *chūken* Horio Hiroko scoring a single *men*. With the two captains also fighting to a scoreless draw, this narrow margin was sufficient to take the trophy to Nara.

The full results are as follows :

## *Individual events:*
**18–29**
1st Fujiyama Eriko (Osaka)
2nd Tedai Mika (Hyogo)
3rd Torii Yūko (Nara)
  Hirayama Arika (Osaka).

**30–39**
1st Sugimoto Saeko (Okayama)
2nd Horio Hiroko (Nara)
3rd Iga Hitomi (Tokyo)
  Nishimura Natsuko (Mie).

**40–49**
1st Inoue Natsuko (Mie)
2nd Tani Hitomi (Tokyo)
3rd Ogita Hiromi (Gifu)
  Takamoto Toshie (Osaka).

**50–59**
1st Takeuchi Kayoko (Tokushima)
2nd Miyazaki Yayoi (Gifu)
3rd Tsuneishi Chizuyo (Kochi)
  Shimosaka Miwa (Kochi).

**60 and over**
1st Tomotsugu Fumiko (Okayama)
2nd Shimizu Taeko (Tokyo)
3rd Kabahara Chizuko (Osaka)
  Takahashi Naoko (Toyama).

## *Team events.*
**Up to 100**
1st Panasonic Denko Sunx A (Aichi)
2nd Panasonic Denko Honsha (Osaka)
3rd Nihon Taisanbin Kogyo Kabushiki Gaisha (Gifu)
  Keishicho Kendo Club (Tokyo).

**101+**
1st Nara-Ken Kendo Renmei (Nara)
2nd Kasamatsu Keimsho A (Gifu)
3rd Kyoin Team (Nara)
  Yamaguchi-Ken (Yamaguchi).

With a total of just under 600 *kenshi* taking part in the various categories, including triple the number of entrants in the "60 and over" division compared to five years ago, the 10th "Otsū-Hai" Taikai serves as solid evidence of the strength of women's kendo in Japan and the interest it holds for women competitors from overseas.

# The History of WOMEN'S KENDO
## Part One

by Ozawa Hiroshi – Tokyo University of Science
Translated by Michael Ishimatsu-Prime

### Introduction

The fourth biggest earthquake in world history occurred on March 11, 2011. The seismic centre was off the Sanriku coast. It was named the "Tōhoku Kantō Great Earthquake" or the "Great East Japan Earthquake". The damage was enormous, and the number of victims was horrifying. This vicious earthquake and its aftermath will remain in the minds of Japanese people for many generations to come.

The greatest impression that remains with me was the calm acceptance of the situation, and the quiet composure shown by almost all of the people who were affected by the disaster. There was no looting of supermarkets and convenience stores to speak of – people still orderly queued up to shop. I wonder where this strength of mind comes from. How were they able to stay calm to that extent?

In the June edition of the *Shinchō 45* magazine last year, I had a discussion with Uchida Tatsuru called, "Dialogue on Bushidō". I shared his opinion that "When one encounters a crisis, 'courage' is the most important thing for survival."

"*Bushidō* is an ethos originally based on killing, but can also be interpreted as embodying knowledge to enable survival in a critical situation. The type of strength necessary to live through an ordeal is not just speed or physical power. In a crisis, it is not muscles, a strong build, or reflexes that will get you through – it is 'courage'."

To encounter such a situation and be able to maintain a calm state of mind, or to not show pleasure or joy to opponents or spectators when you win are characteristics of kendo. If you are awarded a point in a kendo match and you raise your fist in celebration, the point will be taken away. This characteristic is not common in other budo or sports. Not showing your emotions, keeping them hidden inside while exhibiting consideration to your opponent is a virtue peculiar to kendo. It is this self-control that contributes to the cultivation of character.

The topic I will address in this article is "What sort of character should women seek through doing kendo?" Simply put, I believe the answer to this question is to forge "*tanryoku*", or courage. This is not only limited to women of course, but this essay will look at how women's kendo came about, and what significance women's kendo holds.

## The Beginnings of Women's Kendo

The real beginning of women's kendo was after the Second World War. Immediately after the war, kendo was banned by GHQ, but on October 17, 1952, the All Japan Kendo Federation was inaugurated ending kendo's hiatus. Almost six decades have passed since the AJKF's formation. I am not sure whether this should be considered a long time or not, but in any case, it has been during this sixty years that women started to do kendo in earnest, and the number of female practitioners has continued to rise. Who were the first women to do kendo? I think it is a great point of interest why some women chose to take up kendo over naginata or some other budo arts.

According to Ōtsuka Mayumi in *The Encyclopaedia of Kendō*, "The sudden rise of women's kendo occurred in the 1960s and '70s. Until then, most women who did budo did naginata, and only a few women *kenshi* were able to find an environment conducive to their study of kendo."[1]

In the book *Tales of 101 Women Who Lived in the Bakumatsu Period*, it states that Sakamoto Ryōma, a famous warrior from the Tosa domain, studied the Hokushin Ittō-ryū style of swordsmanship at Chiba Shūsaku's dojo in Edo (now Tokyo). When he wrote a letter back to his hometown in Tosa, he made mention of Chiba Sana, the eldest daughter of the dojo master. "She is called Sana, …… she can ride a horse, and also use a sword and a naginata. She is stronger than most boys. To give an example, she has the same ability as Gin, a woman who used to work for us."[2] Of course, this was no ordinary family as her father was a celebrated dojo master who taught *kenjutsu*.

There is another description of a woman skilled in swordsmanship. "It can be said that Ikuko, the daughter of Nanbu Toshihisa, the daimyo of Morioka, excelled in the arts of calligraphy, poetry, court music and tea, and also at horse riding, *kenjutsu*, archery, and other martial arts."[3] Nevertheless, it was rare for women of military families in the Bakumatsu period to be skilled in the martial arts.

Photo 1: In 1952 Ōwada Eiko from Urawa, entered the Fukushima National Sports Meet as a representative of Saitama, and won the women's title. She is pictured with the manager, Ozawa Takashi.

### The Pioneers of Women's Kendo

Ozawa Takashi, my father, wrote in his autobiography *Eighty Years in Kendo* an entry titled "About Women's Kendo".

"Before the war, women's kendo was rarely, if ever, seen – naginata was the main budo. Conversely, men did kendo and judo, and there were very few who did naginata. However, because *shinai-kyōgi* [a hybrid sporting version of kendo introduced after the war] was not so rigorous and there were no injuries, women also started to practise it. At the National Sports Meet in Fukushima (1952), the women's *shinai-kyōgi* title was won by Ōwada Eiko who represented Saitama… She was also a 3-dan in kendo."[4]

It is not known exactly for how long Ōwada learned kendo, but her grade in 1952 was 3-dan, so it is clear that she had been doing it since before the war.

Takano Hatsue-sensei was a notable female *kenshi* being the first woman to be conferred the grade of 7-dan since the inauguration of the AJKF (according to the membership list of the Shūdōgakuin – Takano Sasaburō's dojo – for 1974 and 1976).

Tajima Tsuguo was the Shūdōgakuin secretary, and I had many opportunities to ask him about the dojo and Hatsue-sensei. Tajima-san recalled, "Hatsue-sensei's *keiko* was mannish and intense, and she was physically strong. She would grapple with male *kenshi* of the same age and younger, hurling them away with an arm throw, and driving them away to the skirting boards with her *taiatari*."

I was born after the war, so I do not really know what pre-war kendo was like. Generally speaking, men were at the centre of the kendo world, but there was Hatsue-sensei at the forefront of the Shūdōgakuin, a dojo known for its many hard-hitting *kenshi*. It is hard to imagine how tough this world must have been.

Also, Hatsue-sensei often did *de-geiko* (visiting other dojo). This photo from 1957 is of Hatsue-sensei in Kawaguchi City, Saitama, at the Kōdōkan Fifth Anniversary Competition with her eldest daughter Yōko-sensei, who was a high school student at the time. They entered the tournament together.

As a married couple, Takano Takeshi-

Photo 2: Hatsue-sensei and her eldest daughter, Yōko-sensei, in 1957.

Photo 3: Takano Dojo in front of Kanazawa-bunko Station (January, 2011)

sensei and Hatsue-sensei founded a dojo in 1952 in front of Kanazawa-bunko Station on the Keikyū Line. Many police officers, teachers and regular members gathered for its popular *keiko* and learned their kendo there.

On January 8, 2011, I was invited for the first time to the Takano Dojo and took part in *keiko* and a reunion. At that time, seated next to me were former pupils from many years ago – the current honorary president of Minami Ward, Yokohama City Kendo Federation, Kobayashi Saburō-sensei, the president of Kamakura City Kendo Federation, Okazaki Hideaki-sensei, and a Kanagawa Police old-boy, Sakurai Akio-sensei. I asked them about their memories of Hatsue-sensei. Kobayashi-sensei is now 68 years old, and still practises with the utmost enthusiasm. He attended the Takano Dojo from junior high school third grade to the end of high school during the mid to late 1950s.

"When I attacked Hatsue-sensei and did *taiatari*, she often knocked me over; and even when I stood firm, her *taiatari* sent me flying from the entrance into the road. Now there are many cars that go past so you can't do that, but in those days I was frequently bundled out of the dojo into the street. People used to find this very amusing. 'It happened again' they would say, laughing after *keiko* had finished." As I listened to those three *sensei* speaking, I came to picture the scene of a strict, but warm *keiko* environment.

## Conclusion

Coming face to face with the great disaster that happened recently made me think of many different things. I thought of the books I have read which outline what is necessary to survive in the face of adversity. These books include *The Women of Military Families* by Yamakawa Kikue, *A Daughter of a Samurai*, by Sugimoto Etsuko (translated by Ōiwa Miyo), *The Posture of People in Meiji Japan*, by Sakurai Yoshiko, who read *A Daughter of a Samurai*, and Isabella Bird's *Unbeaten Tracks in Japan*.

Both Yamakawa and Sugimoto were the children of samurai, and received a strict samurai education. From these books it is possible to deduce what style of education Japanese women received in the Edo and Meiji periods. Mothers raised their children, who in turn went on to modernise Japanese society from the Meiji period onwards. The Japanese of this era were people who valued dignity. Books centred on this virtue have become popular in Japan recently, and the origin of much of their content can be traced back to the era in which Yamakawa and Sugimoto lived.

Also, Isabella Bird, a British woman who came to Japan in 1878, wrote of her impressions of the Japanese as diligent, ingenuous and well-mannered people. Recently, the number of foreigners who practise kendo has increased. A reason for this, in addition to the appeal of kendo itself, is the attraction of the underlying spirit of Japan that Yamakawa and Sugimoto lived by, and impressions of Japanese virtues that Bird wrote about in her travels. These virtues are borderless and genderless, and can be learned through kendo.

(Endnotes)
1 Ōtsuka Mayumi, *The Encyclopaedia of Kendo*, The Japanese Academy of Budo – Kendo Division, 2009, p.162
2 *The Tale of 101 Women Who Lived in the Edo Period*, Shin-Jinbutsuōraisha, 2010 p.15
3 Ibid. p.159
4 Ozawa Takashi, *Eighty Years in Kendo* pp.130-131

# Smile Kids Japan

Trevor Chapman
(Dojo Leader – Kashi-no-ki Kenyukai, UK)

I am aware of no one that was not moved by the devastation that took place in Japan on March 11, 2011 at 14:46 hours (Japan time). I remember my wife waking me in the early hours and telling me about the earthquake and tsunami that had hit Japan.

As we watched the devastation unfold through the media coverage, I remembered the many trips that I had made to Japan over the last 18 years in my pursuit of kendo, and the people that I had met and made many friends with.

As the days passed and the true scale of the devastation became known worldwide, I remember thinking about the disaster. I had spent 31 years in the Ambulance service as a front line Paramedic, and felt that I wanted to go to Japan and help with the rescue, but I knew this was not possible as I had not had any training in urban rescue.

In April, I saw a TV programme about a charity called "Smile Kids Japan". It was about a charity helping orphaned children, many whom had been orphaned and traumatised by the tsunami. Some of the children talked about their fear and their harrowing experience. They had lost their homes, belongings, toys, family and friends. It was clear that they would need serious support with counselling to return to some sort of normal life. I was so moved by this program that I felt that my dojo Kashi-no-ki Kenyukai UK could in some way raise money for this charity. In March we had already raised £2,000 for the Japanese Red Cross earthquake and Tsunami appeal.

I talked with my friend in Japan about the TV program, and he informed me that the Tōhoku area was still suffering hardship. Having looked at the smile Kids Japan web site, I found they were raising funds for the Tōhoku Orphans Tohoku Kids Project.

In February, just before the quake, we were very fortunate to have had Tashiro Jun'ichi-sensei (Kyōshi 8-dan) visit out club. He spent one morning talking with seminar candidates about his kendo life and experiences. He told us that "when someone passes a *dan* grade, they get a *menjo* with the *dan* on it. This is an act of receiving. At this point, the meaning of *dan* turns around to mean 'giving'. Each *dan* grade awarded carries a responsibility to be generous." Remembering Tashiro-sensei's words, and reflecting on how I experienced so much help and kind hospitality during my visits to Japan, I felt that if I could raise funds for the "Smile Kids Japan" charity, this would be a small way of repaying the kindness shown to me over the years. These children are a part of Japan's future, and they needed help.

My teacher Ozawa Hiroshi-sensei in Tokyo, and the members of Kobukan raised funds for the Japanese Red Cross by organising a 1000-*suburi* charity event. I talked with my club members, and suggested that we organise a similar event as the Kobukan, and

I asked them to ask for sponsorship from their friends, family and work colleagues. Everyone agreed, and we planned the event for Sunday, May 22.

I decided to write to some of the high-ranking Japanese *sensei* I knew to ask them if they would kindly donate some kendo items to set up an auction site on eBay. I was a little apprehensive about this, as I felt that my request may be a little impolite. After conferring with Miss Matsuda Kazuyo (6-dan), she kindly offered to help me by translating my letters.

Soon I was receiving donated items from Ozawa Hiroshi-sensei, Sumi Masatake-sensei, Chiba Masashi-sensei, Takizawa Kenji-sensei, Tashiro Jun'ichi-sensei and the Japanese Kendo Team; we received *shinai* bags, books, *tenugui*, and many other items. Ozawa-sensei kindly donated some *tenugui* that his father had designed. He signed the *tenugui* with the date of the earthquake and tsunami.

The morning of the event came, and I confess to being quite nervous driving to the dojo. I was thinking that the situation in Japan had in some way taken a back seat in the UK media, and wondered if we would be able to raise the same amount of £2,000 that we had raised in March for the Japanese Red Cross. I had asked my dojo members to take part in this event, as well as some of Japan's most senior *kendōka*, so I wanted the event to be a success.

I had decided that morning to use a *shinai* that had been given to me and had belonged to the late Andō Kōzō-sensei (Hanshi 8-dan), from Kobukan Tokyo to do my 1000-*suburi*. I received it following his death in 2003. This *shinai* had his name embossed on the *tsuka*. I know that this may sound strange, but I felt that by using this *shinai*, Andō-sensei's spirit would in some way be taking part in the event and contribute to its success.

There were eighteen of us in total (including two children). We started the event with a minute of silence in respect for all the children who had lost their lives in the earthquake and tsunami. I then read out a letter received from Chiba-sensei thanking every one taking part for their efforts. After an hour, everyone had completed the challenge, and participants handed in their sponsor monies. I was amazed when I totalled up the sponsor forms of the participants. We had raised a total of £1,422.35 and we still had the auction to go.

I spent a considerable amount of time photographing and translating *tenugui*, and our secretary, Daniel Lavrick, posted the donated items on eBay. Soon, people in Australia, America and across Europe were making bids on these items. I was quite excited that the auction had attracted so much attention around the world. Then again, all of the senior Japanese *sensei* that I had written to were well-known around the kendo world, and had for many years given their time and commitment in building international relations.

Generally, winning bids were from across Europe, the furthest being Sweden. The auction raised £1,234.00, and we also received £250 in donations from *kendōka* and friends. In total, we raised £2,906.00.

I would like to say a special thank you to all the *sensei* who donated items for the auction. Also, thanks goes to Daniel Lavrick for all his hard work with the auction, and to Miss Matsuda Kazuyo for her assistance in Japanese translation. Thank you also to my dojo members, and to the many people who helped and supported the project, both in Japan and the UK.

# A Reflection on *Reigi*

By Taylor Winter

The strong presence of *reigi* in kendo is indisputable. It forms a basis for learning by providing a safe environment, regimen, and structure. It sets out a strict set of rules and guidelines that stop kendo from degrading from an art form or sport, to a bunch of crazies beating each other senseless with sticks. I am told that *reigi* encompasses the actions and formalities which show respect towards our training environment, *sensei*, and training partners. The physical actions provide a vessel which serves to facilitate humility, respect, and control of other emotions such as aggression. Without this facilitation, we see recklessness, lack of self-control, and lack of respect in the dojo ultimately leading to unrefined and untamed kendo.

So, why an amateurish ramble of what I think of *reigi*? Recently, I have been thinking of how *reigi* differs between dojo, and even countries. In addition, I have also been asking questions as to the reasons why certain things are done in certain ways. *Reigi* can be very abstract, or at least seem to be. Take how you lean a *shinai* on the wall for example; it's well known that the *shinai* should be tip up. Or is it? Recently I learned that an oiled *katana* would be put tip-up so that the coat of oil applied would remain even, as opposed to the oil pooling in the bottom of the *saya* (scabbard) if it were placed tip-down. As the *shinai* should be treated as a sword, correctly observing this point shows respect for our kendo equipment, and also focuses our serious mind-set by making the association to a real weapon. I mention this example because it has been pointed out to me that this used to be the norm. Nowadays, we often see *shinai* leaning against a wall tip-down, or simply strewn across the dojo floor.

What does this change in attitude indicate for kendo? Some may say that there is no harm in neglecting such a minor detail. Yet it is the broader changes, or fading away of adherence to traditional protocols, that interest me. I have attended Japanese universities in which students do not even bow to the *shōmen* when entering and leaving the dojo. As all serious martial

artists know, showing respect to your place of training is a fundamental aspect of *reigi*. My point here is that the very same students would surely have been severely reprimanded by their teachers at their high schools or *machi-dōjō* for such a blatant transgression of accepted protocol. But, they seem not to care so much anymore. So, what could be behind this change in acknowledgement of *reigi*? Does this mean that many students in Japanese university kendo clubs no longer have respect for their training space or the people in it?

A more ambiguous example is sitting whilst putting on *bōgu*. This rule is seldom followed by my Japanese peers, but I have always been taught that it is a significant form of accepted *reigi* in the dojo. Nevertheless, if we look back in history before the advent of modern kendo, we might struggle to see how this particular procedure came to fruition. When a warrior donned his armour before battle, he would be standing, with an assistant strapping each piece to his body. However, modern kendo decorum dictates that we sit in that excruciating kneeling position, *seiza*, as we put on our protective equipment. I have been informed that the reason for this is that sitting calmly in *seiza* while putting on your *bōgu* mentally prepares you for training in the same manner as *mokusō*. I have yet to hear any other explanation other than "because it's traditional"… I am curious to see if this aspect of *reigi* is going to continue as I even see *sensei* who do not to comply.

Lastly, a clear cut example which got me started on this tangent is when we line up before *keiko*. I am sure topic least 95 per cent of people reading this article would line up before training starts, sit down in *seiza*, and place their *shinai* at their left side. A somewhat famous, or rather, infamous lot of *kendōka* known as the Tokyo Riot Police are different. They place their *shinai* down on their right side; this means they cannot "draw it as easily", thus showing respect for their training partners. My university dojo also follows this rule. When asking one of my *sensei* about this he simply said "We do it with a *bokutō*, so why not with *shinai*?" In other words, placing the *shinai* down on the right side when sitting, as opposed to the standard left side, is more in tune with traditional protocol for placing a *katana*.

It was all of these points I had noticed in my trainings at various dojo that motivated me to find out more about why we do things the way we do. I was curious as to how these aspects of *reigi* were changing, or even disappearing. Upon asking the top *sensei* at my university, he took only a second of pondering before launching into one of his 'Yoda' like explanations which usually leave me more confused. He explained the significance of *reigi* and why things are certain ways, and why it's important we follow these points diligently. He said changes occur when two concepts clash. The clashes, he continued, were usually between "tradition" and "convenience".

The example he relayed to me concerned the *shinai*; of course, it is convenient to place the *shinai* on the left so you can simply stand up and be ready to draw your sword, but this is not tradition. Traditionally the sword would be on the right side out of respect for training partners, and to add a sense of reality to the idea of the *shinai* being a sword. In this case, convenience has taken a point against tradition. In a similar manner it is tradition to bow to the *shōmen*, but it's much more convenient to walk straight into the room without the bothersome need to stop and bow. Seeing this conflict between tradition and convenience is an interesting problem, but is undoubtedly exacerbated by the fact that many people no longer know why a given tradition exists. Much of it has become forgotten knowledge, and when you question it, it is hard to justify adherence if nobody knows how it came about.

The main question I have about this is how it affects our ability to practise kendo. Can neglecting certain nebulous aspects of *reigi* decrease our respect in the dojo? Does it alter our psychological mind-set in kendo? A greater concern is the safety of practitioners in the dojo. An important aspect of *reigi* is that it serves to guide our behaviour in the dojo and helps us understand and maintain order. Thus, by turning a blind eye to others neglecting *reigi*, or failing to strictly practise *reigi* ourselves, could we actually be introducing increased risk and danger to the dojo? In any case, I certainly do not have any profound answers to the dichotomy of convenience and tradition as it relates to *reigi* in the dojo, other than to say that it behooves kendo practitioners to at least make an effort to understand what various forms of *reigi* mean, where they came from, and why they are necessary.

# HISTORICAL SIGHTSEEING

Text and photographs by Bruce Flanagan

## Part 06
# THE SHINSEN-GUMI 新選組

Mibu Temple in Kyoto served as one of the bases of operations for the Shinsen-gumi in their patrols of the capital

The lives and deeds of the members of the Shinsen-gumi will ever remain a source of controversy, intrigue, romance and swashbuckling drama for aficionados of Japanese history. Cloak-and-dagger accounts of espionage, assassination, political alliances, violent raids and sword duels abound, occasionally obscuring the line between fact and hearsay. To some they were a security force nobly working to keep the peace in chaotic times, while to others they were merely a recruited band of bloodthirsty assassins.

The initial catalyst in the development of this highly feared unit was the arrival of Commodore Perry and his terror-inspiring warships in Edo (Tokyo) Bay in 1853 bearing a written request from President Fillmore that Japan enter a trade treaty with the United States. Since the 1630s Japan had been isolated from contact with the rest of the world under seclusion orders (*sakoku*) from the Tokugawa shogunate. Being ignorant of world affairs and foreign technology, Japan was now split into two factions with the appearance of these 'foreign barbarians' (*gaii*) in their 'black ships' (*kurofune*). The first faction was against foreign intervention in Japanese dealings with their slogan of 'expel the barbarians' (*jōi*). The second faction supported the influx of foreign influence and ending Japan's isolation with their slogan of 'open our country' (*kaikoku*).

Left: Kondō Isami (1834-1868)
Shinsen-gumi Commander - *Kyoku-chō*

Right: Hijikata Toshizō (1835-1869)
Shinsen-gumi Vice-Commander - *Fuku-chō*

Portraits courtesy of the National Diet Library

The issue was further complicated by the presence of two institutions that vied for power and divided the loyalties of the nation. On one side stood the shogunate military government (Bakufu) wielding control under the iron fist of the shogun, Tokugawa Iesada, based in Edo. The Tokugawa line had controlled the realm since their decisive victory at the Battle of Sekigahara in 1600 and had since implemented the social class system (*shi-nō-kō-shō*) dominated by the samurai. On the other side of the power struggle was the imperial court (*chōtei*) headed at the time by Emperor Kōmei in Kyō (Kyoto) which had held hereditary power since ancient times. These turbulent and ultimately final years of the Tokugawa shogunate effectively began with Perry's arrival in 1853 and ended with the formation of the Meiji Government in 1868. This period of approximately fifteen years is now referred to as the end of the Bakufu (Bakumatsu period). Many well-known figures such as Saigō Takamori and Sakamoto Ryōma rose to prominence in this time; individuals who helped catapult the rapidly modernising nation onto the world stage. The Shinsen-gumi, largely consisting of adamant supporters of the Bakufu, made every effort to protect the livelihood of Japan's military government, and so it would not be an exaggeration to say that they fought to preserve the bushi way of life.

## Political dissension

Perry's arrival and the potential threat of foreign encroachment sent shockwaves through the nation's echelons of power. Lords of the feudal domains had already been divided in their support of the emperor and his imperial court, but now advocates of imperial rule rallied anew under the banner of 'revere the emperor' (*sonnō*) while others amongst them afraid of foreign meddling in domestic affairs propounded 'revere the emperor and expel the barbarians' (*sonnō-jōi*).

Being unable to present a united front to foreign trade powers was a terrifying notion and it was even suggested that the Bakufu and the imperial court unite and rule the nation under a system known as *kōbu-gattai*. Due to a division of interests however, the policy never saw fruition. Kyoto was the seat of imperial power at the time and it was here that masterless samurai (*rōshi*) banded together in support of the emperor and foreign exclusion. They committed acts of terrorism against the bureaucrats, warriors and merchants that were aligned with the Bakufu (the *sabaku-ha* faction). Acts of assassination became so prevalent in Kyoto that the police force of the time could not handle the situation and, consequently, fanatic supporters of imperial rule began to take over the reins of the imperial court.

In order to regain control of the capital in the name of the Bakufu, Matsudaira Shungaku, a feudal lord in Fukui, convinced Matsudaira Katamori, the lord of Aizu domain, to post employment offers for a new security force intended to quell the rising tide of terrorism and political unrest in Kyoto. The powerful and influential Aizu domain, which had held a long alliance with the Tokugawa Bakufu, declared that the security force would be called the Rōshi-gumi and would be charged with upholding *bakufu* authority by any means necessary. Bakufu Isami, hailing from Musashi Province near Edo and master of the Shieikan dojo[1], rose to the call, as did other members of his dojo. The Rōshi-gumi's role would be to crack down on supporters of imperial power who were anti-Bakufu activists (the *tōbaku-ha* faction), however Kiyokawa

The red and white standard of the Shinsen-gumi featuring the character for sincerity (*makoto*)

The Yagi-ke residence, one of the main quarters (*tonsho*) used by the Shinsen-gumi in Kyoto

Sanjō Ōhashi, the bridge travellers from eastern Japan and Edo crossed when arriving in Kyoto

Hachirō, the individual in charge of assembling the group, was secretly scheming to take charge and use it to his own ends as an imperialist task force to support the emperor. After Kiyokawa led his team of recruits from Edo to Kyoto and openly declared his intentions, Kondō Isami led a faction of the group to join with Serizawa Kamo (a Mito domain *rōshi*) under Aizu domain control to preserve their original goal of supporting the Bakufu. They called themselves the Mibu-rōshi-gumi, severed connections with Kiyokawa and their new group became the forerunner of the Shinsen-gumi.

In their surprisingly short yet eventful six years of duty, the Shinsen-gumi fought in many battles and carried out numerous operations in the name of the Edo Bakufu. Their travels took them from Kyoto to Edo to Aizu, and as far away as Hakodate in Ezochi (modern-day Hokkaidō).

## Prowling packs of wolves

Initially twelve members of the Shieikan dojo applied to join the Rōshi-gumi, including Kondō Isami, Hijikata Toshizō, Okita Sōji and Nagakura Shinpachi. A total of 234 Kantō-based warriors were recruited through Kiyokawa Hachirō's call to arms. Kiyokawa, with his secret imperialist alignment, had been advertising for troops under placards of 'loyalty and patriotism' but had actually been employing individuals who were loyal to the emperor. In effect, he had amassed a formidably sized personal army consisting mostly of pro-emperor warriors. Once the newly established Rōshi-gumi was assembled, Kiyokawa led them to Kyoto with the bogus objectives of upholding peace and Bakufu power and serving as the shogun's bodyguards during any visits he would make from Edo. They arrived in Mibu Village in Kyoto on February 23, 1863 where Shintokuji Temple would serve as their headquarters. Kiyokawa announced his ulterior agenda for the unit and persuaded over 200 of the *rōshi* to return immediately with him to Edo to perform terrorist acts in support of the emperor and the expulsion of foreigners. Despite assembling large forces in Edo with the support of his pro-emperor allies, his ambitious plans were halted one day when, drunk and walking home alone, he was cut down by a pro-Bakufu assassin.

Under the leadership of Kondō Isami and Serizawa Kamo, 24 members of the group had remained in Kyoto, calling themselves the Mibu-rōshi-gumi and supporting the *baku* Bakufu *fu* under Aizu domain supervision. They had been opposed to Kiyokawa's plans of imperial support from the outset. In joint operations with police and another security group called the Mimawari-gumi, they patrolled the streets of the capital with pro-Bakufu objectives. Their skills in swordsmanship, strict rules, and devotion to their cause made them a force to be reckoned with. Night and day they launched raids on suspected anti-Bakufu activists in Kyoto's narrow paths, lanes, shops and residences, wearing body armour and wielding swords and spears in close quarter combat. Their cutthroat efficiency earned them the nickname Mibu Wolves (*Mibu-rō*). When raiding a building they would generally operate in four-man entry groups and often wore pale blue *haori* coats with white triangular patterns around the cuffs. Their unit flag was coloured red with the same white triangular pattern and was emblazoned with the characters for *makoto* or *sei-jitsu* (sincerity).

> The Shinsen-gumi devised a code of five prohibitions (*kyokuchū-hatto*) that all members were required to follow under threat of *seppuku*.
>
> 1. Do not turn your back on the way of the warrior (*shidō*)
> 2. Do not abandon your duties
> 3. Do not raise funds privately
> 4. Do not deal in legal affairs
> 5. Do not engage in personal conflicts

A chain mail shirt (*kusari-katabira*) that belonged to Kondō Isami weighing approximately 6kg

## Simplified timeline of Shinsen-gumi related events

| | | |
|---|---|---|
| Kyoto (Kyoto) | Feb 23, 1863 | The Rōshi-gumi is assembled in Kyoto. |
| | Mar 12, 1863 | Kondō establishes the Mibu-rōshi-gumi. |
| | Aug, 1863 | The Shinsen-gumi is officially formed following the coup d'état of August 18. |
| | Jun 5, 1864 | Ikeda-ya incident. |
| | Jun 10, 1867 | Shinsen-gumi members are awarded *hatamoto* retainer status. |
| | Jan 3, 1868 | Battle of Toba-Fushimi. |
| Edo (Tōkyoto) | Mar 6, 1868 | The Shinsen-gumi is reorganised into the Kōyō-chinbu-tai but is defeated at the Battle of Kōshū-Katsunuma. |
| | Apr 2, 1868 | Battle formation at Nagare-yama. |
| | Apr 3, 1868 | Kondō surrenders to the new government forces. |
| | Apr 11, 1868 | Hijikata joins forces with the former shogunate's army. |
| | Apr 19, 1868 | Utsunomiya Castle is captured. |
| | Apr 25, 1868 | Kondō is executed (beheading). |
| Aizu | Apr 5, 1868 | Former Shinsen-gumi members join forces with other troops and leave for battle from Shirakawa. |
| | Aug 21, 1868 | Defeat and retreat at the Battle of Bonari Pass. |
| Hakodate | Oct 20, 1868 | Arrival in Ezochi (Hokkaidō). |
| | Dec 15, 1868 | Government commences in Hakodate. |
| | Mar 25, 1869 | Naval Battle of Miyako Bay. |
| | Apr 13, 1869 | Hijikata's troops join the Battle of Futamata-guchi. |
| | May 11, 1869 | Hijikata is killed by gunshot in combat. |
| | May 15, 1869 | Remaining members of the Shinsen-gumi surrender. |

Their daily regimen consisted of rising early, cleaning their quarters, and then indoor or outdoor *keiko* followed by breakfast. The day's work allocations would then be announced during a line-up (*chōrei*). Those with no allocation were free to do as they pleased, and there was no restriction that they stay on the premises. Off-duty troops were permitted to visit the town and Shinsen-gumi members were noted as frequent patrons of the nearby Shimabara entertainment and pleasure district (*yūkaku-gai*). Those on duty would patrol the outskirts of central Kyoto in day and night shifts.

Although under the patronage of the Aizu domain, the group was also known to extort money from anti-Bakufu establishments by force, and to strike deals with merchants, medical practitioners, and others who could provide them with goods and services. The fundamentals of their *bujutsu* training came from the curriculum of Tennen Rishin-ryū which was the *ryūha* practised at Kondō's Shieikan dojo in Edo. It was a comprehensive art consisting of *kenjutsu*, *jūjutsu*, *konbō-jutsu* and *kiai-jutsu* although individuals proficient in swordsmanship were welcomed regardless of the style they practised. With the swelling of their numbers to over seventy soon after the Ikeda-ya incident (see next section), the group enjoyed unchallenged authority over the city's streets, while the ample nightlife continued to provide members with the chance to temporarily forget about their gory work.

At last the Bakufu was achieving its goal of wrangling power back from the imperial court and its supporters. One dilemma that the Shinsen-gumi faced however was that, just because an establishment or group openly supported the Emperor, this did not necessarily mean that they also actively sought to overthrow the Bakufu. Clashes as a result of political misunderstandings ensued, and inner rivalry between Kondō-aligned and Serizawa-aligned groups of Shinsen-gumi troops only intensified the problem. However, despite these smaller goings-on, more significant changes were occurring across the realm. Trade agreements ratified with various foreign powers saw influential domains such as Tosa, Chōshū, Satsuma and Saga, as well as the imperial court aristocracy (*kuge*), begin to vie for control in Japan's inevitable course of participation in foreign trade. Further conflicts of a larger scale now lay in store for the Shinsen-gumi.

## Fateful actions

The quintessential raid and slaughter of anti-Bakufu conspirators by the Shinsen-gumi occurred on June 5, 1864, in the Ikeda-ya, a *ryokan* in Kyoto. Vice-Commander Hijikata Toshizō abducted and tortured[2] a *rōshi* of the Chōshū domain on suspicion of plotting against the Emperor in order to threaten the shogun. Under the duress of torture, Furudaka Shuntarō revealed that he and up to 250 of his companions were planning to set fires around Kyoto, kidnap the emperor in the chaos, and assassinate the head of city security when he attempted to rescue the emperor. He also confessed that many of the conspirators were lodging around the Kawara-machi area. Deductions about the man's business connections obtained from Shinsen-gumi spies lead the group to carry out inspections of certain entertainment and accommodation facilities in Kawara-machi at the beginning of the Gion Festival. When Kondō led

The Ikeda-ya premises is now an *izakaya* standing on Kyoto's Sanjō-dōri

Kyoto Imperial Palace (Kyototo Gosho), former location of the imperial court and Emperor Kōmei's residence

Nijō Castle (Nijō-jō), former Tokugawa shogun residence in Kyoto and Mimawari-gumi security base

nine men to inspect the Ikeda-ya *ryokan*, they discovered firearms and spears and could hear drunken activity on the second floor; the Emperor's would-be kidnappers were in a merry state discussing their plans upstairs. Reports differ as to the total number of conspirators involved but Kondō himself wrote that 11 of them died in the ensuing combat and suicides, and 23 were captured. The Shinsen-gumi only lost three members, but the Ikeda-ya incident spread their reputation as a force not to be trifled with. Incidentally, an individual named Katsura Kogorō, who went under many aliases, managed to escape from the melee via the inn's roof and went on to became Kido Takayoshi, one of the "Three Heroes" of the Meiji Restoration (*Ishin no Sanketsu*) alongside Saigō Takamori and Ōkubo Toshimichi.

Anti-foreign ideology thrived at this time, and amongst the political upheaval Emperor Kōmei appointed Tokugawa Yoshinobu as the new shogun in 1866 after Tokugawa Iemochi passed away from illness. Emperor Kōmei then died shortly after in the same year leaving the imperial throne to his son, Emperor Meiji. Despite strong opposition against opening Japan to foreign trade, progressive anti-Bakufu domains such as Satsuma and Chōshū were already opening their ports, sending officials on overseas visits, and availing themselves of the latest in foreign technology and military know-how. The two domains had even created a military union known as the Satsuma Chōshū Alliance (*Sacchō Meiyaku*).

Due to internal and external pressures Yoshinobu tendered his role as shogun and stepped down in deference to the Emperor in 1867 effectively leaving Emperor Meiji to lead Japan in its new era of Westernisation. However, despite his official resignation, death threats continued to be made against Yoshinobu from his many domain-based adversaries. Still being in command of the former-Bakufu armies, he defiantly declared war on the Satsuma and Chōshū domains and their supporters.

Animosities culminated at the Battle of Toba-Fushimi beginning Jan 3, 1868 in the area of Fushimi between Kyoto and Osaka. Yoshinobu's former-Bakufu army (including Hijikata Toshizō) armed with traditional weaponry faced off against Saigō Takamori's Satsuma forces armed with modern firearms and artillery. The former-Bakufu army had the advantage of numbers, but was defeated and forced to retreat when supposed-ally Tsu domain ordered its troops to open fire on Yoshinobu's positions. With the realisation of this betrayal, Yoshinobu fled to Edo where he surrendered himself and Edo Castle to imperial forces. Despite his surrender, die-hard partisans of the Bakufu formed pockets of resistance against the Satsuma and Chōshū-led imperial forces which now threatened to sweep the length of the country from west to east in support of Emperor Meiji and diplomacy and trade with foreign countries. Lingering hostilities erupted into a series of battles, effectively of civil proportions, collectively known as the Boshin War (*Boshin Sensō*).

The Shinsen-gumi continued to fight for the shogun and, after Kondō was captured and beheaded by imperial troops, remaining members of the Shinsen-gumi joined Hijikata and Saitō Hajime (formerly a Shinsen-gumi unit captain) in various battles and skirmishes. These Boshin War conflicts took them further to the north-east of the country where they teamed up with remnants of Aizu domain's armies but faced further defeats.

In preparation for further armed revolt, supporters of the shogun in the regions of Tōhoku and Echigo created an ill-fated group of domains in 1868 entitled the Alliance of Northern Domains (*Oūetsu Reppan Dōmei*). Their loyalty to the shogun and the samurai way of life was fierce but their thinning numbers and lack of organization saw their under-manned and under-equipped forces lose to the imperial armies. With the backing of navy admiral Enomoto Takeaki, the Bakufu forces made naval sorties which even saw Shinsen-gumi members executing death-defying pirate manoeuvres from ship deck to ship deck with the support of military strategists from France.[3] Their last stand was made in Ezo (Hokkaidō) in the port city of Hakodate where they received reinforcement from like-minded shogun supporters of the Ezo Republic (*Ezo Kyotowa-koku*) who hoped that Ezo could become a self-governing samurai

Goryōkaku fort in Hakodate City, Hokkaidō

A statue of Kondō Isami and the graves of Serizawa Kamo and various members of the Shinsen-gumi at Mibu Temple in Kyoto

state unaffected by imperial control. The star-shaped fortress Goryōkaku, consisting of five points of land around a central base surrounded by a moat system, formed one of the main fighting posts. Despite the site being strategically designed to allow cannon fire in all directions, droves of imperial (now Meiji government) troops began to land in Hakodate from navy ships and quickly defeated the final ranks of the former-Bakufu soldiers. Remaining Shinsen-gumi troops surrendered to the new Meiji government's army on May 15, 1869, four days after Hijikata was killed by gunshot in combat. The battle drew to a close quickly thereafter.

## Dawn of a new age

With this resistance eliminated, the bushi class was no longer a viable power and Emperor Meiji moved his new government to Edo which was renamed Tokyo or eastern capital. In 1871 domains were abolished and prefectures were established (*haihan-chiken*), and in 1877 samurai were no longer recognised financially by the government. The heyday of the samurai had drawn to an end. Various surviving members of the Shinsen-gumi returned to ordinary occupations such as Nagakura Shinpachi and Shimada Kai who taught *kenjutsu* and Saitō Hajime who became a police officer in Tokyo. The Shinsen-gumi left an indelible mark on Japanese history and their strong ideology and cold ferocity in battle lives on through the plethora of movies, literature, cartoons, comics, games and merchandise that their lives and deeds have inspired.

The main *bujutsu ryūha* practised by the Shinsen-gumi was Tennen Rishin-ryū. Kondō Isami was the third head of the school and its teachings survive today in *koryū* form as recognised by the Nihon Kobudō Kyotokai.

Left: members of the *ryū* perform in the annual *enbu taikai* at the Meiji Jingū shrine in TōKyoto

Photograph courtesy of Jeff Broderick

### Notes

1. The Shieikan dojo is believed to have been located in the area that is now Shinjuku-ku.
2. The loft where Furudaka was suspended by rope over a three-storey drop and tortured in the Maekawa-tei quarters is still preserved today.
3. An increasing reliance on foreign military technology and weaponry saw many experts from abroad called to service in Japan.

### Bibliography

1. *Shinsen-gumi Shiseki Kikō (Zusetsu)*, Hagio M., Gakken, 2003.
2. *Rekishi Gunzō Shiri-zu 31 - Kessei Shinsen-gumi*, Futomaru N. (ed), Gakken, 2003.
3. *Shinsen-gumi no koto ga omoshiroi hodo wakaru hon*, Nakami T., Chukei Publishing Co., 2004 (timeline adapted from page 15).
4. *A Brief History of the Samurai*, Clements J., Running Press, 2010.
5. *Shinsengumi - The Shogun's Last Samurai Corps*, Hillsborough R., Tuttle Publishing, 2010.
6. *Dictionary of Battles and Sieges*, Jaques T., Greenwood Press, 2007.
7. *Kōjien Dai-go-Han*, Iwanami Shoten, 2004.

### Related websites

- www.mibudera.com
- www.mibu-yagike.jp
- kyu-maekawatei.com
- r.gnavi.co.jp/k781330
- www.ryozen-museum.or.jp
- www.city.hino.tokyo.jp/shinsenr
- www.tennenrishinryu.com

### Coming up

The next instalment of Historical Sightseeing will delve into the long and violent history of the province of Owari, birthplace of Oda Nobunaga and Toyotomi Hideyoshi, which now forms the western half of Aichi Prefecture and Nagoya.

About the author:

Bruce Flanagan is a lecturer at Ritsumeikan University in Kyoto. He holds a Master of Arts in interpreting and translation studies from the University of New South Wales in Sydney and practises kendo, iaido, karate, naginata and jodo.

# Argentina
## New Kendo Wave & Why it Matters

Gabriel Weitzner (Canada)

Occupying most of the southern portion of South America, Argentina extends 3460 km (2150 miles) from the Northern tip of the country to Tierra del Fuego. It would be fair to mention that Argentina is much larger than Spain, France and Germany combined. This fact facilitates an understanding of the challenge in covering kendo practice over the vast Argentine territory.

In Argentina, the practice of kendo started around the 1970s. It was introduced at the "Asociacion Japonesa Argentina" (AJA) by the late Miyagi Masakatsu-sensei, later on joined by the late Sakae Eizo-sensei.

Some of the first kendo students, among others, were Ernesto Kimura, Carlos Alberto Pascual and Oscar Cirone. In July 1978, Argentina received a visit by Kasahara-sensei (FIK secretary general), and Onuma-sensei (Tokyo Police), Hanshi and Kyōshi 8-dan respectively.

National Championship 2011

Ladies Seminar

Carlos Alberto Pascual and Oscar Cirone both started kendo at AJA, and represented Argentina at the 4th Kendo World Championship in Sapporo in 1979 for the first time. Since then, Argentina has participated in almost every WKC.

In 1985 the Argentine Kendo Federation FAK, was created, with the AJA as a founding member of the federation. In 1988, Fukumoto Shūji-sensei visited Argentina for over a month promoting kendo in Buenos Aires, Mar del Plata, Cordoba, Mendoza and Corrientes. Until 1985, the practice of kendo in Argentina was centred in Buenos Aires.

Due to the efforts of Ernesto Kimura, kendo had a chance to prosper in Cordoba with Gustavo Adolfo Ramos. He took responsibility for the creation of the Asociacion Cordobesa de Kendo in 1993. Ernesto Kimura helped kendo in Mendoza as well. During the '80s and '90s, Argentine kendo was growing slowly but steadily, due to individual strong efforts and the new communication media – e-mail and the internet – which created new channels for the expansion of kendo.

Oscar Cirone
– President - Confederacion de Kendo de la Republica Argentina

In the last few years, something remarkable has taken place, and the constant efforts put in place in the past have started to pay off. Kendo expanded to the provinces of La Pampa, Catamarca and La Rioja thanks in great part to Gustavo Adolfo Ramos. Please keep in mind the distances (over a thousand km) between these places to truly understand the tremendous efforts to develop kendo there.

Gustavo Jacinto, who started kendo with Oscar Cirone, was able to expand the art not only in the Palermo area, but he also managed to introduce kendo to the Military, more precisely a place called Circulo Militar, as well as Buenos Aires University and the very prestigious Buenos Aires College (Colegio Nacional Buenos Aires).

Another remarkable event took place when Chief of Police Jorge Venturini, who started kendo with Oscar Cirone, created two clubs – one in La Plata, and another in Mar del Plata, both in the province of Buenos Aires, four-hundred kilometres apart. Several years later, in collaboration with Juan Fuster and Gustavo Jacinto, they introduced kendo to the Police Academy, where it was taught to over seven-hundred police cadets.

What of women in Argentine kendo? The Ramos family is a very special one. Not only does Gustavo practise Kendo, but his wife Monica Arioni and two of their three daughters also train. Natilia and Ximena Ramos both started kendo at eleven and eight years of age respectively.

Police Academy Kendo

By now they have an impressive collection of first places in individual and team competitions over the last decade.

The female kendo population has seen exponential growth in Cordoba, and all the other regions. The Cordoba's Ladies Team was twice visited by Pernilla Nordwall from the Swedish Kendo Team. Penny, as her friends in Argentina call her, spent some time immersing herself in Argentine culture and the Spanish language.

Recently, through the sponsorship of Ernesto Kimura and Gustavo Ramos, Asuncion Gonzalez, a 5-dan from Madrid, Spain, went to Cordoba to conduct the very first kendo seminar for women in Argentina. The event was a resounding success.

During the first weekend of September 2011, the National Kendo Tournament took place in Argentina. The cities of Buenos Aires, La Plata, Mar del Plata, Cordoba, Mendoza, Rosario, La Pampa, Neuquen, and special invitees from the neighbouring country Republica Oriental del Uruguay, gathered in Buenos Aires for the championship. All those cities were represented by about 13 clubs with more than 130 competitors.

How is it possible to accomplish such exponential growth and the introduction to important institutions? The answer is the strong collaboration among all the people across Argentina, who possess the common goal of preserving kendo's values.

In 2011, the Argentine Kendo Confederation (Confederacion de Kendo de la Republica Argentina) will be officially inaugurated. This event will be another milestone for the growth of kendo in Argentina. If you plan to visit Argentina, and would like to train, please contact the following people:

- **Confederacion de Kendo de la Republica Argentina**
  **Oscar Cirone** – President -

- **Asociacion Cordobesa de Kendo - Cordoba**
  Contact: **Gustavo Ramos**   gustavo_adolfo_ramos@hotmail.com

- **Asociacion Argentina de Kendo - Buenos Aires**
  Contact: **Oscar Cirone**    oscarcirone@hotmail.com

- **Asociacion Japonesa Argentina - Buenos Aires**
  Contact: **Ernesto Kimura**  ernestokimura@yahoo.com.ar
           **Daisuke Miura**    miuradai45@hotmail.com

- **Asociacion Yoishinkan - Mar del Plata - La Plata**
  Contact: **Jorge Venturini**  liderrojo1@hotmail.com
           **Juan Fuster**      argfuster@gmail.com

- **Asociacion Kenmukan - Buenos Aires**
  Contact: **Gustavo Jacinto**  gustavojacinto@gmail.com

- **Asociacion Dai Shin Kai - Buenos Aires**
  Contact: **Gustavo Manini**   genbudo@fibertel.com.ar

- **Asociacion Mendocina de Kendo - Mendoza**
  Contact: **Nicolas del Solar**

- **Asociacion Rosarina de Kendo - Santa Fe**
  Contact: **Jose Luis Zanotti** joseluis@rosariokendo.com.ar

- **Asociacion Chun Mu Dang - Buenos Aires**
  Contact: **Pedro Seo**        kendoseo@hotmail.com

- **Dojo La Pampa - La Pampa**
  Contact: **Sergio Reale**

- **Asociacion Hanin - Buenos Aires**
  Contact: **Soojin Baik**      drbaik.soojin@gmail.com

# KURIKARA: THE SWORD AND THE SERPENT

By John Maki Evans

Review by Taylor Winter

"In *Mikkyo*—Japanese esoteric Buddhism—the dragon Kurikara symbolizes the internal energy developed through sword practice. Kurikara is a manifestation of the fierce bodhisattva Fudo Myo O, the patron of ascetics and warriors in Japan, who uses his sword to destroy delusions and sever attachments. Fudo's sword represents the gaining of discriminative power and decisiveness—the ability to cut through illusion and attachment. This leads to the development of an inner energy that allows one to 'burn up' all obstacles to spiritual freedom."

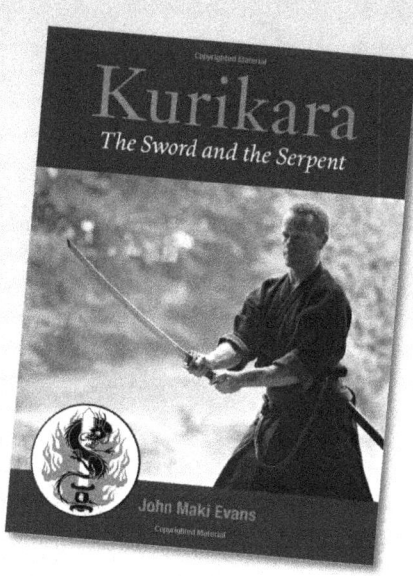

*Kurikara: The Sword and the Serpent* by John Maki Evans, shares a wealth of experiences and ideas the author has collected over his years practising *koryū* sword forms. The author teaches yoga and *battōdō* in London. He is also the director of the Islington Yoga School, and heads the Fudokan Battodo dojo which is affiliated with the International Battodo Federation. He was taught by the *yamabushi* (mountain ascetics), or esoteric Buddhist monks who lived and trained deep in the mountains of Japan. His latest book is an easy read which gives an overview of general *kenjutsu* philosophy and training. He is able to explain the technical and spiritual elements of swordsmanship in a way that is informative and accessible, giving readers an overall concept of *koryū* teachings.

The descriptions are simple and to the point. This makes it a book with appeal to any reader, regardless of *koryū* experience. The content follows a chronological description, including an explanation of the stages of swordsmanship which relate to elements in some *ryūha* (schools). A reader who studies *koryū* will definitely feel moments that cause pieces of the puzzle to fall into place. I experienced this when reading the section explaining the stages a swordsman moves through when working towards *ki-ken-tai-itchi*.

I assume that many people reading this review are kendo practitioners. The *kendōka* will have moments ranging from "I can't make heads or tails of this" to "oh, of course, why didn't I think of that." Topics relating to the latter would include ideas on movement, the importance of the legs in swordsmanship, and breathing. A topic which may cause some confusion will be the author's ideas on *tanren*, or use of core exercises that meld "inner" and "outer" power, but this is a crucial concept in the study of modern kendo, so is very useful to reread many times. As a *kendōka*, reading this little volume will allow you to see the general ideas of *koryū kenjutsu*, and how they apply to the study of modern kendo. Many of the ideas in the book directly relate to kendo, although it might not seem so at first.

The section I found particularly interesting was on *tameshi-giri* – practice cutting with a live blade. As an area of swordsmanship I have never had experience in before, I found the author's explanation to be fascinating. He first describes the basic ideas behind *tameshi-giri*, and then expands into more detail. The reasons offered for training in specific ways are an important feature throughout the book, and the author offers logical reasoning for why other alternative methods of training are inferior, and thus are not often seen in *koryū* schools.

As stated earlier in the review, most ideas are based on the author's experiences. The ideas are all well supported and references are provided to substantiate his writing. For *kenjutsu* practitioners, or people who want an informative source of information for the background of modern kendo, *Kurikara: The Sword and the Serpent* is an ideal introduction.

**Paperback:** 160 pages
**Publisher:** Blue Snake Books; 1 edition (December 7, 2010)
**Language:** English
**ISBN-10:** 1583942440
**ISBN-13:** 978-1583942444

# Jukendo no Kata

## – Final part: TANKEN TAI TŌ NO KATA –

*Tanken*: Fujita Hirō, K8-dan
*Tō*: Endō Mamoru, H8-dan

by Baptiste Tavernier

The Tankendo-no-Kata's ultimate purpose is to impart the essence of tankendo. The forms combine the basic techniques with a fixed order, and through learning the combination of techniques, students of tankendo develop a strong spirit, good posture and technical ability. The practitioner learns to understand and judge correct *maai*, identify opportunities for thrusting, polish their technique, and experience the exquisiteness of *zanshin*. The student must try to understand the principles underlying the technical combinations and postures, rather than just going through the motions superficially. It is also important to train with the purpose of cultivating mind and body. The role of *uchikata* is to highlight the techniques of *shikata*. It is particularly important to execute the techniques with powerful *kiai* and maintain the symbiotic relationship between *uchikata* and *shikata*.

The Tanken-tai-Tō-no-Kata consists of six sets, which can be divided into two groups of three. From *ippon-me* to *sanbon-me*, the detached bayonet overcomes the sword. From *yohon-me* to *roppon-me*, the sword prevails.

## About TANKENDO:

Tankendo literally means the way of the short sword. It is in fact the art of detached bayonet, as devised by the Japanese army during the Taishō period. Tankendo is nowadays an allied discipline of jukendo, within the All Japan Jukendo Federation. It encompasses *kata* and *bōgu* practice. Interestingly, during the Shōwa period tankendo eventually fell under the influence of some high-ranked kendo instructors: the use of curved *kodachi* with *tsuba* instead of straight wooden bayonet became widespread; a few techniques were modified to look more kendo-ish, and *kirikaeshi* was introduced as well. Although this trend is still present in modern tankendo, practitioners must never forget that their actual weapon is a *chokutō*, a straight blade with no *tsuba*, and that rather than cutting, the main technique in tankendo is thrusting.

*Irimi* is a term used by tankendo exponents to denote an offensive action where the attacker enters into the *maai* of his opponent and stabs him at close quarters. *Irimi* generally consists of several phases: entering into the *maai*; suppressing the opponent's weapon or controlling the opponent's wrist; grabbing the forearm or the elbow of the opponent, then breaking his balance; and finaly stabbing to the torso.

## Kamae

Although there are four standard *kamae* in tankendo, only two are demonstrated in the Tanken-tai-Tō-no-Kata: *chūdan-no-kamae* and *chūdan-irimi-no-kamae*.

## Ippon-me: nodo no tsuki - sen

*Uchikata* (*tō*) and *shikata* (*tanken*) are facing each other, separated by a distance of nine steps. After bowing, both assume *chūdan-no-kamae* (photo ❷). Then, vigilantly, *uchikata* lowers his weapon into *gedan-no-kamae* while *shikata* assumes *chūdan-irimi-no-kamae* (Photo ❸).

Starting from the front foot, *uchikata* and *shikata* take three big steps forward. As soon as they enter into the *maai* for attack (photo ❹), *shikata* takes the initiative, suppresses *uchikata*'s sword by pushing it downward (Photo ❺) and immediately thrusts at *uchikata*'s *nodo* (Photo ❻).

While taking a big step backwards, *shikata* pulls his *tanken* back strongly, and immediately shows *zanshin* by taking a small step forward keeping the tip pointed at *uchikata*.(Photo ❼).

*Uchikata* leads *shikata* back to *chūdan-no-kamae*. They both disengage their weapons to close the *kata* (Photo ❽). From the rear foot, both take five small steps and return to their original starting positions (Photo ❾).

### Nihon-me: seitai do no tsuki - sensen no sen

*Uchikata* (*tō*) is in *gedan-no-kamae* and *shikata* (*tanken*) in *chūdan-irimi-no-kamae*. Starting from the front foot, both take three big steps forward, but *uchikata* shortens his last step and stops out of *maai* (Photo ❷).

*Shikata* moves in (*irimi*) and tries to suppress *uchikata*'s sword by pushing it to the right (Photo ❸), but *uchikata* evades by stepping backwards and thrusts immediately at *shikata*'s torso.

However, *shikata* suppresses *uchikata*'s sword by pushing it to the left/downward (Photo ❹), then grabs and locks *uchikata*'s left arm and breaks his balance (Photo ❺). Finally, *shikata* stabs *uchikata* in the torso (Photo ❻).

*Shikata* withdraws cautiously with *zanshin* (Photo ❼). *Uchikata* and *shikata* then go back to *chūdan-no-kamae*. They disengage their weapons to close the *kata* (Photo ❽), and from the rear foot, both take five small steps and return to their original starting positions.

## Sanbon-me: men wo fusegi seitai-zuki - sensen no sen

*Uchikata* (*tō*) assumes *gedan-no-kamae* while *shikata* (*tanken*) assumes *chūdan-irimi-no-kamae*. Starting from the front foot, *uchikata* and *shikata* take three big steps forward, but *uchikata* shortens his last step and stops out of *maai* (photo ❷).

*Shikata* moves in (*irimi*) and tries to suppress *uchikata*'s sword by pushing it downward, but *uchikata* evades, stepping backwards while assuming *wakigamae* (Photo ❸) and immediately strikes *men* (Photos ❹ & ❺). However, *shikata* blocks the sword, making a cross with his arms (Photo ❺) so he can grab *uchikata*'s left arm (Photo ❻) and break his balance (Photo ❼) - note the *fumikae-ashi* footwork here.

Finally, *shikata* stabs *uchikata* in the torso (Photo ❽).

*Shikata* withdraws cautiously with *zanshin*. *Uchikata* and *shikata* then go back to *chūdan-no-kamae*. They disengage their weapons to close the *kata*, and from the rear foot, both take five small steps and return to the original starting position.

## Yonhon-me: nodo no tsuki - sen

*Uchikata* (*tanken*) assumes *chūdan-irimi-no-kamae* and *shikata* (*tō*) assumes *gedan-no-kamae*. Starting from the front foot, both take three big steps forward.

As soon as they enter into the *maai* for attack (photo ❷), *uchikata* moves in (*irimi*) in order to suppress *shikata*'s sword from the left, but *shikata* evades by stepping backwards diagonally to the right (Photo ❸) and thrusts immediately at *shikata*'s *nodo* (Photo ❹).

While taking a big step backwards, *shikata* pulls his sword back strongly, and demonstrates *zanshin*. *Uchikata* and *shikata* go back to *chūdan-no-kamae*. They disengage their weapons to close the *kata*, and from the rear foot, both take five small steps and return to the original starting position.
(Photos ❺, ❻ & ❼).

## Gohon-me: Irimi ni tai suru men no uchi - Go no sen

*Uchikata* (*tanken*) assumes *chūdan-irimi-no-kamae* and *shikata* (*tō*) goes into *gedan-no-kamae*. Starting from the front foot, both take three big steps forward, but *uchikata* shortens his last step and stops out of *maai* (photo ❷).

*Uchikata* moves in (*irimi*) and tries to suppress *shikata*'s sword by pushing it downwards, but *shikata* evades by stepping backwards diagonally to the right (Photo ❸) and immediately strikes *uchikata*'s men (Photos ❹ & ❺).

*Shikata* demonstrates *zanshin*, and takes a big step backwards while assuming *hidari-jōdan*. *Uchikata* and *shikata* then go back to *chūdan-no-kamae*. They disengage their weapons to close the *kata*, and from the rear foot, both take five small steps and return to the original starting position.
(Photos ❻, ❼ & ❽).

# Roppon-me: Jodan kara no Men Uchi - Go no Sen

*Shikata* (*tō*) assumes *hidari-jōdan* and *uchikata* (*tanken*) responds by pointing his *kensen* towards *shikata*'s left wrist. Starting from the front foot, both take three big steps forward.

As soon as they enter into the *maai* for attack, taking the initiative *uchikata* moves in (*irimi*) and pressures *shikata*'s left wrist (Photo ❷), but *shikata* evades by stepping backwards diagonally to the right (Photo ❸) and immediately strikes *uchikata*'s men (Photo ❹).

*Shikata* withdraws cautiously with *zanshin*. *Uchikata* and *shikata* then go back to *chūdan-no-kamae*. They disengage their weapons to close the *kata* (Photos ❺ & ❻), and from the rear foot, both take five small steps and return to the original starting position.

Finally, *uchikata* and *shikata* perform *osame-tō* and both bow to conclude the Tanken-tai-Tō-no-Kata.

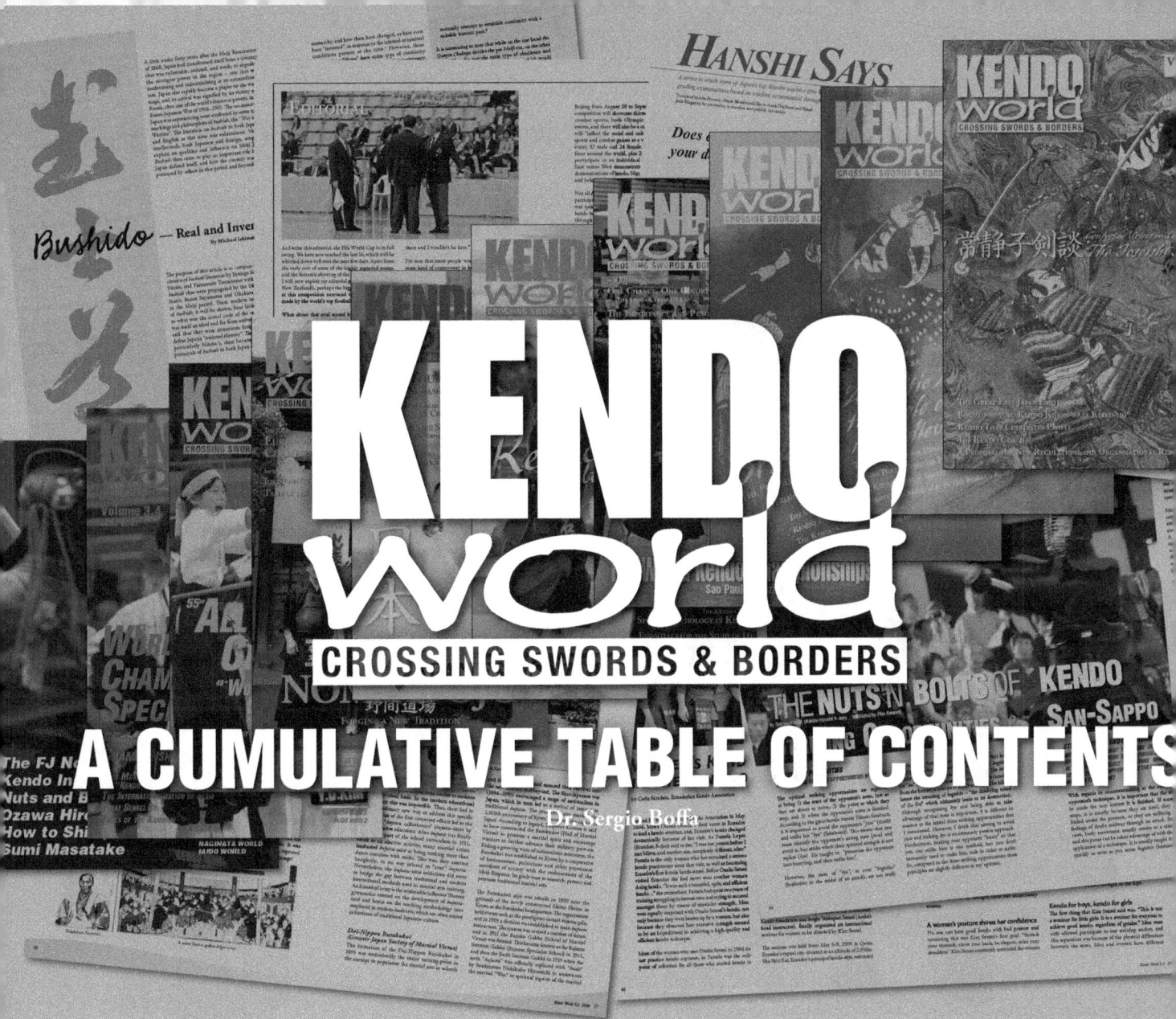

# KENDO world
## CROSSING SWORDS & BORDERS
## A CUMULATIVE TABLE OF CONTENTS
### Dr Sergio Boffa

## Introduction

When I decided to make a cumulative table of contents for the five first volumes of your favourite magazine, I had several things in mind. First, I knew that it would help me a lot in my own research as I figured it would help me quickly find a useful article that has been lost for years in the maze of my memory. Since others might also be willing to access the wealth of information disseminated over the last twenty issues of Kendo World – that is 2153 pages – I decided to offer the fruits of my work for everybody's benefit. I am sure it will be useful to many a kendo aficionado. At least it should be... It could make the difference in your next 8-dan grading! Second, I mistakenly thought that it would be an easy and quick job to do, and might even be another line in my CV. I was wrong about the second point, and it took me a much longer time to complete than I could have ever envisioned. But, as Confucius said to his disciples: "No pain, no gain!"

This general table of contents would normally be followed by an index, but would have made the work three times bigger. I decided, for the sake of the Amazonian Forest, not to go that far. Instead, I have classified the articles under general and/or precise categories. In some cases, the same article has been placed under different headings. That should help the reader to quickly find an article of interest. In some cases, I had to change the original title due to the odd slight inconsistency.

Thus, the first objective of this table of contents is to allow readers to find articles of interest. It is NOT a bibliography where the references can just be copied and used elsewhere. In this case, you should always crosscheck my references with the original title of the article. I also refrained from mentioning the translator's or the photographer's names. This does not mean that I do not respect their work. Far from it! I decided on this option to make the table shorter and clearer. Again, I ask the reader to go to the original paper to find all of the relevant information.

# A CUMULATIVE TABLE OF CONTENTS

## History

### Bushido, Budo, Philosophy & Spirituality

- An., *Defining Budo*, 2009, Vol. 4-4, p. 3.
- Abe Tetsushi, *Cultural Friction in Budo*, 2005, Vol. 3-2, pp. 8-17.
- Bennett, Alex, *Editorial*, 2004, Vol. 2-4, pp. 4-5 [about the Budo Charter].
- Bennett, Alex, *The Beginner's Guide to Bushido*, 2004, Vol. 2-4, pp. 50-56.
- Hellman, Christopher, *Confucian Voices in Swordsmanship, The Jōseishi Kendan*, 2011, Vol. 5-4, pp. 67-71.
- Inoue, Yoshihiko, *Hokkai-Join and Reflections on the Meaning of Mokuso*, 2001, Vol. 1-1, pp. 13-16.
- Ishimatsu-Prime, Michael, *Celebrating the Dead*, 2009, Vol. 5-1, pp. 64-65 [about 47 rōnin].
- Ishimatsu-Prime, Michael, *Bushido - Real and Invented*, 2010, Vol. 5-2, pp. 4-11.
- Kirchner, Thomas, *Zen & the Martial Arts*, 2010, Vol. 5-2, pp. 107-109.
- Maeder, Stephan, *The Adventure of the Way of the Sword in the 21st Century, Part 5: Bushido - Just Another Anachronism?*, 2010, Vol. 5-2, p. 47.
- Moate, Sarah, *Zen Calligraphy and Painting of Yamaoka Tesshû at the V&A*, 2008, Vol. 4-2, pp. 15-17.
- Moate, Sarah, *Bushido, The Zen Calligraphy of Katsu Kaishû and Takahashi Deishû*, 2008, Vol. 4-3, pp. 84-87.
- Moate, Sarah, *Suigetsu, "The Moon in Water", The Zen calligraphy of Yamaoka Tesshû and Terayama Tanchû*, 2009, Vol. 4-4, pp. 98-101.
- Nagy, Stephen Robert, *Internationalization of Budo Culture, Important Question for the Future of Budo*, 2007, Vol. 3-4, pp. 84-90.
- Rothmar, Tyler, *Kendo in Context*, 2007, Vol. 3-4, pp. 154-156.
- Takemura, Eiji and Ishimatsu-Prime, Michael, *The Role of Confucianism and Swordsmanship in the Bakumatsu Period*, 2008, Vol. 4-3, pp. 56-57.
- Tanaka, Mamoru, *Budo in an Age of Diversification*, 2004, Vol. 2-4, pp. 63-68.
- Uozumi, Takashi, *Ryuha Kenjutsu, The Formation of Japanese Budo Culture*, 2007, Vol. 3-4, pp. 68-75.
- Wells, Ken, *Budo & Business*, 2003, Vol. 2-1, pp. 34-35.

### Bushido in the Past and in the Present (by John Toshimichi Imai (1906) and introduced by Alex Bennett).

- *Part 1: Bushido - What it is, and what it is not*, 2007, Vol. 3-4, pp. 114-117.
- *Part 2: Bushido as Represented by a Typical Master*, 2007, Vol. 4-1, pp. 44-49.
- *Part 3: Bushido as Represented in the Historic Dramas*, 2008, Vol. 4-2, pp. 76-83.
- *Part 4: Bushido in the Present*, 2008, Vol. 4-3, pp. 78-82.

### Tales of the Samurai (by Miyamori A. (1920))

- *Chapter 1: Ungo-Zenji*, 2004, Vol. 3-1, pp. 22-27.
- *Chapter 2: The Loyalty of a Boy Samurai*, 2005, Vol. 3-2, pp. 52-55.
- *Chapter 3: Katsuno's Revenge*, 2006, Vol. 3-3, pp. 122-135.
- *Chapter 4: A Wedding Present*, 2007, Vol. 3-4, pp. 118-126.
- *Chapter 5: The Heroism of Torii Katsutaka*, 2007, Vol. 4-1, pp. 126-132.
- *Chapter 6: The Wrestling of a Daimyo*, 2008, Vol. 4-2, pp. 48-53.
- *Chapter 7: The Story of Kimura Shigenari*, 2008, Vol. 4-3, pp. 88-98.
- *Chapter 8: Honest Kyûsuke*, 2009, Vol. 4-4, pp. 50-58.

### Historical Sightseeing (by Bruce Flanagan)

- *N° 001, Itsukushima Island*, 2006, Vol. 3-3, pp. 118-121.
- *N° 002, Unganzenji Temple*, 2007, Vol. 4-1, pp. 40-42.
- *N° 003, Meiji-Mura Museum*, 2008, Vol. 4-2, pp. 94-96.
- *N° 004, Sekigahara Town, Ancient battlefield sites*, 2009, Vol. 5-1, pp. 126-129.
- *N° 005, Hokuriku Region*, 2010, Vol. 5-3, pp. 14-17.

### Kendo (Pre-Meiji)

- Bennett, Alex and Ishimatsu-Prime, Michael, *The Asiatic Society of Japan Lecture, Spiritual Sports, The "Civilising Process" of Japanese Martial Arts during the Tokugawa Period and Beyond*, 2008, Vol. 4-2, pp. 84-87.
- Bennett, Alex, *Spiritual Sports, The Cultural Evolution of Japanese Swordsmanship*, 2009, Vol. 5-1, pp. 59-63 [from Tokugawa to Meiji].
- Bennett, Alex, *"Aesthetic Asceticism" & the Role of Swordsmanship in Medieval Japan*, 2010, Vol. 5-3, pp. 18-27.
- Cundy, Antony, *The 31st Nihon Kobudo Enbu Taikai*, 2008, Vol. 4-2, pp. 110-112.
- Cundy, Antony, *The 75th Anniversary Demonstration of the Nihon Kobudo Shinkokai*, 2010, Vol. 5-3, pp. 90-91.
- Hellman, Christopher, *Confucian Voices in*

- Swordsmanship, *The Jōseishi Kendan*, 2011, Vol. 5-4, pp. 67-71.
- Nakamura, Tamio, *The History of Bogu*, 2001, Vol. 1-1, pp. 3-12.
- Takemura, Eiji and Ishimatsu-Prime, Michael, *The Role of Confucianism and Swordsmanship in the Bakumatsu Period*, 2008, Vol. 4-3, pp. 56-57.
- Tanaka, Mamoru, *The Value of Classical Martial Arts Texts*, 2004, Vol. 2-3, pp. 56-59.
- Tavernier, Baptiste, *Old Scrolls, Bokuden Matsugo-ryû*, 2009, Vol. 4-4, pp. 39-45.
- Uozumi, Takashi, *Ryuha Kenjutsu, The Formation of Japanese Budo Culture*, 2007, Vol. 3-4, pp. 68-75.

### Tradition & Transmission (by Antony Cundy)

- *Tenshin Shoden Katori Shinto-Ryu*, 2001, Vol. 1-1, pp. 40-45.
- *The Maniwa Nen-Ryu*, 2002, Vol. 1-2, pp. 66-71.
- *Yagyu Shinkage Ryu Hyoho*, 2002, Vol. 1-3, pp. 73-78.
- *Kashima Shinden Jikishinkage-Ryu*, 2002, Vol. 1-4, pp. 55-61.
- *Bichu Den Takeuchi Ryu*, 2003, Vol. 2-1, pp. 70-75.
- *Suio Ryu*, 2003, Vol. 2-2, pp. 52-61.
- *Kobori-Ryu*, 2004, Vol. 2-3, pp. 20-26.
- *Shindo Munen Ryu*, 2004, Vol. 2-4, pp. 72-79.
- *Morishige-Ryu*, 2004, Vol. 3-1, pp. 64-71.
- *Hoki-Ryu Iaijutsu (Hoshino-Ha)*, 2005, Vol. 3-2, pp. 72-77.

### Swords of Wisdom
### (from the book *Kenshi no Meigon* by Tobe Shinjûrō (1998) translated by Alex Bennett)

- *The Way of War is the Way of Peace - Hyōhō wa heihō nari (Iizasa Choisai)*, 2002, Vol. 1-2, pp. 64-65.
- *Horses Kick! - Uma no haneru mono (Tsukahara Bokuden)*, 2002, Vol. 1-3, pp. 64-65.
- *Win by Making Them Speculate! - Korashite katsu (Tsukahara Bokuden)*, 2002, Vol. 1-4, pp. 25-26.
- *It shouldn't make any difference what tools you use... - Emono wo erabazu (Tsukahara Bokuden)*, 2003, Vol. 2-1, pp. 76-77.
- *Stand out from the Crowd, be the Aspiration of Others - Hito no Hyoteki Tare (Saito Denkibo)*, 2003, Vol. 2-2, pp. 70-71.
- *Become an evil Spirit - Akuryo to naran (Iwama Kokuma & Tsuchiko Doronosuke)*, 2004, Vol. 2-3, pp. 68-69.
- *Devotion to the Way of the Arts - Geido Hitotsuji (Kamiizumi Ise-no-Kami)*, 2004, Vol. 2-4, pp. 70-71.
- *Indestructible Mind- Horobosenu Kokoro (Kamiizumi Ise-no-Kami)*, 2004, Vol. 3-1, pp. 72-73.
- *Man of Sincerity - Shinjitsu no Hito (Yagyu Sekishusai Muneyoshi)*, 2005, Vol. 3-2, pp. 58-59.
- *Return the Mind - Kokoro wo Kaesu Koto (Yagyu Tajima no Kami Munenori)*, 2006, Vol. 3-3, pp. 90-91.
- *The Sword for Ruling a Peaceful Realm - Hei-Tenka-no-Ken (Yagyu Tajima no Kami Munenori)*, 2007, Vol. 3-4, pp. 50-51.
- *Listen to the Sound of the Wind and the Water... (Yagyu Jubei Mitsuyoshi*, 2007, Vol. 4-1, pp. 74-75.
- *Upright posture - Tsuttatta-Mi (Yagyu Hyogonosuke Toshitoshi)*, 2008, Vol. 4-2, pp. 28-29.
- *Offence and defence are inseparably linked - Ken-Tai Ichinyo (Marume Kurando Nagayoshi)*, 2008, Vol. 4-3, pp. 102-103.
- *The Precision of the Short-Sword - Kodachi no Sae*, 2009, Vol. 4-4, pp. 24-25.
- *Stealing the Sword with Savoir-faire - Kiten no Muto-Dori (Toda Echigo-no-Kami Shigemasa)*, 2009, Vol. 5-1, pp. 122-123.
- *The Sword of no-contemplation - Muso-no-Ken (Itō Ittōsai)*, 2010, Vol. 5-2, pp. 96-97.
- *The Mind of Abandonment (Itō Ittōsai)*, 2010, Vol. 5-3, pp. 60-61.
- *No need for the Strength of demons (Ono Jirōemon Tadaaki)*, 2011, Vol. 5-4, pp. 24-25.

### Miyamoto Musashi

- Boffa, Sergio, *Miyamoto Musashi (1584-1645), the Gorin-no-Sho and Modern Kendo*, 2004, Vol. 2-4, pp. 18-20.
- Flanagan, Bruce, *N° 002, Unganzenji Temple*, 2007, Vol. 4-1, pp. 40-42.
- Hellman, Christopher, *The Last Manga Exhibition: Musashi Gets the Ending he Deserves*, 2010, Vol. 5-3, pp. 54-55 [about Inoue Takehiko and the *Vagabond*].
- Uozumi, Takashi, *Research into Miyamoto Musashi's Gorin no Sho*, 2002, Vol. 1-2, pp. 7-19.

### Kendo (Meiji to WWII)

- Bennett, Alex, *A Brief Synopsis of the History of Modern Kendo*, 2004, Vol. 3-1, pp. 6-15 [from Meiji to now].
- Bennett, Alex and Ishimatsu-Prime, Michael, *The Asiatic Society of Japan Lecture, Spiritual Sports, The "Civilising Process" of Japanese Martial Arts during the Tokugawa Period and Beyond*, 2008, Vol. 4-2, pp. 84-87.
- Bennett, Alex, *The "Civilising Process" of Japanese Swordsmanship from the Tokugawa Period and Beyond*, 2010, Vol. 5-2, pp. 15-21 [from Meiji to now].
- Kobayashi, Luiz, *A Brief Overview of Pre-WWII*

- *Kendo in Brazil, Part 1*, 2010, Vol. 5-2, pp. 26-28.
- Kobayashi, Luiz, *A Brief Overview of Pre-WWII Kendo in Brazil, Part 2*, 2010, Vol. 5-3, pp. 62-64.
- Martin, Paul, *Noma Dōjō, Forging a New Tradition*, 2008, Vol. 4-2, pp. 4-11.
- Moriyama, Ryōtsuku, *Waseda University Kendo Club & Takano Sasaburo Sensei*, 2008, Vol. 4-3, pp. 99-101.
- Norman, F.J., *"Kenjutsu" or Japanese Fencing*, 2002, Vol. 1-3, pp. 15-22.
- Takemura, Eiji and Ishimatsu-Prime, Michael, *The Role of Confucianism and Swordsmanship in the Bakumatsu Period*, 2008, Vol. 4-3, pp. 56-57.

### F.J. Norman

- An., *The F.J. Saga Continues...*, 2002, Vol. 1-4, p. 33 [about F.J. Norman].
- Bennett, Alex, *Feature: The Search for FJ Norman: Western Kendo Pioneer*, 2002, Vol. 1-3, pp. 12-14.
- Bennett, Alex, *F.J. Norman: The Saga Continues*, 2003, Vol. 2-1, pp. 50-51.
- Bennett, Alex, *The FJ Norman Saga - The Final Chapter?*, 2006, Vol. 3-3, pp. 8-15.
- Norman, F.J., *"Kenjutsu" or Japanese Fencing*, 2002, Vol. 1-3, pp. 15-22.

### Kendo (after WWII)

- Abramo, Caio, *The Current Status of Kendo in Brazil*, 2009, Vol. 4-4, pp. 10-13.
- Bennett, Alex, *A Brief Synopsis of the History of Modern Kendo*, 2004, Vol. 3-1, pp. 6-15 [from Meiji to now].
- Bennett, Alex, *The "Civilising Process" of Japanese Swordsmanship from the Tokugawa Period and Beyond*, 2010, Vol. 5-2, pp. 15-21 [from Meiji to now].
- Bennett, Alex, *The "Shinai-Kyōgi" Experiment*, 2011, Vol. 5-4, pp. 26-30.
- Lissabet, Ernest and Seto, Donald, *Cherry Blossom Kendo, A Short History of Kendo in Washington D.C.*, 2008, Vol. 4-2, pp. 38-45.
- Martin, Paul, *Noma Dōjō, Forging a New Tradition*, 2008, Vol. 4-2, pp. 4-11.
- McCall, George, *Kendo in Scotland*, 2003, Vol. 2-2, pp. 85-87.
- Nowakowski, Witold, *Kendo in Poland, From the Beginning...*, 2003, Vol. 2-1, pp. 78-79.
- Nowakowski, Witold, *Lietuvos Kendo - Kendo in Lithuania*, 2006, Vol. 3-3, pp. 80-81.
- Peterson, Bryan, *Malawi Kendo*, 2006, Vol. 3-3, pp. 64-65.
- Peterson, Bryan, *Wenzhou Kendo*, 2006, Vol. 3-3, pp. 84-89.
- Yoshida, Yasumasa, *A Brief History of Russian Kendo*, 2002, Vol. 1-2, pp. 44-45.
- Weiss, Eyal, *The Informal History of Kendo in Israel*, 2002, Vol. 1-4, pp. 53-54.
- Weitzner, Gabriel, *From Brazil '82 to Brazil '09, VII South American Championship*, 2008, Vol. 4-3, pp. 46-49.

## Techniques

### Techniques - General

- Baba, Kinji, *Getting to the Point - Tsuki*, 2002, Vol. 1-2, pp. 20-26.
- Bennett, Alex, *Bokuto-ni-Yoru Kendo Kihon-Waza Keiko-Ho, Training Method for Fundamental Kendo Techniques with a Bokuto*, 2011, Vol. 5-4, pp. 40-43.
- Boffa, Sergio, *Kendo & Violence*, 2009, Vol. 5-1, pp. 88-89.
- Chiba, Masashi, *Know your Opponent*, 2008, Vol. 4-3, pp. 16-19.
- Edo, Kōkichi, Tsumura, Kōsaku, Shizawa, Kunio, Yano, Hiroshi and Watanabe, Kaoru, *Practical Kendo, The Comprehensive Q&A Guide to the Art of Japanese Fencing*, 2008, Vol. 4-3, pp. 24-31.
- Gibson, Stuart, *At the Sharp End*, 2008, Vol. 4-3, p. 23 [about *mukae-zuki*].
- Gibson, Stuart, *It's not the Hokey Cokey*, 2010, Vol. 5-2, pp. 94-95 [about *seme*].
- Harwood, Steven, *Breathing*, 2008, Vol. 4-2, pp. 56-59.
- Inoue, Yoshihiko, *Hokkai-Join and Reflections on the Meaning of Mokuso*, 2001, Vol. 1-1, pp. 13-16.
- Marsten, Jeff, *The Wrong Warm-Up*, 2004, Vol. 2-3, pp. 60-61.
- Ōya, Minoru, *The Technical and Psychological Methodology of Kendo, Part 1*, 2002, Vol. 1-4, pp. 5-9.
- Ōya, Minoru, *The Technical and Psychological Methodology of Kendo, Part 2*, 2003, Vol. 2-1, pp. 24-27.
- Ozawa, Hiroshi, *Essence of Training in Japanese Culture: Technique Acquirement and Secret of Kendo*, 2006, Vol. 3-3, pp. 17-23.
- Rothmar, Tyler, *What Senseis Do*, 2007, Vol. 3-4, pp. 130-133.
- Rothmar, Tyler, *Motodachi*, 2008, Vol. 4-2, pp. 92-93 [interview with Yamamoto Kazuhide].
- Shimokawa, Mika, *Learning and Enjoying Kendo*, 2010, Vol. 5-3, p. 34.
- Takenaka, Kentarō, *The Importance and Practicality*

*of Maintaining Chudan as a Form of Defence in Kendo*, 2009, Vol. 5-1, pp. 31-37.
- Tsurumaru, Juichi, *The Theory of Kendo*, 2004, Vol. 3-1, pp. 40-43.
- Winter, Taylor, *Becoming One with the Sword*, 2011, Vol. 5-4, pp. 64-65.

### The Role of Breath Control (by Steven Harwood)

- *The Role of Breath Control in Kendo: Part 1*, 2001, Vol. 1-1, pp. 21-22.
- *The Role of Breath Control in Kendo, Part 2*, 2002, Vol. 1-2, pp. 60-63.
- *The Role of Breath Control in Kendo, Part 3*, 2002, Vol. 1-3, pp. 53-56.
- *The Role of Breath Control in Kendo, Part 4*, 2002, Vol. 1-4, pp. 50-52.
- *The Role of Breath Control in Kendo, Part 5*, 2003, Vol. 2-1, pp. 52-54.
- *The Role of Breath Control in Kendo, Part 6*, 2003, Vol. 2-2, pp. 49-51.
- *The Role of Breath Control in Kendo, Part 7*, 2004, Vol. 2-3, p. 32.
- *The Role of Breath Control in Kendo, Part 8*, 2004, Vol. 2-4, pp. 61-62.
- *The Role of Breath Control in Kendo, Part 9*, 2004, Vol. 3-1, pp. 58-60.
- *The Role of Breath Control in Kendo, Part 10*, 2005, Vol. 3-2, pp. 92-94.
- *The Role of Breath Control in Kendo, Part 11*, 2006, Vol. 3-3, pp. 96-99.
- *Breathing in Kendo Kata*, 2007, Vol. 4-1, pp. 50-54.
- *Breathing*, 2008, Vol. 4-2, pp. 56-59.

### The Nuts and Bolts of Kendo (from *Kendo Jotatsu no Hiketsu* by Nakano Yasoji and translated by Alex Bennett)

- *Men Waza*, 2002, Vol. 1-3, pp. 26-30.
- *Kote, Do, Tsuki*, 2002, Vol. 1-4, pp. 34-39.
- *Harai-Waza*, 2003, Vol. 2-1, pp. 14-20.
- *Ni/San-Dan-Waza*, 2003, Vol. 2-2, pp. 37-41.
- *The Principles of Debana-Waza*, 2004, Vol. 2-3, pp. 14-18.
- *The Principles of Hiki-Waza*, 2004, Vol. 2-4, pp. 57-60.
- *The Principles of Katsugi-Waza*, 2004, Vol. 3-1, pp. 16-17.
- *The Principles of Katate-Waza*, 2005, Vol. 3-2, pp. 48-49.
- *Suriage-Waza*, 2006, Vol. 3-3, pp. 42-45.
- *Nuki-Waza*, 2007, Vol. 3-4, pp. 42-46.
- *Kaeshi-Waza, Uchiotoshi-Waza*, 2007, Vol. 4-1, pp. 104-109.
- *What is Seme?*, 2008, Vol. 4-3, pp. 14-15.
- *What are the Principles of Maai*, 2009, Vol. 5-1, pp. 28-30.
- *Striking Opportunities & San-Sappo*, 2010, Vol. 5-2, pp. 66-68.
- *Tsuba-Zeriai & Tai-Atari*, 2010, Vol. 5-3, pp. 9-11.
- *Yuko Datotsu - The Valid Strike*, 2011, Vol. 5-4, pp. 14-16.

### Reidan Jichi (by Ōya Minoru, translated by Alex Bennett)

- *Chapter 1: The Greater Meaning of Kendo*, 2004, Vol. 3-1, pp. 30-31.
- *Chapter 2: How to Learn Kendo*, 2005, Vol. 3-2, p. 19.
- *Chapter 3: The Aims and Ideals of Training*, 2006, Vol. 3-3, pp. 50-51.
- *Chapter 4: Training*, 2007, Vol. 3-4, pp. 48-49.
- *Chapter 5: About "Ki"*, 2007, Vol. 4-1, pp. 56-57.
- *Chapter 6: Rei*, 2008, Vol. 4-2, pp. 26-27.
- *Chapter 7: The Technical Theory of Kendo*, 2008, Vol. 4-3, pp. 20-22.
- *Chapter 8: Kamae*, 2009, Vol. 4-4, pp. 22-23.
- *Chapter 9: Kamae*, 2009, Vol. 5-1, pp. 56-58.
- *Chapter 10: Various Issues Surrounding Seme*, 2010, Vol. 5-2, pp. 22-25.
- *Chapter 11: Maai*, 2010, Vol. 5-3, pp. 12-13.
- *Chapter 12: Striking*, 2011, Vol. 5-4, pp. 17-21.

### Kendo Inside Out (by Honda Sōtarō)

- *Part 1: A Comparison of Circumstance*, 2005, Vol. 3-2, pp. 40-44.
- *Part 2: Footwork and Cutting*, 2006, Vol. 3-3, pp. 52-55.
- *Part 3: Kûkan-datotsu and Kihon-uchi*, 2007, Vol. 3-4, pp. 91-94.
- *Part 4: Kirikaeshi and Uchikomi-geiko*, 2007, Vol. 3-4, pp. 95-97.
- *Part 5: Waza-Geiko*, 2007, Vol. 4-1, pp. 78-83.
- *Part 6: Kakari-Geiko*, 2008, Vol. 4-2, pp. 23-25.

### Kendo that Cultivates People (by Sumi Masatake and translated by Honda Sōtarō)

- *Part 1: The Themes of the Articles*, 2006, Vol. 3-3, pp. 40-41.
- *Part 2: Teaching Children at Nyûmon-ki Level*, 2007, Vol. 3-4, pp. 76-81.
- *Part 3: Adolescence, Good Time for Physical and Mental Forging*, 2007, Vol. 4-1, pp. 112-115.
- *Part 4: The Role of Keiko at Tanren-Ki Level, Physical and Mental Forging Stage*, 2008, Vol. 4-2, pp. 88-91.
- *Part 5: The Role of Keiko at Tanren-Ki Level*, 2008,

Vol. 4-3, pp. 3-9.
- *Part 6: The Role of Keiko at Tanren-Ki Level*, 2009, Vol. 4-4, pp. 66-69.
- *Part 7: The Role of Keiko at Tanren-Ki Level*, 2009, Vol. 5-1, pp. 40-43.
- *Part 8: The Role of Keiko at Tanren-Ki Level*, 2010, Vol. 5-2, pp. 69-71.
- *Part 9: The Conclusion of Tanren-Ki and Preparation for Seijuku-Ki (Maturity)*, 2010, Vol. 5-3, pp. 35-37.
- *Part 10: Further Development*, 2011, Vol. 5-4, pp. 53-59.

## Nito (by Yamaguchi Masato)
- *Part 1: The Basics*, 2005, Vol. 3-2, pp. 20-27.
- *Part 2: The Basics*, 2006, Vol. 3-3, pp. 46-47.
- *Part 3: Fundamental Techniques*, 2007, Vol. 3-4, pp. 106-111.
- *Part 4: Basic Techniques*, 2007, Vol. 4-1, pp. 84-95.
- *Part 5: Applied Techniques (1)*, 2009, Vol. 4-4, pp. 28-31.
- *Part 6: Applied Techniques (2)*, 2009, Vol. 5-1, pp. 116-121.
- *Part 7: Applied Techniques (3)*, 2010, Vol. 5-3, pp. 92-103.

## Reigi
- Inoue, Yoshihiko, *Hokkai-Join and Reflections on the Meaning of Mokuso*, 2001, Vol. 1-1, pp. 13-16.
- Ishimatsu-Prime, Michael, *Ishimatsu Shugyo Trip, A play on Words, The Keiko? - Za-Keiko!*, 2007, Vol. 4-1, p. 17.
- Oya, Minoru, *Reidan-Jichi, Chapter 6: Rei*, 2008, Vol. 4-2, pp. 26-27.
- Ozawa, Hiroshi, *Essence of Training in Japanese Culture: Technique Acquirement and Secret of Kendo*, 2006, Vol. 3-3, pp. 17-23.
- Robison, Hamish and Bennett, Alex, *Kendo World Survey No. 3: Rei*, 2002, Vol. 1-3, pp. 67-69.

## Kata
- Bennett, Alex, *The Dai Nippon Butokukai Seitei Kenjutsu Kata*, 2010, Vol. 5-2, pp. 29-38.
- Bennett, Alex, *Bokuto-ni-Yoru Kendo Kihon-Waza Keiko-Ho, Training Method for Fundamental Kendo Techniques with a Bokuto*, 2011, Vol. 5-4, pp. 40-43.
- Harwood, Steven, *Breathing in Kendo Kata*, 2007, Vol. 4-1, pp. 50-54.
- Inoue, Yoshihiko, *A Philosophical Look at Kata, Part 1*, 2002, Vol. 1-2, pp. 34-38.
- Inoue, Yoshihiko, *A Philosophical Look at Kata, Part 2*, 2002, Vol. 1-3, pp. 59-63.
- Inoue, Yoshihiko, *A Philosophical Look at Kata, Part 3*, 2002, Vol. 1-4, pp. 13-15.
- Inoue, Yoshihiko, *A Philosophical Look at Kata, Part 4*, 2003, Vol. 2-1, pp. 28-33.
- Lainé, Aurélien, *The Sun and the Sword*, 2007, Vol. 4.1, pp. 63-64.

## Refereeing
- Bennett, Alex, *Judges in Court*, 2003, Vol. 2-2, pp. 6-8.
- Fukumoto, Shuji, *Shinpan from Scratch, Part 1: Where did Rules Come From*, 2002, Vol. 1-2, pp. 27-30.
- Fukumoto, Shuji, *Shinpan from Scratch, Part 2: Correct Judgements in the Correct Frame of Mind*, 2002, Vol. 1-3, pp. 31-34.
- Holt, Terry, *The First Steps to Becoming a Referee*, 2006, Vol. 3-3, pp. 100-111.
- Ōtsuka, Tadayoshi, *A Proposal for New Regulations and Organisational Reform in Kendo, An Attempt to Make Kendo more Comprehensible for the World*, 2011, Vol. 5-4, pp. 77-84.
- Uehara, Kichio, *The Current Kendo Refereeing System, Room for Improvement*, 2007, Vol. 4-1, pp. 14-16.
- Vitalis, Louis, *How to Become a Good Kendo Referee*, 2004, Vol. 2-3, pp. 70-72.

## Grading
- An., *AJKF Shogo Examination, Kyoshi*, 2002, Vol. 1-2, pp. 48-49.
- An., *Kendo World survey No. 2: Gradings*, 2002, Vol. 1-2, pp. 54-59.
- An., *Taking a Grading in Japan*, 2002, Vol. 1-2, p. 59.
- Gibson, Stuart, *It's a Long Hard Road*, 2009, Vol. 4-4, pp. 96-97 [about 4 dan grading].
- Lainé, Aurélien, *The Nidan Grading*, 2009, Vol. 5-1, pp. 72-73.
- Marsten, Jeff, *Seven*, 2002, Vol. 1-2, pp. 46-47.
- Shin, Paul H.B., *Reaching the Pinnacle with Helping Hands from Afar*, 2010, Vol. 5-2, pp. 52-55 [about Kato, Shozo].

## Hanshi Says... (Translated by Alex Bennett)
- *Arimitsu Masaaki*, 2004, Vol. 2-4, pp. 22-25.
- *Furuta Yukitaka*, 2003, Vol. 2-1, pp. 6-9.
- *Harada Genji*, 2003, Vol. 2-2, pp. 29-32.
- *Ishihara Katsutoshi*, 2002, Vol. 1-3, pp. 48-52.
- *Iwatate Saburo*, 2002, Vol. 1-4, pp. 27-30.
- *Kaku Toshihiko*, 2005, Vol. 3-2, pp. 36-39.
- *Kobayashi Hideo*, 2004, Vol. 2-3, pp. 34-37.
- *Kojima Masaru*, 2011, Vol. 5-4, pp. 10-11.
- *Matsumoto Akimasa*, 2009, Vol. 4-4, pp. 7-9.
- *Murayama Keisuke*, 2002, Vol. 1-2, pp. 50-53.

- *Oka Kenjiro*, 2007, Vol. 4-1, pp. 96-98.
- *Okada Yasuo*, 2009, Vol. 5-1, pp. 23-25.
- *Okushima Yoshio*, 2008, Vol. 4-3, pp. 12-13.
- *Okuzono Kuniyoshi*, 2004, Vol. 3-1, pp. 18-21.
- *Ōta Tadanori*, 2010, Vol. 5-2, pp. 12-14.
- *Sato Hironobu*, 2006, Vol. 3-3, pp. 34-37.
- *Satō Nariaki*, 2010, Vol. 5-3, pp. 7-8.
- *Shimano Masahiro*, 2007, Vol. 3-4, pp. 38-41.
- *Sonoda Masaji*, 2008, Vol. 4-2, pp. 20-22.

## Teaching and Coaching

- Boffa, Sergio, *Kendo & Violence*, 2009, Vol. 5-1, pp. 88-89.
- Hanson, Dee, *The Silent Kai, Deaf Students and Kendo, The Kagami Shin Dojo and Tim*, 2010, Vol. 5-3, pp. 52-53.
- Ishimatsu-Prime, Michael, *Teaching in a Foreign Language*, 2007, Vol. 4-1, pp. 26-28 [Interview with Yoshisato Shōji].
- Kanzaki, Hiroshi, *Some Thoughts on the "Art of Kantoku"*, 2010, Vol. 5-3, pp. 38-42.
- Nagy, Stephen Robert, *Pedagogical Opportunities and Challenges of Teaching Budo*, 2011, Vol. 5-4, pp. 31-38.
- Sheppard, Ben, *Teaching Kendo in a non-Japanese High School*, 2008, Vol. 4-2, pp. 70-75.
- Sheppard, Ben, *Teaching Kendo to Children, An Introduction for New Instructors*, 2010, Vol. 5-2, pp. 39-43.

## The Kendo Coach, Sport Psychology in Kendo (by Blake Bennett)

- *Part 1: Developing a Psychological Skills Training (PST) Programme*, 2009, Vol. 4-4, pp. 90-95.
- *Part 2: Coping with Anxiety, An Examination of Arousal and Anxiety and their Effects on Performance*, 2009, Vol. 5-1, pp. 76-87.
- *Part 3: Attentional Focus*, 2010, Vol. 5-2, pp. 80-90.
- *Part 4: Self Confidence and Goal Setting*, 2010, Vol. 5-3, pp. 43-47.
- *Part 5: Literature Review of a Social Psychological Issue: Team Cohesion and Team Goal Setting*, 2011, Vol. 5-4, pp. 60-63.

## Medicine and Health

- Bennett, Alex, *Budo for everyone*, 2002, Vol. 1-4, pp. 44-46 [about people with physical and mental disabilities].
- Carmody-Stephens, Damian, *Kendope?*, 2001, Vol. 1-1, pp. 31-34.
- Hanson, Dee, *The Silent Kai, Deaf Students and Kendo, The Kagami Shin Dojo and Tim*, 2010, Vol. 5-3, pp. 52-53.
- Hitchcock, Karl, *Budo with Bipolar*, 2010, Vol. 5-3, p. 83.

## The Kendo Clinic (Translated by Michael I. Komoto)

- Arima, Saburō, *Achilles Tendon Injuries in Kendo*, 2001, Vol. 1-1, pp. 23-30.
- Arima, Saburō, *Back Injuries*, 2002, Vol. 1-2, pp. 39-43.
- Arima, Saburō, *Kendo and Back Pain*, 2002, Vol. 1-3, pp. 37-47.
- Arima, Saburō, *Friction Blisters & Cracks in Skin*, 2002, Vol. 1-4, pp. 17-24.
- Arima, Saburō, *Rear Foot and Heel Pain in the Kendo Practitioner*, 2003, Vol. 2-1, pp. 36-45.
- Arima, Saburō, *Biomechanics of the Left Leg in the Kendo Attack*, 2003, Vol. 2-2, pp. 42-48.
- Arima, Saburō, *Kendo Elbow: Elbow Extension Posterior Compartment Syndrome in Kendo*, 2004, Vol. 2-3, pp. 42-53.
- Arima, Saburō, *The Inversion Ankle Sprain: Ankle Lateral Ligament Injuries in Kendo*, 2004, Vol. 2-4, pp. 35-46.
- Arima, Saburō, *Toenail Injuries in Kendo: Part One, The Subungual Hematoma*, 2004, Vol. 3-1, pp. 44-47.
- Arima, Saburō, *Toenail Injuries in Kendo: Part Two, Onychocryptosis, The Ingrown Toenail*, 2005, Vol. 3-2, pp. 28-33.
- Arima, Saburō, *Knee Injuries in Kendo: Part One*, 2006, Vol. 3-3, pp. 66-75.
- Arima, Saburō, *Knee Injuries in Kendo; Part Two*, 2007, Vol. 3-4, pp. 52-65.
- Arima, Saburō, *Trigger Finger and Trigger Thumb*, 2008, Vol. 4-3, pp. 32-35.
- Arima, Saburō, *Ganglion the "Bible Cyst"*, 2009, Vol. 4-4, pp. 46-47.
- Arima, Saburō and Komoto, Michael, *Adhesive Capsulitis or "Frozen Shoulder"*, 2010, Vol. 5-3, pp. 31-33.

# Kendo events, Kendo-jo, Kendo personalities

## World Kendo Championship

- Abramo, Caio, *14th WKC and the Shinai Measuring Team*, 2009, Vol. 5-1, pp. 20-22.
- Bennett, Alex, *12th World Kendo Champs*, 2003, Vol. 2-2, pp. 4-5.
- Bennett, Alex, *12th World Kendo Championships*

*report*, 2003, Vol. 2-2, pp. 10-25.
- Bennett, Alex, *The 13th World Kendo Championship, Taiwan 2006 Dec. 8.9.10*, 2007, Vol. 3-4, pp. 4-11.
- Boffa, Sergio, *A Few Thoughts on the 12th World Kendo Championship*, 2003, Vol. 2-2, pp. 26-27.
- Boffa, Sergio, *The Japan Defeat at the 13th WKC (Taipei)*, 2007, Vol. 3-4, pp. 31-32.
- Komoto, Michael, *14th World Kendo Championships, Sao Paulo, Brazil*, 2009, Vol. 5-1, pp. 3-12.
- Shishikura, Masashi "Kan", *Starting Over, USA vs Japan*, 2007, Vol. 3-4, pp. 12-19 [about the 13th WKC].
- Yang, Christopher, *Do you Believe in Miracles?*, 2007, Vol. 4-1, pp. 30-35 [about the 13th WKC].
- Yang, Christopher, *One Chance, One Opportunity, The Story of Team USA*, 2009, Vol. 5-1, pp. 13-19 [about the 14th WKC].
- Yung, Vivian, *For 3 Years, 3 Days, 3 Minutes*, 2007, Vol. 3-4, pp. 28-30 [about the 13th WKC].

### European Championship
- Crane, Caleb, *21st European Kendo Championship*, 2007, Vol. 3-4, pp. 34-37.
- Komoto, Michael, *The 22nd European Kendo Championships*, 2008, Vol. 4-2, pp. 12-13.
- Odinot, Hein, Zago, Lorenzo and Komoto, Michael, *2005 European Championships, The Thrill of Victory & the Agony of the Feet*, 2005, Vol. 3-2, pp. 88-91.

### All Japan Kendo Championship
- An., *49th All Japan Kendo Championship*, 2001, Vol. 1-1, pp. 47-48.
- An., *50th All Japan Kendo Championship Tournament*, 2002, Vol. 1-4, pp. 74-75.
- An., *The 54th All Japan Kendo Championships, 3rd November 2006*, 2006, Vol. 3-3, p. 144.
- Bennett, Alex, *51st All Japan Kendo Championships*, 2004, Vol. 2-3, pp. 6-12.
- Rothmar, Tyler, *55th All Japan Kendo Championship*, 2007, Vol. 4-1, pp. 8-11.
- Yamaguchi, Tamiko, *The poster used to advertise the recently held 49th All Japan Kendo Championship*, 2001, Vol. 1-1, p. 46.

### All Japan Women's Kendo Championships
- Bennett, Alex, *41st All Japan Women's Kendo Championships*, 2002, Vol. 1-4, pp. 69-71.
- Bennett, Alex, *42st All Japan Women's Kendo Championships*, 2004, Vol. 2-3, pp. 28-30.
- Rothmar, Tyler, *Women's All Japan Kendo Championship*, 2007, Vol. 4-1, p. 12.

### Hachidan Taikai
- Bennett, Alex, *Second All Japan Sembatsu Kendo 8th Dan Tournament*, 2004, Vol. 2-4, pp. 26-28.
- Bennett, Alex, *GR8!! Special 8th Dan Tournament*, 2002, Vol. 1-4, pp. 72-74.
- Rothmar, Tyler, *5th Hachidan Taikai Report*, 2007, Vol. 3-4, p. 151.
- Rothmar, Tyler, *2008 Hachidan Taikai Report*, 2008, Vol. 4-2, p. 14.

### Tozai Taiko
- Aatsu, Tadashi, *East vs West, The 53rd Tozai Taiko 2007*, 2007, Vol. 4-1, p. 13.
- Ishimatsu-Prime, Michael, *55th Zen Nihon Tozai Taiko Kendo Taikai, The 55th All Japan East-West Kendo Tournament*, 2009, Vol. 5-1, pp. 26-27.

### Other Championships and Tournaments
- Chen, Eda, *5th Hong Kong & Asian (Regional) Kendo Tournament 2005 Special Administrative Region China*, 2005, Vol. 3-2, pp. 56-57.
- Huehner, Garrett, *West Point, The 1st Kendo Tournament*, 2004, Vol. 3-1, pp. 34-35.
- Jackson, Lockie, *The 1st Otsu Cup*, 2003, Vol. 2-1, pp. 22-23.
- Jones, Trevor, *The 5th Otsû Cup*, 2007, Vol. 3-4, pp. 128-129.
- Komoto, Michael, *Russian Central Region Mini-Seminar & the 8th Annual Moscow Open Tournament*, 2006, Vol. 3-3, pp. 92-95.
- Peterson, Bryan, *I Love China*, 2010, Vol. 5-3, pp. 72-74 [about Sportaccord Combat Games 2010 Beijing].

### Seminars
- An., *Images from the 2003 Budo Seminar*, 2003, Vol. 2-1, pp. 86-95.
- An., *Gedatsukai*, 2004, Vol. 2-4, pp. 94-95 [29th Foreign Kendo Leader's Summer Seminar].
- An., *(British) Army Martial Arts Association, 2nd Novice Kendo Course*, 2005, Vol. 3-2, pp. 78-80.
- An., *Russian Seminar Report, An Assortment of Comments from Club Representatives*, 2008, Vol. 4-2, pp. 100-101.
- Baker, Philip, *The 2005 30th Foreign Kendo Leaders Summer Seminar*, 2005, Vol. 3-2, pp. 68-71.
- Bennett, Alex, *Kendo Amigo: Guatemala*, 2002, Vol. 1-3, pp. 23-25.
- Bennett, Alex, *Bu Way in Norway? Yes Way!*, 2002, Vol. 1-4, p. 47.
- Bennett, Alex, *Iran and did Kendo*, 2004, Vol. 2-4, pp. 6-17.
- Boffa, Sergio, *Kitamoto #27*, 2002, Vol. 1-4, pp.

31-33.
- Channell, Randy, *The International Seminar of Budo Culture*, 2002, Vol. 1-4, pp. 40-43.
- Ellero, Martino, *2007 Foreign Leader's Kendo Summer Seminar*, 2007, Vol. 4-1, pp. 70-73.
- Flanagan, Bruce, *The Nippon Budokan Foundation's Budo Culture Seminar Soon to Turn Twenty*, 2007, Vol. 3-4, p. 153.
- Horita, Carlos, *Democratising Kendo Instruction through Institutional Agreements*, 2008, Vol. 4-3, pp. 42-45 [about Iwatate sensei in Mexico].
- Komoto, Michael I., *26th Foreign Kendo Instructors Summer Kendo Seminar: The Kitamoto Camp*, 2001, Vol. 1-1, pp. 37-39.
- Komoto, Michael and Peterson, Bryan, *Mandal International Martial Arts Summer Camp*, 2007, Vol. 3-4, pp. 112-113.
- Marx, Katie and Sylvester, Kate, *Connecting Oceanic Women, A New Seminar on Aiki*, 2011, Vol. 5-4, pp. 72-73.
- O'Donnell, G., *19th Annual Kodokan International Kendo Seminar*, 2004, Vol. 3-1, pp. 74-79.
- Sanchez, Carla, *Women's Kendo in the Lands of Diversity*, 2010, Vol. 5-2, pp. 48-51 [Miwa Onaka in Ecuador].
- Santos-Pimpao, Laurent, *Kendo Sensei Passing Through Catalunya (South-West France)*, 2009, Vol. 5-1, p. 132.
- Shioiri, Hiroyuki, *Chile Report*, 2008, Vol. 4-2, pp. 98-99.
- Shioiri, Hiroyuki, *The Chilean Kenshi*, 2009, Vol. 4-4, pp. 14-15.
- Stephenson, Alan, *The New Zealand Kendo Federation Annual Kendo Seminar, Waikato University, Hamilton, August 10-12, 2007*, 2007, Vol. 4-1, pp. 60-62.
- Yukovic, Radosh, *Belgrade*, 2004, Vol. 2-3, pp. 38-41 [ZNKR delegation].

### Demonstrations
- Cundy, Antony, *The 31st Nihon Kobudo Enbu Taikai*, 2008, Vol. 4-2, pp. 110-112.
- Cundy, Antony, *The 75th Anniversary Demonstration of the Nihon Kobudo Shinkokai*, 2010, Vol. 5-3, pp. 90-91.
- Horita, Carlos, *Exhibicion de Artes Marciales 2010, Budo Japones en Mexico*, 2010, Vol. 5-3, pp. 65-68.

### Other Kendo Experiences
- An., *Endurance Challenge at Auckland Kendo Club*, 2003, Vol. 2-1, p. 77.
- Castelli, Donatella, *The Kyoto Embu Taikai, The Ultimate Kendo Experience*, 2011, Vol. 5-4, pp. 22-23.
- Dickie, Mure, *The China Connection*, 2007, Vol. 4-1, p. 43.
- Flanagan, Bruce, *2005 Aichi Japan Expo Kendo Festival*, 2005, Vol. 3-2, pp. 82-83.
- Gibson, Stuart, *It's a Long Hard Road*, 2009, Vol. 4-4, pp. 96-97 [about 4 dan grading].
- Hanson, Dee, *Land of the Long White Shinai*, 2009, Vol. 4-4, pp. 20-21 [about New Zealand].
- Hanson, Dee, *Kendo in Kathmandu*, 2009, Vol. 5-1, pp. 44-45.
- Ie, Bryan, *A Gaijin's Path into Kendo*, 2004, Vol. 3-1, pp. 83-85.
- Lainé, Aurélien, *Finding my Way*, 2008, Vol. 4-2, p. 97.
- Lainé, Aurélien, *Do It Yourself Kendo*, 2009, Vol. 5-1, pp. 38-39.
- Lainé, Aurélien, *Building the Garden*, 2011, Vol. 5-4, pp. 44-45.
- Maksay, Arpad, *My Nittaidai Experience*, 2003, Vol. 2-2, pp. 33-36.
- Prime, Michael, *The 2nd Kendo World Gasshuku*, 2006, Vol. 3-3, pp. 142-143.
- Robison, Hamish, *A Year in the Life of an IBU Exchange Student*, 2004, Vol. 2-3, pp. 54-55. Van Rooyen, Peter, *A Beginner in Japan*, 2011, Vol. 5-4, p. 87.
- Tan, Alfred, *Kendo in Shangai*, 2010, Vol. 5-3, pp. 75-78.
- Weitzner, Gabriel, *A Sojourn in the Middle East*, 2009, Vol. 5-1, pp. 94-95.
- Wells, Ken, *The Gogatsu Taikai*, 2004, Vol. 3-1, pp. 62-63.
- Wong, Alicia, *Wow!! Kendo Holiday in Japan*, 2010, Vol. 5-3, pp. 69-71.

### A Duffle Bag & a Bogu Bag (by Imafuji Masahiro)
- *Part 1: Staying Afloat in the Deep End*, 2008, Vol. 4-2, pp. 54-55.
- *Part 2: Diametrically Supposed*, 2008, Vol. 4-3, p. 53.
- *Part 3: Bouncer*, 2009, Vol. 4-4, p. 59.
- *Part 4: Demos!*, 2009, Vol. 5-1, p. 96.
- *Part 5: The Way of the Sword in Guatemala*, 2010, Vol. 5-2, pp. 72-73.
- *Part 6: Brilliant Cultural Boundary Crossover*, 2010, Vol. 5-3, pp. 28-29.
- *Part 7: Promoting Kendo to the World*, 2011, Vol. 5-4, pp. 50-51.

### Talk with your Kensen (by Akita Toshimichi)
- *International Musha Shugyō*, 2007, Vol. 3-4, pp.

138-139.
- *Sekishinkan in Hong Kong*, 2007, Vol. 4-1, p. 29.
- *Bangkok/Bangladesh*, 2008, Vol. 4-2, p. 37.

## The Dojo Files (by various authors)

- An., *An Introduction to the Auckland Kendo Club*, 2002, Vol. 1-3, p. 66.
- An., *Fudoshin Kendo, Melbourne, Australia*, 2002, Vol. 1-4, pp. 67-68.
- An., *Szigetkozi Junior Kendo Klub*, 2004, Vol. 2-3, p. 31.
- An., *May the Fourth be with You*, 2011, Vol. 5-4, pp. 85-87 [Hutt Kendo Club, N.-Z.].
- Abbey, Eric and Kondek, Charlie, *Kendo in Michigan*, 2004, Vol. 3-1, pp. 48-51.
- Eizō, Yoshino, *The Attraction of the Way of the Sword*, 2010, Vol. 5-3, pp. 57-59 [about the Waseda University Kendo Club].
- Holt, Terry, *The History of Mumeishi Kendo Club 1968 to 2002*, 2002, Vol. 1-2, pp. 72-73.
- Komoto, Michael, *Mumeishi Dojo, London Mumeishi Dojo 40th Anniversary*, 2009, Vol. 4-4, pp. 26-27.
- Lainé, Aurélien, *Kendo Clubs in the South of France*, 2008, Vol. 4-2, pp. 46-47.
- MKAU and Peterson, Bryan, *Macau Kendo Association Union*, 2007, Vol. 3-4, pp. 104-105.
- Peterson, Bryan, *Going Postal*, 2007, Vol. 3-4, pp. 134-135 [Closing of the Teishin Dojo].
- Prime, Michael, *The CyberDojo*, 2007, Vol. 3-4, pp. 136-137.
- Prime, Michael, *International Goodwill Kendo Club*, 2007, Vol. 3-4, pp. 140-142.
- Rothmar, Tyler, *Finding Dojo in Japan*, 2006, Vol. 3-3, pp. 112-113.
- Stephenson, Alan, *Auckland Kendo Club, New Zealand, Dojo Relocation 2008*, 2008, Vol. 4-3, pp. 38-41.
- Yamamoto, Jason, *Orange County Buddhist Church Kendo Dojo*, 2003, Vol. 2-1, pp. 68-69.

## Sensei

- Brundage, Greg, *Living your Art, An Interview with Park Yong Chon - Korean Sword Master*, 2007, Vol. 3-4, p. 143.
- Dickie, Mure, *Luan Jujie's Olympic Fencing Dream*, 2008, Vol. 4-3, pp. 54-55.
- Evans, Jeff, *Kendo and the Search for Inner-Peace*, 2009, Vol. 5-1, pp. 90-93 [about Graham Sayer sensei].
- Gibson, Stuart, *The Story of Ozawa Hiroshi*, 2010, Vol. 5-3, pp. 49-51.
- Grounds, Kevin, *Female Touch*, 2003, Vol. 2-1, pp. 58-59 [interview with Karukome Mitsuyo].
- Jones, Adrian, *Far, Far East, Part 1*, 2003, Vol. 2-2, pp. 63-64 [about Don Trent].
- Jones, Adrian, *Far, Far East, Part 2*, 2004, Vol. 2-3, pp. 66-67 [about Don Trent].
- Kustosz, Andrzej, *Master, Ando Kozo Sensei, 1940-2003*, 2004, Vol. 2-4, pp. 30-31.
- Makita, Minoru, *Kendo to Me, The Attraction*, 2007, Vol. 3-4, pp. 66-67 [Makita sensei's presentation at the Nippon Budokan's 19th International Seminar for Budo Culture].
- Peterson, Bryan, *Konishi Sensei, Hanshi 8-dan*, 2008, Vol. 4-3, pp. 50-52.
- Prime, Michael, *Fujikawa Sensei Interview*, 2005, Vol. 3-2, pp. 6-7.
- Rothmar, Tyler, *Motodachi*, 2008, Vol. 4-2, pp. 92-93 [interview with Yamamoto Kazuhide].
- Shin, Paul H.B., *Reaching the Pinnacle with Helping Hands from Afar*, 2010, Vol. 5-2, pp. 52-55 [about Kato Shozo].

## Obituaries

- An., *Obituary, Nishiyama Yasuhiro Hanshi 8th dan*, 2004, Vol. 2-4, p. 17.
- Bennett, Alex and Robison, Hamish, *Obituary, Kawamori Keiko, 19 Oct. 1948-29 Dec. 2002*, 2003, Vol. 2-1, p. 20.
- Dyakov, Alexsei, *Obituary: Late Russian Kendo Federation President Nikolay Yakovlev*, 2002, Vol. 1-2, p. 45.
- Ghijben, Elizabeth Badon and Metselaar, Alphons, *Willem Gerard Ferdinand Bekink, 29 March 1919-9 April 2008*, 2008, Vol. 4-3, pp. 110-111.
- Komoto, Michael, *Hashimoto Ryutaro*, 2006, Vol. 3-3, pp. 6-7.
- Hotovec, Vladimir, *In Memory of Giga Toru Sensei, 28th February-31st August 2002*, 2007, Vol. 3-4, p. 149.
- Schmidt, Richard, *In Memoriam, Dr. (LtCol) Gordon Warner, USMC (Ret.)*, 2010, Vol. 5-3, pp. 4-6.

# Kendo Equipment

## Japanese Sword

- Boffa, Sergio, *When Europeans were Discovering the Japanese Sword*, 2006, Vol. 3-3, pp. 57-59.
- Eien, H.M., *Reflections on the Katana, The Beauty & the Brutality*, 2008, Vol. 4-3, p. 66.
- Ishimatsu-Prime, Michael, *Foreign Correspondents*

*Club of Japan Event, Japanese Swordsmiths, Ohsumi Toshihira and Miyairi Norihiro*, 2007, Vol. 4-1, p. 116.
- Jackson, Lockie and Ozaki, Akiyuki, *Interview with Ozaki Akiyuki – Japanese Sword Polisher*, 2001, Vol. 1-1, pp. 17-20.
- Prime, Michael, *The Japanese Sword Museum & Japan Sword*, 2006, Vol. 3-3, pp. 82-83.
- Sinclaire, Clive, *Concerning Shinken*, 2002, Vol. 1-3, pp. 70-72.
- Sinclaire, Clive, *Spotting a Good Blade!*, 2003, Vol. 2-1, pp. 80-83.
- Sinclaire, Clive, *Brief Notes on Hizen-To*, 2004, Vol. 2-3, pp. 74-76.

### Ideas and History of the Sword (by Ozawa Hiroshi)

- *Part 1: Japanese Myths & the Significance of the Sword*, 2007, Vol. 4-1, pp. 18-25.
- *Part 2 (a): Ancient Japan and the Sword*, 2008, Vol. 4-2, pp. 32-36.
- *Part 2 (b): Ancient Japan and the Sword*, 2008, Vol. 4-3, pp. 58-61.
- *Part 3: Swords in Medieval Japan*, 2009, Vol. 4-4, pp. 32-38.
- *Part 4: Swords in Early-Modern Japan*, 2009, Vol. 5-1, pp. 66-71.

### The Adventure of the Way of the Sword in the 21st Century (by Stefan Maeder)

- *Part 1: Introduction*, 2008, Vol. 4-2, pp. 68-69.
- *Part 2: Enhancing Science by Considering "Principles of the Sword" (1)*, 2008, Vol. 4-3, p. 65.
- *Part 3: Enhancing Science by Considering "Principles of the Sword" (2)*, 2009, Vol. 4-4, p. 77.
- *Part 4: About Strength and the Happiest Face I have ever Seen...*, 2009, Vol. 5-1, p. 115.
- *Part 5: Bushido - Just Another Anachronism?*, 2010, Vol. 5-2, p. 47.

### Forging Japanese Swords, Twenty Years on the Swordsmith's Path (by Sadanao Mikami, translated by Nick Mathys)

- *The Process of Making Japanese Swords, Part 1*, 2008, Vol. 4-3, pp. 62-64.
- *The Process of Making Japanese Swords, Part 2*, 2009, Vol. 4-4, pp. 70-76.
- *The Process of Making Japanese Swords, Part 3*, 2009, Vol. 5-1, pp. 46-55.
- *The Process of Making Japanese Swords, Part 4*, 2010, Vol. 5-2, pp. 56-65.
- 

### Kendogu

- An., *Martial Aids, The Menstacles*, 2002, Vol. 1-2, p. 87 [about kendo glasses].
- An., *Martial Aids, The "Men-Gane Cover"*, 2009, Vol. 4-4, p. 111.
- An., *Looking after your Bogu, Part 1*, 2004, Vol. 3-1, pp. 52-57.
- An., *Looking after your Bogu, Part 2*, 2005, Vol. 3-2, pp. 60-67.
- An., *Tozando's 20th Anniversary*, 2009, Vol. 5-1, pp. 130-131.
- An., *Miyako Kendogu*, 2010, Vol. 5-2, p. 112.
- Bennett, Alex, *Caned with Carbon*, 2002, Vol. 1-3, pp. 57-58 [about the Hasegawa carbon *shinai*].
- Bennett, Alex, *Clearly a Men!*, 2002, Vol. 1-4, pp. 65-66 [about the Hasegawa *Mujun Men*].
- Bennett, Alex, *Bogu, Behind the Scenes, Part 1*, 2003, Vol. 2-1, pp. 60-61 [Mitsuboshi Textile Co.].
- Bennett, Alex and Robison, Hamish, *Kendo World Survey No 4: Shinai*, 2002, Vol. 1-4, pp. 62-64.
- Bennett, Alex, *The Bokuto*, 2007, Vol. 4-1, pp. 4-7.
- Bennett, Alex, *Tozando Shogoin Store, A Fusion of Old and New*, 2008, Vol. 4-2, pp. 18-19.
- Bennett, Alex, *Bogu Pioneer, Sakigake*, 2008, Vol. 4-3, pp. 10-11.
- Bennett, Alex, *A Stitch in Time*, 2009, Vol. 4-4, pp. 4-6 [Discussion between Sakudō Masao sensei and master Tawara Hirofumi].
- Gringras, Mark, Robison, Hamish and Bennett, Alex, *Kendo World Survey No 5: Bogu*, 2003, Vol. 2-1, pp. 62-66.
- Ishimatsu-Prime, Michael, *Tenugui, From Rags to Riches*, 2007, Vol. 4-1, pp. 110-111.
- Ishimatsu-Prime, Michael, *The "Refinement Practice Sword"*, 2011, Vol. 5-4, p. 39 [Sei-Ren-Tō].
- Nagao, Susumu, *Kendo's Not-So Common-Sense: the Hakama*, 2010, Vol. 5-3, p. 56.
- Nakamura, Tamio, *The History of Bogu*, 2001, Vol. 1-1, pp. 3-12.
- Peterson, Bryan, *Tsuki Protector*, 2006, Vol. 3-3, p. 16.
- Tavernier, Baptiste, *Shoryudoh, An Interview with Tanaka Toshikazu*, 2011, Vol. 5-4, pp. 12-13.

### By the Way (by Lockie Jackson)

- *How can I choose the best bogu for me?*, 2003, Vol. 2-1, p. 13.
- *It's not so easy for me to have my kote repalmed...*, 2003, Vol. 2-2, p. 28.
- *I've just bought myself a top knotch keiko-gi*, 2004, Vol. 2-3, p. 19.
- *How do I go about selecting the best shinai in the rack?*, 2004, Vol. 2-4, p. 47.

- *The Frankenstein shinai*, 2004, Vol. 3-1, p. 32.

## Martial Aids (by Greg "Manuke" Robinson)
- Robinson, Greg, *Martial Aids*, 2003, Vol. 2-1, p. 96 [the wooden *bokuto* with *saya*].
- Robinson, Greg, *Martial Aids*, 2003, Vol. 2-2, p. 99 [the scratching bamboo babe].
- Robinson, Greg, *Martial Aids*, 2004, Vol. 2-3, p. 81 [the green grenade].
- Robinson, Greg, *Martial Aids*, 2004, Vol. 2-4, p. 96 [the kote cologne].
- Robinson, Greg, *Martial Aids*, 2004, Vol. 3-1, p. 92 [the x-strap].
- Robinson, Greg, *Martial Aids*, 2005, Vol. 3-2, p. 99 [the sword socks].
- Robinson, Greg, *Martial Aids*, 2006, Vol. 3-3, p. 137 [The wheel with appeals].

## Reviews (Books)
- Amdur, Ellis, *Old School, Essays on Japanese Martial Traditions*, reviewed by Antony Cundy, 2004, Vol. 2-3, pp. 62-63.
- Amdur, Ellis, *Duelling with O-Sensei, Grappling with the Myth of the Warrior Sage*, reviewed by Antony Cundy, 2004, Vol. 2-4, pp. 48-49.
- Broderick, Jeff, *Kendo, The Essential Guide to Mastering the Art*, reviewed by Bruce Flanagan, 2006, Vol. 3-3, p. 136.
- Cleary, Thomas, *Training the Samurai Mind, A Bushido Sourcebook*, reviewed by Michael Ishimatsu-Prime, 2009, Vol. 4-4, p. 103.
- Cleary, Thomas, *Samurai Wisdom, Lesson from Japan's Warrior Culture*, reviewed by Michael Ishimatsu-Prime, 2009, Vol. 5-1, pp. 106-107.
- De Lange, William, *Origins of a Legend, The Real Musashi, The Bushu Denraiki*, reviewed by Jeff Broderick, 2010, Vol. 5-2, pp. 74-75.
- Gruzanski, Charles V., *Try Flyte Martial Arts: DVDs*, reviewed by Antony Cundy, 2004, Vol. 3-1, p. 61.
- Hatsumi, Masaaki, *Japanese Sword Fighting, Secret of the Samurai*, reviewed by Antony Cundy, 2008, Vol. 4-3, p. 112.
- Knutsen, Roald, *Rediscovering Budo from a Swordsman's Perspective*, reviewed by Antony Cundy, 2004, Vol. 3-1, pp. 28-29.
- Lowry, Dave, *Persimmon Wind, A Martial Artist's Journey in Japan*, reviewed by Bruce Flanagan, 2005, Vol. 3-2, pp. 86-87.
- Otake, Risuke, *Katori Shinto-Ryu, Warrior Tradition*, reviewed by Alex Bennett, 2007, Vol. 3-4, p. 47.
- Sidney, James, *The Warrior's Path, Wisdom from Contemporary Martial Arts Master*, reviewed by Tyler Rothmar, 2007, Vol. 3-4, p. 33.
- Tanaka, Fumon, *Samurai Fighting Arts, The Spirit and the Practice*, reviewed by Antony Cundy, 2006, Vol. 3-3, pp. 38-39.
- Tokugawa, Tsuneari, *The Edo Inheritance*, reviewed by M. Ishimatsu-Prime, 2009, Vol. 4-4, p. 112.
- Wilson, William Scott, *The Lone Samurai, The Life of Miyamoto Musashi*, reviewed by Antony Cundy, 2005, Vol. 3-2, pp. 34-35.
- Yoshiyama, Mitsuru, *The Kendo Grading Book, How to Pass Kendo Examination 4-dan to 7-dan*, reviewed by Bryan Peterson, 2007, Vol. 3-4, p. 152.

## Reviews (DVDs and Movies)
- AJKF, *56th All Japan Kendo Championships*, reviewed by Michael Ishimatsu-Prime, 2009, Vol. 4-4, p. 16.
- Empty Mind Films, *Art of the Japanese Sword*, reviewed by Tyler Rothmar, 2011, Vol. 5-4, p. 52.
- Hertz, Chiba Masashi, *Jissen Kendo*, reviewed by Tyler Rothmar, 2008, Vol. 4-2, p. 120.
- NHK DVD, *All Japan Kendo Championships, 1996-1999*, reviewed by Michael Ishimatsu-Prime, 2007, Vol. 4-1, p. 55.
- Perrin, George, *4th Dan*, reviewed by Michael Ishimatsu-Prime, 2010, Vol. 5-2, pp. 44-46.

# Kendo Varia

## Various articles about Kendo
- An., *Online Overhaul, Stratus11.com works with Kendo World magazine to forge a sharp new online presence*, 2003, Vol. 2-2, p. 75.
- An., *KW CrossWord*, 2011, Vol. 5-4, p. 66.
- Abe, Tetsushi and Bennett, Alex, *Chewing the Fat*, 2007, Vol. 3-4, pp. 20-27 [about Japanese and international kendo].
- Bennett, Alex, *Editorial*, 2005, Vol. 3-2, pp. 4-5 [The Pain of Rejection - IKF & GAISF].
- Carmody-Stephens, Damian, *The Winning Edge*, 2003, Vol. 2-1, pp. 10-12 [about fitness].
- Daboo, *Void = Absence, Simplification*, 2007, Vol. 3-4, p. 150.
- Jones, Trevor, *RoboKendo*, 2006, Vol. 3-3, pp. 60-61.
- Pilgrim, Axel, *The Dōjō and the Boardroom Executing Strikes & Decisions*, 2010, Vol. 5-3, pp. 88-89.
- Sylvester, Kate, *Unmasking Japanese Women's Kendo*, 2011, Vol. 5-4, pp. 74-76.
- Takeyasu Yoshimitsu, *Message from the All Japan*

*Kendo Federation*, 2001, Vol. 1-1, p. 2.
- Vitalis, Louis, *Kendo, Iaido & Jodo, A Comparison Between Japan and Europe*, 2003, Vol. 2-2, pp. 65-69.
- Wells, Ken, *Budo & Business*, 2003, Vol. 2-1, pp. 34-35.

### Kendo World Survey (by various authors)
- An., *Kendo World Survey No. 1: Kendo and the Olympics*, 2001, Vol. 1-1, pp. 51-55.
- An., *Kendo World Survey No. 2: Gradings*, 2002, Vol. 1-2, pp. 54-59.
- Bennett, Alex and Robison, Hamish, *Kendo World Survey No 4: Shinai*, 2002, Vol. 1-4, pp. 62-64.
- Gringras, Mark, Robison, Hamish and Bennett, Alex, *Kendo World Survey No 5: Bogu*, 2003, Vol. 2-1, pp. 62-66.
- Robison, Hamish and Bennett, Alex, *Kendo World Survey No. 3: Rei*, 2002, Vol. 1-3, pp. 67-69.

### Japanese Academy of Budo (by various authors)
- An., *Japanese Academy of Budo*, 2001, Vol. 1-1, pp. 49-50.
- An., *Japanese Academy of Budo*, 2002, Vol. 1-2, p. 53.
- An., *Japanese Academy of Budo*, 2002, Vol. 1-3, p. 52.
- An., *Japanese Academy of Budo*, 2002, Vol. 1-4, p. 24.
- An., *Japanese Academy of Budo*, 2005, Vol. 3-2, p. 50.
- An., *It's Academic: Note from the Japanese Academy of Budo*, 2011, Vol. 5-4, pp. 46-47.

## Other Martial Arts

### Kumdo
- An., *Road to the Olympics? Formation of World Kendo Federation in Korea?*, 2002, Vol. 1-3, pp. 7-11.
- Brundage, Greg, *Living your Art, An Interview with Park Yong Chon - Korean Sword Master*, 2007, Vol. 3-4, p. 143.
- Katō, Jun'ichi, *From Korea, The Internationalisation of Kumdo, Part 1*, 2007, Vol. 4-1, pp. 99-103.
- Katō, Jun'ichi, *From Korea, The Internationalisation of Kumdo, Part 2*, 2008, Vol. 4-3, pp. 67-71.
- Katō, Jun'ichi, *From Korea, The Internationalisation of Kumdo, Part 3*, 2009, Vol. 4-4, pp. 17-19.
- Katō, Jun'ichi, *Current Circumstances in the Korean Kumdo Association*, 2010, Vol. 5-3, pp. 79-82.
- Lainé, Aurélien, *Kumdo Demystified*, 2010, Vol. 5-2, pp. 98-99.

### Iaido
- An., *AJKF Shogo Examination, Kyoshi*, 2002, Vol. 1-2, pp. 48-49.
- An., *Iai-Jinx*, 2002, Vol. 1-3, pp. 51, 56.
- An., *Taking a Slash at the Title: The 37th All Japan Iaido Championships*, 2002, Vol. 1-4, p. 94.
- An., *Martial Aids*, 2002, Vol. 1-4, p. 95 [about cardboard cutting dummies].
- All Japan Kendo Federation Iaido, *New Instructional Points*, 2010, Vol. 5-3, pp. 111-112.
- Bennett, Alexander, *Martial Aids*, 2001, Vol. 1-1, p. 72.
- Broderick, Jeff, *40th All Japan Iai Championships, October 15th, 2005*, 2006, Vol. 3-3, pp. 48-49.
- Channell, Randall V., *Kumi-Himo, The Art of Traditional Japanese Braiding*, 2007, Vol. 3-4, p. 127 [*Sageo*].
- Eura, Kazunori, *Zen Meditation Experience*, 2007, Vol. 4-1, pp. 76-77.
- Goodman, Fay, *At the Cutting Edge*, 2003, Vol. 2-2, pp. 76-77.
- Hickey, David, *Trafalgar Square and Iai in the Sky*, 2009, Vol. 5-1, pp. 74-75.
- Ishimatsu-Prime, Michael, *Diplomacy, Budo and Love, Interview with Eli Cohen - Former Israeli Ambassador to Japan*, 2007, Vol. 4-1, pp. 36-39.
- Jones, Adrian, *Gentleman and a Scholar - Kaneda Kazuhisa, Part 1*, 2002, Vol. 1-4, pp. 48-49.
- Jones, Adrian, *Gentleman and a Scholar - Kaneda Kazuhisa, Part 2*, 2003, Vol. 2-1, pp. 46-49.
- Kaneda, Kazuhisa, *Iaido as a University Subject, Part 1*, 2006, Vol. 3-3, pp. 138-141.
- Katsuse, Mitsuyasu Kagemasa, *Essentials for the Study of Iai*, 2009, Vol. 4-4, pp. 78-87.
- Nagy, Stephen, *The 2005 June Iaido Regional Training Seminar*, 2006, Vol. 3-3, pp. 31-33.
- Nagy, Stephen Robert, *Classical Iai Seminar, Are All Styles Created Equal?*, 2008, Vol. 4-2, pp. 106-109.
- Taylor, Kim, *Haruna Sensei Remembered*, 2002, Vol. 1-4, pp. 81-82.

### Iaido World (by Trevor Jones)
- Jones, Trevor, *Iaido World*, 2001, Vol. 1-1, pp. 56-68 [about Sogiri and Nuki Uchi].
- Jones, Trevor, *Iaido World*, 2002, Vol. 1-2, pp. 74-76 [about importing and exporting swords in Japan].
- Jones, Trevor, *Iaido World*, 2002, Vol. 1-3, pp. 79-80 [about organisations, gradings and competitions in Japan].
- Jones, Trevor, *Iaido World*, 2002, Vol. 1-4, pp. 76-

# A CUMULATIVE TABLE OF CONTENTS

- 81 [about Haruna Matsuo].
- Jones, Trevor, *Iaido World*, 2003, Vol. 2-2, pp. 78-81 [A Conversation with Fay Goodman].
- Jones, Trevor, *Iaido World*, 2005, Vol. 3-2, p. 81 [World Iaido Championship].

## Cutting-Edge, Iaido (by Kaneda Kazuhisa)

- Kaneda, Kazuhisa, *Cutting-Edge, Iaido*, 2007, Vol. 3-4, pp. 101-103 [general technical elements].
- Kaneda, Kazuhisa, *Cutting-Edge, Iaido*, 2007, Vol. 4-1, pp. 65-69 [AJKF Iai 1-6].
- Kaneda, Kazuhisa, *Cutting-Edge, Iaido*, 2008, Vol. 4-2, pp. 102-105 [AJKF Iai 7-10].
- Kaneda, Kazuhisa, *Cutting-Edge, Iaido*, 2009, Vol. 4-4, pp. 88-89 [AJKF Iai 11-12].

## Jodo

- An., *AJKF Shogo Examination, Kyoshi*, 2002, Vol. 1-2, pp. 48-49.
- An., *Interview with Nakanishi Yasushi*, 2002, Vol. 1-4, pp. 83-87.
- An., *Koshukai*, 2003, Vol. 2-1, p. 61.
- James, T.H., *Jodo World*, 2001, Vol. 1-1, pp. 69-70.
- Pickering, Anthony and Lee-Steere, Marcus, *The Australian Iaido & Jodo Seminar & Championships 2004*, 2004, Vol. 2-4, pp. 88-91.
- Taylor, Kim, *A Brief History of ZNKR Jodo*, 2002, Vol. 1-2, pp. 80-86.
- Taylor, Kim, *Jodo World, The Place of Jodo in the Kendo Federation*, 2002, Vol. 1-3, pp. 81-83.

## Naginata

- Amdur, Ellis, *An Overview of the Way of Naginata, The Perspective of a Traditionalist*, 2009, Vol. 4-4, pp. 106-110.
- Bennett, Alex, *All Japan Naginata Champs*, 2002, Vol. 1-2, pp. 78-79.
- Bennett, Alex, *Naginata Shiai*, 2002, Vol. 1-3, pp. 86-87.
- Bennett, Alex, *Shikake-Oji*, 2002, Vol. 1-4, pp. 90-93.
- Bennett, Alex, *Naginata Kata*, 2003, Vol. 2-1, pp. 84-85.
- Bennett, Alex, *Great Naginata Masters of Modern Times, Part 1*, 2003, Vol. 2-2, pp. 82-84 [about Mitamura Chiyo].
- Bennett, Alex, *Great Naginata Masters of Modern Times, Part 2*, 2004, Vol. 2-3, pp. 78-80 [about Sonobe Hideo].
- Bennett, Alex, *The History of Naginata*, 2004, Vol. 2-4, pp. 82-87.
- Bennett, Alex, *Ishu-Jiai*, 2004, Vol. 3-1, pp. 80-81.
- Bennett, Alex, *Rhythm Naginata*, 2005, Vol. 3-2, p. 85.
- Bennett, Alex, *4th World Naginata Championships in Brussels*, 2007, Vol. 4-1, pp. 118-122.
- Funahara, Shizue, *The Importance of Kihon*, 2001, Vol. 1-1, pp. 70-71.
- Lainé, Aurélien, *International Naginata Federation Seminar 2008 in New Zealand*, 2008, Vol. 4-3, pp. 72-73.
- May Yien, Jean, *A Godan Experience*, 2003, Vol. 2-2, pp. 88-92.
- Peterson, Bryan, *"In the Deep End"*, 2004, Vol. 2-4, pp. 80-81 [Shimpan].
- Peterson, Bryan, *Joto High School Naginata Club*, 2008, Vol. 4-2, pp. 116-117.

## Naginata Technical Special: Shikake-Oji (by Alex Bennett)

- *Part 1: Ippon-Me*, 2006, Vol. 3-3, pp. 76-78.
- *Part 2: Nihon-Me*, 2007, Vol. 3-4, pp. 98-100.
- *Part3: Sanbon-Me*, 2007, Vol. 4-1, pp. 123-125.
- *Part 4: Yonhon-Me*, 2008, Vol. 4-2, pp. 114-115.
- *Part 5: Gohon-Me*, 2008, Vol. 4-3, pp. 74-76.
- *Part 6: Roppon-Me*, 2009, Vol. 4-4, pp. 104-105.
- *Part 7: Nanahon-Me*, 2009, Vol. 5-1, pp. 112-114.
- *Part 8: Hachihon-Me*, 2010, Vol. 5-2, pp. 91-93.

## Jukendo

- Kelsey, Steve, *Jukendo World*, 2002, Vol. 1-2, p. 77.
- Kelsey, Steve, *It's all in the Heart*, 2002, Vol. 1-3, pp. 84-85.
- Kelsey, Steve, *Retreating in Jukendo*, 2002, Vol. 1-4, pp. 88-89.
- Kelsey, Steve, *Tankendo*, 2003, Vol. 2-1, p. 67.
- Kelsey, Steve, *Jukendo and Cross Training*, 2003, Vol. 2-2, p. 93.
- Kelsey, Steve, *Cutting the Corners*, 2004, Vol. 2-3, pp. 82-83.
- Kelsey, Steve, *Jukendo Kata - The Third Pillar*, 2004, Vol. 2-4, pp. 92-93.
- Kelsey, Steve, *Jukendo's Simplicity*, 2004, Vol. 3-1, p. 82.
- Kelsey, Steve, *Jukendo World*, 2005, Vol. 3-2, p. 84.
- Kelsey, Steve, *Looking Back*, 2007, Vol. 3-4, pp. 144-145.
- Kelsey, Steve, *Touch and Go!!*, 2008, Vol. 4-2, p. 113.
- Tavernier, Baptiste, *16th All Japan Jukendo Championship*, 2008, Vol. 4-3, p. 77.
- Tavernier, Baptiste, *From Jukenjutsu to Jukendo, An Interview with Kobayashi Sensei*, 2009, Vol. 4-4, pp. 64-65.

### Jukendo no Kata (by Baptiste Tavernier)
- *Part 1: Jukendo no Kata*, 2009, Vol. 5-1, pp. 97-105.
- *Part 2: Mokujû Tai Tô no Kata*, 2010, Vol. 5-2, pp. 100-106.
- *Part 3: Mokujû Tai Tanken no Kata*, 2010, Vol. 5-3, pp. 104-110.
- *Part 4: Tankendo no Kata*, 2011, Vol. 5-4, pp. 92-99.

## Japanese Culture

### Japanese Culture - Generality
- Cundy, Antony, *A Call to Arms: What Martial Artists can do for Japan*, 2011, Vol. 5-4, p. 9 [about the earthquake and tsunami].
- Hellman, Christopher, *The Last Manga Exhibition: Musashi Gets the Ending he Deserves*, 2010, Vol. 5-3, pp. 54-55 [about Inoue Takehiko and the *Vagabond*].
- Ishimatsu-Prime, Michael, *Yasukuni*, 2008, Vol. 4-2, pp. 118-119.
- Ishimatsu-Prime, Michael, *Celebrating the Dead*, 2009, Vol. 5-1, pp. 64-65 [about 47 rōnin].
- Ishimatsu-Prime, Michael, *The Great East Japan Earthquake*, 2011, Vol. 5-4, pp. 4-8.
- Lainé, Aurélien, *The Art of Devotion*, 2009, Vol. 4-4, p. 63 [about calligraphy].
- Moate, Sarah, *Zen Calligraphy and Painting of Yamaoka Tesshû at the V&A*, 2008, Vol. 4-2, pp. 15-17.
- Moate, Sarah, *Bushido, The Zen Calligraphy of Katsu Kaishû and Takahashi Deishû*, 2008, Vol. 4-3, pp. 84-87.
- Moate, Sarah, *Suigetsu, "The Moon in Water", The Zen calligraphy of Yamaoka Tesshû and Terayama Tanchû*, 2009, Vol. 4-4, pp. 98-101.
- Prime, Michael, *The Way*, 2006, Vol. 3-3, pp. 24-30 [Chado - Tea Ceremony].
- Prime, Michael, *The Experts*, 2006, Vol. 3-3, pp. 114-117 [I am *NipponJin*].

### Unlocking Japan (by Lockie Jackson)
- *Part 1: "Special Guest" or "One of the Rest"*, 2001, Vol. 1-1, pp. 35-36.
- *Part 2: Dojos, Here and There*, 2002, Vol. 1-2, pp. 31-33.
- *Part 3: Do you know Ray?*, 2002, Vol. 1-3, pp. 35-36.
- *Part 4: Getting Practical*, 2002, Vol. 1-4, pp. 10-12.
- *Part 5: Making Sense out of "sensei"*, 2003, Vol. 2-1, pp. 55-57.
- *Part 6: Ken's Story...*, 2003, Vol. 2-2, pp. 72-74.
- *Part 7: The Crying Game*, 2004, Vol. 2-3, pp. 64-65.
- *Part 8: The Funeral*, 2004, Vol. 2-4, pp. 32-34.
- *Part 9: The Way of the Bath*, 2004, Vol. 3-1, pp. 36-37.
- *Part 10: Eezii Raidaa!*, 2005, Vol. 3-2, pp. 45-47.
- *Part 11: The Barber Shop*, 2006, Vol. 3-3, pp. 62-63.
- *Part 12: When in Rome*, 2007, Vol. 3-4, pp. 82-83.
- *Part 13: The Real Santa*, 2007, Vol. 4-1, pp. 58-59.
- *Part 14: Thug School*, 2008, Vol. 4-2, pp. 30-31.
- *Part 15: Expats and Mates*, 2008, Vol. 4-3, pp. 36-37.
- *Part 16: Lifers*, 2009, Vol. 4-4, pp. 48-49.
- *Part 17: The Safe Country?*, 2009, Vol. 5-1, pp. 124-125.
- *Part 18: The Idiot Box*, 2010, Vol. 5-2, pp. 110-111.
- *Part 19: Budgie Boys*, 2010, Vol. 5-3, p. 30.
- *Part 20: Lessons Learned*, 2011, Vol. 5-4, pp. 48-49.

### Shinai Sagas (by Charlie Kondek)
- *Long Day*, 2003, Vol. 2-2, pp. 94-98.
- *A Mountain in the Mists*, 2004, Vol. 2-3, pp. 84-87.
- *The Invaders*, 2004, Vol. 3-1, pp. 86-89.
- *Shinken Shobu*, 2005, Vol. 3-2, pp. 95-98.
- *The Longest Enchō*, 2007, Vol. 3-4, pp. 146-148.
- *The Contenders*, 2008, Vol. 4-2, pp. 60-67.
- *Some Invisible Someone*, 2008, Vol. 4-3, pp. 104-109.
- *Three Ronin*, 2009, Vol. 4-4, pp. 60-62.
- *I'm Different Now...*, 2009, Vol. 5-1, pp. 108-111.
- *The Fifth Poison*, 2010, Vol. 5-2, pp. 76-79.
- *You Know What to Do*, 2010, Vol. 5-3, pp. 84-87.
- *The Coming of Spring*, 2011, Vol. 5-4, pp. 88-91.

### Humour
- Broderick, Jeff, *Iai-Jinx*, 2002, Vol. 1-3, pp. 51, 56.
- Broderick, Jeff, *Iai-Jinx*, 2002, Vol. 1-4, p. 24.
- Broderick, Jeff, *Iai-Jinx*, 2003, Vol. 2-1, pp. 45, 66.
- Broderick, Jeff, *Iai-Jinx*, 2003, Vol. 2-2, p. 5.
- Broderick, Jeff, *Iai-Jinx*, 2004, Vol. 2-3, p. 77.
- Broderick, Jeff, *Iai-Jinx*, 2005, Vol. 3-2, pp. 39, 87.
- Broderick, Jeff, *Iai-Jinx*, 2006, Vol. 3-3, p. 39.
- Doran, Kirk, *Kirk's Zodiac Zone*, 2002, Vol. 1-4, p. 16.
- Doran, Kirk, *Kirk's Zodiac Zone*, 2003, Vol. 2-1, p. 21.
- Doran, Kirk, *Kirk's Zodiac Zone*, 2003, Vol. 2-2, p. 62.
- Doran, Kirk, *Kirk's Zodiac Zone*, 2004, Vol. 2-3, p. 73.
- Doran, Kirk, *Kirk's Zodiac Zone*, 2004, Vol. 2-4, p. 69.
- Doran, Kirk, *Kirk's Zodiac Zone*, 2004, Vol. 3-1, p. 38.
- Doran, Kirk, *Kirk's Zodiac Zone*, 2005, Vol. 3-2, p. 51.
- Doran, Kirk, *Kirk's Zodiac Zone*, 2006, Vol. 3-3, p. 56.

www.ingramcontent.com/pod-product-compliance
Lightning Source LLC
Chambersburg PA
CBHW080856090426
42735CB00014B/3165